Public Assembly Facility Management: Principles and Practices

Second Edition

PUBLIC ASSEMBLY FACILITY MANAGEMENT: PRINCIPLES AND PRACTICES

Lee A. Esckilsen, CFE
Johnson & Wales University, Providence, RI

Frank E. Russo, Jr. CFE
Global Spectrum, Glastonbury, CT

Robert J. Stewart, CFE
Johnson & Wales University, Providence, RI

Contributing Editors
Peter J. Graham, Ed.D.
University of South Carolina, Columbia, SC

Don Hancock, Ph.D., CAE

Ray Ward, CFE

International Association of
Venue Managers, Inc.

Printed and Published by
International Association of
Venue Managers, Inc.
635 Fritz Drive, Suite 100
Coppell, TX 75019
www.iavm.org

Printed in the United States of America.

"This publication is designed to provide accurate and
authoritative information in regard to the subject
matter covered. It is sold with the understanding
that the publisher is not engaged in rendering legal
advice, accounting or other professional service. If
legal advice or other expert advice is required, the
services of a competent professional person should
be sought."

-from Declaration of Principles jointly
adopted by Committee of American Bar
Association and Committee of Publishers
and Associations

ISBN 978-0-9841303-0-6

Second Edition

CONTENTS

PREFACE...vii

IAAM FOUNDATION ACKNOWLEDGEMENT.............................ix

CHAPTER ONE
OWNERSHIP AND GOVERNANCE OF PUBLIC ASSEMBLY FACILITIES..........1

CHAPTER TWO
ORGANIZATION AND MANAGEMENT....................................23

CHAPTER THREE
SCHEDULING FACILITIES AND BOOKING EVENTS.............................47

CHAPTER FOUR
SALES AND MARKETING..69

CHAPTER FIVE
TICKETING AND ACCESS MANAGEMENT................................95

CHAPTER SIX
BUSINESS AND FINANCIAL MANAGEMENT.................................129

CHAPTER SEVEN
EVENT AND ANCILLARY REVENUE SOURCES...............................157

CHAPTER EIGHT
EVENT MANAGEMENT...189

CHAPTER NINE
FACILITY OPERATIONS AND EVENT SERVICES...............................225

APPENDIX A
ILLUSTRATIONS...253

APPENDIX B
CORE COMPETENCIES...271

APPENDIX C
CONTRACT COMPONENTS...281

APPENDIX D
RELATED ORGANIZATIONS..287

APPENDIX E
GLOSSARY...299

INDEX..313

PREFACE

Public Assembly Facility Management is increasingly being recognized as a vital and rewarding profession by private facility owners, governmental elected and administrative officials, and a growing body of stakeholders worldwide. In order to continually enhance the expertise and professionalism of its members, the IAAM and the IAAM Foundation committed substantial financial resources to create a written "Body of Knowledge."

IAAM's leadership created a Body of Knowledge Task Force (BOK) in 1999 with the purpose of documenting the body of knowledge in the industry through creation of the "core competencies" for public assembly facility management. The Body of Knowledge Task Force then took the "core competencies" to the next level as a textbook outline. The outline was also used to create a template for a master's degree in public assembly facility management. The first edition of the textbook, published in 2003, has been adopted for classroom use by 55 colleges and universities.

As a key component to its commitment to professionalism, the IAAM has also developed an extensive network of relationships with colleges and universities that now offer graduate and undergraduate courses and degree programs in public assembly facility management. Further, the IAAM has created a special "Student" membership category and an "Associate" membership category for college/university faculty members. What IAAM has achieved is an ever increasing number of academically trained and educated mid-level managers that show great promise in raising the bar of professionalism for the entire industry.

The IAAM's success on this front is the reason why there has been such widespread demand for this new, updated second edition of *Public Assembly Facility Management: Principles and Practices.*

The innumerable hours the Body of Knowledge Task Force volunteered in creating and crafting the core competencies came to fruition with the publication of the first edition of *Public Assembly Facility Management: Principles and Practices.* Dr. Peter J. Graham, Professor for the Department of Sport & Entertainment Management, University of South Carolina, Columbia, SC, served as the Principal Writer for the textbook and

Ray Ward, CFE, President, Dakota Enterprises, Inc., Granite Bay, CA as Executive Editor. Other University of South Carolina faculty instrumental in development of the first edition were Dr. Laura Sawyer, John Bolin, and Dr. Tom Regan.

IAAM's Body of Knowledge Task Force was appointed in 1999 and was funded by a grant from the IAAM Foundation. Body of Knowledge Task Force members from 1999-2005 who oversaw the textbook project were Frank E. Russo, Jr., CFE, chair, Global Spectrum, Glastonbury, CT; Patrick K. Fitzgerald, CFE, past chair, CAVS/Gund Arena Company, Cleveland, OH; Debbie Kling, formerly of Bank of America Centre, Boise, ID; Lynda Reinhart, CFE, Stephen C. O'Connell Center, University of Florida, Gainesville, FL; Robert E. Seitz, CFE, formerly of Topeka Center for the Performing Arts, Topeka, KS; Rodney J. Smith, CFE, formerly of Denver Performing Arts Complex, Denver, CO; Robert J. Stewart, CFE, formerly of Lawlor Events Center, University of Nevada, Reno, NV; and Dexter G. King, CFE, IAAM Executive Director, formerly of BSU Pavilion, Boise, ID.

This second edition was extensively revised and expanded by Lee A. Esckilsen, CFE, Associate Professor in The Center for Sports, Entertainment & Event Management, Johnson & Wales University, Providence, RI, Frank E. Russo, Jr., CFE, of Global Spectrum, and Robert J. Stewart, CFE, Assistant Professor in The Center for Sports, Entertainment & Event Management, Johnson & Wales University, Providence, RI, Don Hancock, Ph.D, CAE, from the IAAM staff served as managing editor of the revision.

In August 2008, IAAM formed an Ad Hoc Textbook Task Force to assist with the final review and editing of this second edition. IAAM and the second edition authors owe thanks to the many IAAM members who have provided technical review and contribution of materials to the second edition. Members of the Ad Hoc Textbook Task Force (2008-09) included Patrick Donnelly; Bobby Goldwater; Wendy Gregus; Adonis "Sporty" Jeralds, CFE; Bob LeBarron, CFE; Michael Norton; Lynda Reinhart, CFE; Philip Rothschild, Ph.D; Dan Saunders, CFE; Bill Squires; Rodney Smith, CFE; Cheryl Swanson, CFE; and Scott Wysong, Ph.D.

ACKNOWLEDGMENT

Financial support for the Public Assembly Facility Management: Principles and Practices has been provided by the International Association of Assembly Managers Foundation. Without their support, this textbook would not have been possible.

The Foundation is committed to raising funds to support the public assembly facility profession through programs of research, professional development and education.

The following IAAM Foundation Board of Trustees, past and present, provided leadership and vision for this project.

CHAPTER 1

OWNERSHIP AND GOVERNANCE OF PUBLIC ASSEMBLY FACILITIES

CHAPTER OUTLINE

INTRODUCTION
TYPES OF PUBLIC ASSEMBLY FACILITIES
GOVERNANCE OF PUBLIC ASSEMBLY FACILITIES
FINANCIAL PERFORMANCE EXPECTATIONS
PUBLIC PRIVATE MANAGEMENT
- THE PRIVATE MANAGEMENT ALTERNATIVE
- AUTHORITIES/COMMISSIONS
- ACADEMIC INSTITUTIONS AND NON-PROFITS ORGANIZATIONS
CHARACTERISTICS OF GOVERNING BODIES
COMMON OPERATING DYNAMICS
SUMMARY
REFERENCES AND ADDITIONAL READINGS

INTRODUCTION

Public assembly facilities (PAFs) have in some respects become the modern day version of the cathedral of middle ages Europe or the hippodrome, stadium, or theatre of ancient Rome and Greece. Many cities and towns build them as the focal point of their communities. Whether or not the huge investment of public funds can be truly cost-justified, government leaders, in most cases, build them simply because they want them. Why? To attract or retain one or more professional sports franchises. To put their city "on-the-map." To enhance the quality of life. To attract conventions and tradeshows and thus stimulate the local economy.

For whatever reason, more and more are being built at an ever increasing cost to the public in the name of competing for sports and entertainment events as well as conventions, tradeshows, meetings and conferences.

Public assembly facilities such as arenas, stadiums, civic and convention centers, and theaters evolved out of the need by social communities to build permanent structures for public assembly – for political and commercial activities, religious gatherings, sports spectacles, artistic expression, and for commercial and educational assemblies. On any given day, literally thousands of public assembly facilities worldwide are open and serving the public because their communities responded to the need and/or desire.

Very few public assembly facilities operate at a financial surplus or profit, especially when debt service (principal and interest payments on the cost of construction) is calculated. And, many, if not most require some level of operating subsidy. Given the often staggering cost of modern arenas, stadiums, convention centers, and even performing arts venues, it is little wonder that public rather than private financing is necessary to get these facilities built and operational.

Governance of a public assembly facility therefore typically involves ownership and management by city, county, or state government. There are also a number of examples where a facility is owned and operated by a private corporation. Examples include Madison Square Garden, Portland's Rose Garden, the Wachovia Complex in Philadelphia and the American Airlines arenas in both Miami and Dallas. A private non-profit foundation owns the Bradley Center in Milwaukee. Many colleges and universities, both public and private, also own arenas. The vast majority of all PAFs, by pure economic necessity, are owned by government.

Government by its very nature often is not well suited to operate what is essentially a sales and marketing oriented enterprise rather than a typical taxpayer service. This is not to say that some governmental entities do not operate in a business-like manner, but for the most part government does have trouble effectively managing a public assembly facility for the following reasons:

- Government provides required services but always in the context of controlling costs to minimize the impact on property taxes. PAFs must spend money to make money and do not easily fit into bureaucratic budget constraints.

- Taxpayers have no realistic choice with respect to the services provided and their costs except periodically when they vote. PAFs must compete within a broad geographic region for both events and ticketbuyers or attendees. Expenditures of necessary dollars for sales and marketing, advertising and promotion, "wining and dining," gifts and the like do not go over well in a purely public context, especially when publicized by the media.

- PAFs cannot usually cope with across-the-board budget cuts, hiring freezes, residency requirements, non-performance-based compensation plans, and other such attempts by government to place a straight-jacket of conformity on a facility that competes daily and sells its uniqueness in the marketplace.

This book is intended to help guide all owners and managers and serve as a resource for educators and students on the best principles and practices necessary to protect, preserve, and enhance the public assembly facility. One of the very first steps, of course, is to define the public purpose of the facility. This is necessary in order to establish realistic operating policies, budgets, and overall community expectation levels. Unfortunately, very often there is a lack of definition of the public purpose/mission of the facility. It is a community asset, but is it intended to be a

- Civic center for community events?
- Sports and entertainment center?
- Convention center/trade show center/attraction?
- Economic impact driver?
- Quality of life enhancement?
- All of the above?

At what cost is the community willing to build and operate a public assembly facility? Is it to be a

- Net income generator (usually exclusive of debt service and long-term capital improvement fund)?
- Break-even operation?
- Subsidized operation?

Does public policy match the public's willingness to subsidize? Is there a clear and realistic determination of intentions that provides community leaders with answers to questions on whether or not to build a facility in the first place and how to govern, manage, and operate them? Each public assembly facility is a partner in the larger industries of sports and entertainment, including the arts as well as meetings, conventions, consumer shows, and trade shows.

Each public assembly facility must find its place within the local, regional, national, or international markets in which it competes. These markets often are intensely competitive. And though there may exist a dramatic variation in size, function, and purpose for each venue, their primary purpose remains constant: providing service to the public. (NOTE: The terms venue and facility are synonymous and are frequently used interchangeably.) This chapter addresses basic concepts, governance of public assembly facilities, and introductory management issues.

TYPES OF PUBLIC ASSEMBLY FACILITIES

There are many different types of public assembly facilities. Therefore, in the discussion that follows, the term public assembly facility (ies) will refer to all public and private facilities designed to accommodate people that assemble for a common purpose. Thus, the term public assembly facility includes, but is not limited to, amphitheatres, arenas, auditoriums, conference centers, congress centers, convention centers, complexes, exhibition halls, performing arts theatres, stadiums, and special event facilities. The following definitions are drawn from the IAAM's Industry Profile Surveys (IPS):

AMPHITHEATRE - an open-air facility with a stage, usually some permanent seating, and some lawn seating area. **Typical Events** - concerts, stage presentations, community events, and miscellaneous other events.

ARENA - an indoor facility with fixed and/or portable seats surrounding an open floor area, which can be set with different event configurations. May have a permanent stage or use portable staging when necessary. **Typical Events** - basketball, hockey, other sports, concerts, ice shows, circuses, other family shows, and miscellaneous other major events. These facilities may also have occasional conventions, trade shows, and meetings, but they are not primarily convention and exhibition centers, as defined in the IPS.

COMPLEX - a combination of two or more of the facility types, presenting typical events as indicated. Typically, a complex has single management and combined financial reporting.

CONFERENCE CENTERS - primarily designed for small-scale meetings and conferences. They typically provide state-of-the-art educational meeting rooms and may also provide sleeping rooms.

CONGRESS CENTER - generally are found in Europe where conventions are referred to as congresses. Most of these centers do not have special-purpose or dedicated exhibit space. However, because they are designed to accommodate multiple-hosting duties, they normally contain one or more raked, sloped or ascending floor, fixed-seat theatres.

CONVENTION CENTER/EXPO CENTER/TRADE SHOW CENTER - an indoor facility with large exhibit areas, supplemented by various sized meeting rooms. **Typical Events** - conventions, trade shows, consumer shows (e.g. boat, home, auto, etc.), banquets, receptions, meetings, major local events, and others. Trade fairs may also own and tour shows. In the IPS questionnaires, a distinction was made between those facilities that were primarily convention centers and those exhibit halls that were part of a complex.

Exhibition halls are most often part of a convention center and may contain up to 1,000,000 or more square feet of contiguous flat-floor space and ceilings 25 to 35 feet in height. However, the vast majority are more likely to have floor space in the 60,000 to 200,000 square foot range.

PERFORMING ARTS FACILITIES: AUDITORIUMS/CONCERT HALLS/ THEATRES - an indoor performing arts facility or concert hall usually with some type of permanent stage and permanent seats on a raked (sloped) floor, or may have a center or thrust stage with either permanent and/or portable seating. **Typical Events** - concerts, symphony, drama, dance, touring Broadway shows, ballet, opera, stage presentations, and other community events. These facilities may also have conventions, trade shows, and meetings, but they are not primarily convention and exhibition centers, as defined in the IPS.

SPECIAL EVENT FACILITIES - such as tennis stadiums, velodromes, curling rinks, horse and dog racetracks, and motor speedways are examples of structures designed to accommodate a specific activity or event. These facility types like all public assembly facilities are on occasion used to host activities or events not related to their primary purpose.

STADIUM - a large facility, either open-aired or domed, with fixed seats, or bleachers surrounding a "field area." **Typical Events** - baseball, football, soccer, major concerts, spectacles, major civic events, and others. A large domed facility with full-field football/soccer capability is considered a stadium even though its event schedule may include exhibits, basketball, family shows, and other arena-type events.

GOVERNANCE OF PUBLIC ASSEMBLY FACILITIES

Public bodies finance, construct, and manage the majority of public assembly facilities, and thus this form of ownership is by far the most common. (See Figure 1-1) Management and governance of a public assembly facility varies from city to city but usually place the general manager reporting to a city or county manager, chief administrative officer, and in some cases to the chief elected official, usually the mayor. Alternatively, some cities establish authorities, boards, or commissions to oversee the facility's operations and, through state-enabling legislation, allow for more operating flexibility than other governmental departments.

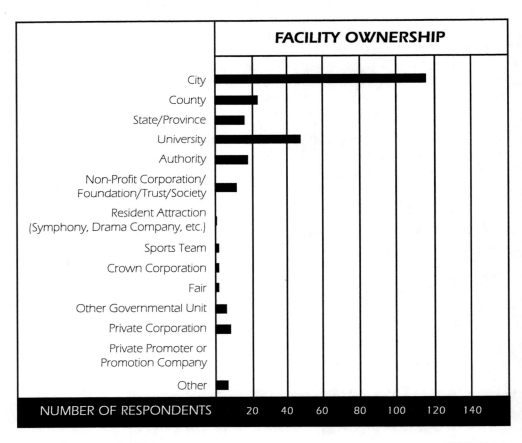

2006 IAAM Industry Profile Survey

FIGURE 1-1

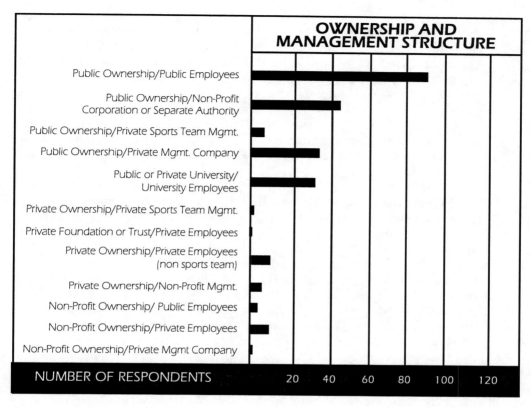

OWNERSHIP AND MANAGEMENT STRUCTURE

Ownership Type	Number of Respondents
Public Ownership/Public Employees	
Public Ownership/Non-Profit Corporation or Separate Authority	
Public Ownership/Private Sports Team Mgmt.	
Public Ownership/Private Mgmt. Company	
Public or Private University/ University Employees	
Private Ownership/Private Sports Team Mgmt.	
Private Foundation or Trust/Private Employees	
Private Ownership/Private Employees (non sports team)	
Private Ownership/Non-Profit Mgmt.	
Non-Profit Ownership/ Public Employees	
Non-Profit Ownership/Private Employees	
Non-Profit Ownership/Private Mgmt Company	

NUMBER OF RESPONDENTS   20   40   60   80   100   120

2006 IAAM Industry Profile Survey   **FIGURE 1-2**

While there are a variety of possibilities for the ownership, governance, and day-to-day operating management of public assembly facilities, these can be described in certain basic formats. (See Figure 1-2). There are five basic forms of governance of public assembly facilities:

- **Elected public body** (e.g., city council, county supervisors, recreation districts, fair, districts, etc.). While the reporting lines may be through an appointed official (e.g., city manager, department head), it is the city council or elected governing body that makes the final policy decisions such as operating and capital budgets, booking and scheduling policies, rates, long-term leases with a prime tenant(s), and major contracts.

- **Elected public body with an independent board** (e.g., authority, board, commission, facilities district, etc.). The board would likely be appointed by the public body, receive its authority from the public body, and have some reporting responsibilities (and perhaps some approvals such as budget) to that body.

- **Public non-profit or not-for-profit corporation or commission or authority.** This arrangement might typically have more independent authority yet would have to have at least an operating agreement with the owner (the public body). This structure is most common to performing arts centers and theaters.

- **Private non-profit corporation.** This arrangement involves the creation of the private corporation that then enters into a legal agreement with the owner. The board of directors is elected internally by the corporation, as are replacements.

- **Private corporation, limited liability company or partnership, public company.** Typical examples are MLB parks, NFL stadiums, and NASCAR tracks.

Under each of the governance forms, the responsible entity can hire employees directly to manage and operate the facility. They also have the option of contracting with a private management company, sport team, or some other entity to manage and operate the facility. In most arrangements, concessionaires or third-party vendors may be contracted to provide services such as food and beverage concessions and catering, parking operations, cleaning, general facility maintenance, and/or smaller more specialized services like elevator and scoreboard maintenance.

In order to be effective, all forms of governance and management should be philosophically entrepreneurial and oriented toward achieving the best possible bottom line given the mission statement. In governmental and non-profit operations, different terminology may be used, but profit is nearly always desired, if not stated as an objective. Public agencies may describe this objective to be self-sustaining or to obtain a net operating surplus.

FINANCIAL PERFORMANCE EXPECTATIONS

Figure 1-3 displays the results of the 2006 IAAM Industry Profile Survey addressing the expectations of the facility owner regarding facility financial performance. The results are aggregated to include all facility types and sizes. Simply, the results go from an expectation that the operating expenses will be (1) subsidized to (2) operating break-even to (3) operating break-even plus debt service but no profit to (4) operating profit to (5) operating break-even plus debt service and making a profit.

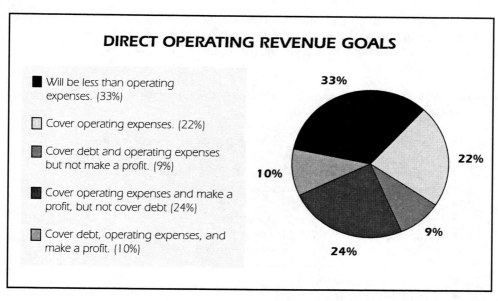

DIRECT OPERATING REVENUE GOALS

- Will be less than operating expenses. (33%)
- Cover operating expenses. (22%)
- Cover debt and operating expenses but not make a profit. (9%)
- Cover operating expenses and make a profit, but not cover debt (24%)
- Cover debt, operating expenses, and make a profit. (10%)

33%
22%
10%
9%
24%

FIGURE 1-3

A facility's financial performance depends on several factors, such as

- Competition from similar venues within the same market
- Capacity (seats, exhibit space, etc.)
- Rigging capacity for lighting, sound, and other theatrical/concert equipment
- Willingness to take financial risks by co-promoting or in-house promoting
- Ability to generate high amounts of nonevent revenue from advertising signage, premium seating, naming and beverage rights, and other commercial rights
- Adequate points-of-sale to maximize fast food concession and merchandise sales
- Labor rates and work rules as they affect the net revenue of promoter/ show producers to maximize their profits
- Ease of access for load-in and load-out of events
- Cooperative media
- Cooperative convention and visitors bureau, chamber of commerce, and other community stakeholders
- Ability to offer exceptional guest services
- Ability to provide a safe and clean environment
- Amount of safe and affordable parking within close proximity to the facility

It is the responsibility of any facility's governing body to understand that unlike other governmental/taxpayer services, a PAF operates in a highly competitive environment for events, for attendees, for commercial rights buyers, and for other income producers.

Some of the facility performance evaluation criteria by which facility management is evaluated include

- Facility bookings and financial results meet the expectations of the owner
- Well rounded schedule of events and number of event days booked
- Positive bottom line/financial results
- Economic impact
- Quality of sales and marketing efforts
- Increased hotel room night sales
- First class asset protection and maintenance
- Customer/client evaluation
- Community involvement
- Ability to pay off debt service

PUBLIC OR PRIVATE MANAGEMENT OF PUBLIC ASSEMBLY FACILITIES?

There are no automatic answers as to the issue of whether a facility should be publicly or privately managed. Each situation is unique. The governing body has to make the hard decisions as to what it wants its facilities to be and how much control it is willing to delegate to another entity. The public body has to determine if the return for the expenditure necessary to have a private firm manage the facility is cost effective in terms of dollars, activity, program, and fulfilling the facility's public purpose.

In some cases, private owners, usually major league sport franchise owners, invest substantial amounts of their own capital to build a new arena or stadium. In such cases, local governments may assist with the development of these privately owned facilities by granting reduced tax liabilities and providing other incentives, including financial investment of public funds and infrastructure development. In these cases, the team usually has full management control of the venue.

When a public assembly facility is government owned but privately managed, the governance arrangement and relationship applied will be defined by the contract agreement between the two parties. Generally, the owner will delegate administration of the contract to a contract administrator (city manager, department head, etc.) or group (authority, commission, non-profit organization, etc.) to provide oversight. The purpose of this oversight is for communication and accountability, but not for dictating specifically how private management will be carried out. The contract for private management services will stipulate the term, conditions, scope of service, and consideration of the agreement. In situations of this nature, a strong working relationship is maintained between the management firm and the representative(s) of the owner or the governing body. If not, the remedy may be to contract with a different firm or to take the management operations in-house.

(Figure 1-4 presents examples of public assembly facilities that exist within the various forms of ownership and governance). Despite the differences of ownership and operation described above, the public assembly facility manager almost always reports to a higher authority, i.e., an organization or body that represents the ultimate owner. There is a clear need in the public assembly facility industry for each facility to have some type of a board that offers policy guidance, funding, community advocacy and public relations, performance reviews, and counsel and advice in key areas of facility management.

EXAMPLES OF OWNERSHIP AND GOVERNANCE

DEPARTMENT OF A CITY/ COUNTY/STATE GOVERNMENT

- Denver Performing Arts Complex (Denver, CO)
- Dallas Convention Center (Dallas, TX)
- Rose Bowl (Pasadena, CA)
- Indiana Convention Center (Indianapolis, IN)
- Springfield Civic Center (Springfield, MA)
- Cintermex Convention and Exposition Facility (Monterrey, Mexico)

AS A PUBLIC AUTHORITY OR COMMISSION

- Georgia World Congress Center (Atlanta, GA)
- Charlotte Coliseum (Charlotte, NC)
- Cumberland County Civic Center (Portland, ME)
- Spokane Arena (Spokane, WA)

NON-PROFIT ORGANIZATIONS OR FOUNDATIONS

- Embassy Theatre (Fort Wayne, IN)
- Wisconsin Exposition Center (West Allis, WI)

GOVERNMENT OWNED BUT PRIVATELY MANAGED OPERATION

- Sovereign Bank Arena (Trenton, NJ)
- Bakersfield Arena and Civic Center (Bakersfield, CA)
- Everett Regional Events Center (Everett, WA)
- Eagan Convention Center (Anchorage, AK)

PRIVATELY OWNED AND OPERATED

- Bass Hall (Ft. Worth, TX)
- Madison Square Garden (New York City, NY)
- MCI Center (Washington, DC)
- Staples Center (Los Angeles, CA)
- Bank of America Centre (Boise, ID)

WITHIN A UNIVERSITY

(Managed by a private management company)
- Dean Dome, University of North Carolina (Chapel Hill, NC)

(Managed as a university department)
- Joyce Center, Notre Dame University (South Bend, IN)
- Frank Erwin Center, University of Texas (Austin, TX)

FIGURE 1-4

The Management of Public Assembly Facilities by Private Companies

When achieving operating objectives becomes difficult with public management, private management companies may be able to assist the owner/public leaders achieve the desired results. These results may be to achieve an actual operating profit, to minimize actual operating losses, and/or to provide a more desired schedule of event programming. The base management fee and incentive income the private management company receives are expenses of the facility's operating budget. A private management agreement often includes the potential for earning incentive income if the firm exceeds predetermined financial and operational benchmarks which would include one or more of the following:

- Increasing operating revenue over an agreed dollar amount
- Decreasing operating losses under an agreed dollar amount
- Increasing annual attendance
- Increasing gross concessions sales
- Increasing hotel/motel sales tax revenue
- Maintaining the facility in superior condition
- Positive customer satisfaction surveys

If a facility has been financed with tax exempt bonds, bond counsel should review a private management agreement to be sure there are no violations of IRS provisions.

There are a variety of reasons why government may decide to privatize the management of their facility. According to Frank E. Russo, Jr., Senior Vice President, Global Spectrum, the conditions that prompt consideration of private management vary, but most share the following characteristics:

- Bureaucratic controls over the budget that are contrary to a free-market thinking.
- Financial losses caused by local economic problems; intense competition for new facilities in the area; difficulties with managing a sales and marketing enterprise with rules that apply to governmental taxpayer services; customer and tenant dissatisfaction; physical deterioration of the plant and equipment; and onerous labor agreements.
- The demand for more event activity, especially for facilities in secondary and tertiary markets.
- The need for investment dollars for renovation, expansion, and/or equipment purchases.
- The simple desire for a clean sweep and a new beginning.
- The need for experienced, professional direction for new facilities from planning, to grand opening, to day-today operations.

Private management companies can risk venture capital in the development or promotion of events and activities that might not otherwise be presented in facilities operated by governmental entities. In any case, private management offers government, universities, and sports teams an effective and proven alternative to the operation of their own facilities.

A misconception about private management is that the owner loses control of the facility operation. This is simply not the case. In most private management arrangements, the owner retains control of all major areas of responsibility including approval of the following:

- Annual operating and capital budgets
- The general manager candidate
- The booking and scheduling policies and rental rates
- Long-term and prime tenant leases
- Major contracts
- Co-promotions and/or in-house promotions that involve financial risk to the facility
- Financial and facility audits

If a private management company invests capital and/or takes on the risk of possible operating deficits, there are typically a set of terms and conditions that give the private manager more control than if he/she is working simply for a base management fee and possible incentive income based on exceeding performance benchmarks. Private management companies have grown their penetration among government-owned facilities over the last 20 years, especially among city-owned mid-sized and large arenas, stadiums, and convention centers

The Management of Public Assembly Facilities by Professional Sports Teams

A related trend is takeover of management of sports arenas and stadiums by team ownership. Through the last half of the twentieth century, cities, counties, and state governments frequently built and managed the sports arenas and stadiums that major league teams played in. Sports teams in city after city have taken over management of the next generation of sports venues, which offer the ancillary revenues from luxury seating, enhanced food and beverage, and other services teams need to remain competitive and make profits for team owners. Figure 1.5 summarizes these changes by major sports league.

Figure 1.5

(Public refers to government owned and operated, *private* refers to team management, and *private management* refers to government owned facilities that are, by contract, managed by for-profit companies.)

NBA
- 1990
  - o   12 public
  - o   12 private (professional sports teams)
  - o   2 public w/ private management
- 2008
  - o   3 public
  - o   24 private (professional sports teams)
  - o   3 public w/ private management

NFL
- 1990
  - o   20 public
  - o   5 private (professional sports teams)
  - o   2 public w/ private management
- 2008
  - o   10 public
  - o   15 private (professional sports teams)
  - o   6 public w/ private management

NHL
- 1990
  - o   5 public
  - o   13 private (professional sports teams)
  - o   2 public w/ private management
- 2008
  - o   28 private (professional sports teams)
  - o   2 public w/ private management

MLB
- 1990
  - o   14 public
  - o   9 private (professional sports teams)
  - o   2 public w/ private management
  - o   1 city and team
- 2008
  - o   2 public
  - o   27 private (professional sports teams)
  - o   1 city and team

Data courtesy of CSL, International, and IAAM staff research

AUTHORITIES/COMMISSIONS

Many publicly owned PAFs are governed by an authority or commission created by the government entity, usually set up under state enabling legislation. The facility's owner generally makes appointments to the governing body. This governing format is valuable in that it enables the facility management to operate with greater flexibility and effectiveness, especially in the areas of personnel management, payroll, purchasing, contract negotiations, sales and marketing, and authority to negotiate competitive "deals."

Given proper authority, these types of boards usually attract dedicated community leaders who bring needed business expertise and bottom-line perspective to the process. In the operating agreements with various types of independent boards (there may also be state enabling legislation that allows local municipal ordinances), public agencies can establish policies and controls that protect the public's rights while at the same time developing the framework for effective management. In many cases, state enabling legislation allows an authority/commission to establish more entrepreneurial operating policies consistent with the needs of competitive business.

Of principal concern with any type of public governing structure is the authority that is granted to the board to conduct the business of the facility. If a powerless advisory board were created, one that must depend upon "city hall" for virtually every decision, then it would be better for "city hall" to directly manage the facility rather than carry on the facade of independent management. Many qualified business leaders and citizens are reluctant to devote their time and energy to public bodies if their input is meaningless.

ACADEMIC INSTITUTIONS AND NON-PROFIT ORGANIZATIONS

Academic institutions such as colleges and universities, whether public or private, own and operate on-campus facilities such as performing arts centers, stadiums, arenas, and conference centers. Although administrative responsibility of specific facilities may be aligned under applicable departments (e.g., student affairs, auxiliary services, business and finance, or athletics), governance of collegiate facilities may also be delegated to an advisory committee comprised of elected and/or appointed representatives of the faculty, administration, and student body. However, ultimate governance authority rests in the hands of the university's president and governing board.

Some public assembly facilities, particularly performing arts centers, may be owned and operated by private non-profit organizations. With this type of ownership and management, governance is dictated by the organization's membership. It is important to realize when discussing non-profit organization's bylaws and/or that the non-profit designation is only a tax status. The true nature of many venue non-profit organizations is to serve as an organization dedicated to presenting cultural entertainment as a part of the overall quality of life in a community. Symphonies, opera and ballet companies, chamber orchestras, and other such entertainment, including Broadway plays and musicals, do not enjoy mass appeal and yet they are critical elements in our society and must be presented. Non-profit organizations find ways to close the financial gap by generating revenue through grants, donations, and sponsorships

CHARACTERISTICS OF GOVERNING BODIES

Whether a public assembly facility manager's governing body is a city council, county commission, non-profit organization, separately appointed or elected governmental authority, or a private board, the manager needs certain types of expertise at the board level to help guide the organization by establishing policies at least in the following areas:

- Internal and external audits
- Budgeting and financial management and reporting
- Human resource/performance evaluation /compensation
- Advertising and marketing
- Legal issues
- Communications/public relations

A valuable asset for any governing board is access to the "movers and shakers" in the community. Sometimes, a simple telephone contact can initiate a solution, stop a problem, or at least create a contact point for beginning discussions on an issue.

Fundamentally, public assembly facility managers working for a public body must effectively deal with an administrative department or some form of governing board in order to be effective — and to survive. In many cases this is much easier said than done due to the fact that most governmental offices or boards consist of members elected by the community or appointed by the local legislative bodies (e.g., city councils) for a specified time period. Thus, the public assembly facility manager is always striving to develop positive relationships with new members while maintaining established relationships with continuing members. Given the nature of politics, this can at times prove to be a very difficult and delicate task.

While most PAFs act as some form of economic drivers for the community, many of them can be mired in a straight-jacket of government rules and regulations that render them impotent and ineffective in their mission and role and unable to successfully compete. The bureaucratic processes that may work effectively for departments delivering only taxpayer services (e.g., street repairs) are more often than not totally inappropriate for managers who must deal with issues concerning sales, marketing, customer satisfaction, and intense competition.

Regardless of the facility's governance structure, achieving the public purpose through successful management outcomes is dependent upon effectively earning client and public confidence. Whether publicly or privately managed, facilities must be competitively focused and able to respond and adjust to market shifts. It takes extraordinary skill, dedication, and perseverance to cost-effectively manage a public assembly facility. Facility managers often serve as the "lightening rod" that deflects a number of governance issues so that the overall organization can effectively deal with their day-to-day, event-related responsibilities. The general manager's focus may often be on dealing with and managing the external forces that affect the facility's day-to-day operations.

COMMON OPERATING DYNAMICS

Common threads of operating dynamics exist among all facilities. Some of these commonalities are event booking and scheduling, event management, parking, crowd management, ticketing, advertising, concessions and catering, facility maintenance, and marketing and sales. Thus, regardless of a facility's size, mission, governance, management, or organizational structure, clear similarities in operating dynamics exist. For example, the manager of an arena and the manager of a performing arts center are both concerned with crowd management and risk management. Some of these commonalities date back to ancient history. Many of the operational areas considered vital by the manager of the Flavian Amphitheatre (Roman Colosseum) when staging gladiatorial combat in A.D. 80 are also considered vital to the manager responsible for staging a rock concert in a modern amphitheatre, or other type of public assembly facility.

Public assembly facilities usually operate within the scope of a written statement of purpose or a mission statement. For instance, the Georgia World Congress Center and Georgia Dome in Atlanta were created through legislation of the Georgia legislature with this purpose:

> These facilities exist for the primary purpose of promoting and facilitating events and activities that generate economic benefits to the citizens of the State of Georgia and the City of Atlanta as well as enhance the quality of life for every Georgian.

PAFs also often create vision and mission statements to help governing boards, management, and staff maintain focus on central goals and objectives. Mission statements often identify the purpose of the facility and provide a basis for making policy decisions regarding issues of scheduling, booking priorities, tenant oversight, reporting, and budget development. (Figure 1-6 provides examples of facility mission statements.)

Figure 1-6   EXAMPLES OF MISSION STATEMENTS

THE AIR CANADA CENTRE, TORONTO, CANADA
Vision and Values

At Maple Leaf Sports & Entertainment our vision is to WIN: to Excite Every Fan, Inspire Our People, be Dedicated to Our Teams and be Leaders in our Community.

Win
Excite every **fan.**
Inspire our **people.**
Dedicated to our **teams.**
Leaders in our **community.**

HONG KONG CONVENTION AND EXHIBITION CENTRE
Mission Statement
We live and work by a vision and mission "centred" on you.

Our Vision:
To be the best exhibition and convention centre in Asia internationally renowned for excellence and hosting the world's greatest events.

Our Mission:
To enable HKCEC's customers to consistently experience value and levels of service beyond their expectations through individual and team commitment to quality using innovative and creative operating techniques.

ORANGE COUNTY PERFORMING ARTS CENTER
Mission Statement

The Orange County Performing Arts Center exists to present a wide variety of the most significant national and international productions of music, dance and theater to the people of Southern California. We believe that experiencing the best in the performing arts adds meaningfully to the quality of life in our community and are committed to providing an unsurpassed attendance experience. In conjunction with its artistic mission, the Center is also entrusted with stewardship of its world class facilities which provide the performance base for its resident companies.

By 2025, the world's finest artists and companies will seek to perform first on our stages because we have cultivated the nation's most enthusiastic, loyal and knowledgeable audiences for important music, dance and theater. The caliber of our presentations will be second to none, complemented by innovative programs of community education and engagement. By bringing together existing and new audiences to experience programs that excite the creative tension between tradition and innovation, the Center will be recognized by everyone as the dynamic cultural and civic center of our community. Infused with an engaging energy and welcoming to all, the Center will stand as a national model for an artistically ambitious, financially sustainable performing arts center.

Rarely does a PAF operate in a single purpose environment. Twenty-first century governing bodies and managers, therefore, need a commanding knowledge of how these operating dynamics affect their facility as well as understanding the effect they have on their competitors.

Successful facility governance demands diligence and creativity. Recognizing the financial impact that public assembly facilities provide, some communities create special taxes or taxing districts to subsidize operating budgets of public assembly facilities. An example of such an approach is the hotel/motel "bed" or transient occupancy tax (TOT). Another approach is an entertainment district tax or Tax Increment Financing Districts (TIF). Regardless of the method, these supplemental funding approaches reflect a recognition by the community that there are other far-reaching, "quality-of-life" values that the facility provides to community members.

PAF managers and their governing boards must be willing to consider a reasoned gamble based on their risk tolerance level and legal requirements. Thus, like other entrepreneurs, the facility manager might be allowed to organize, operate, and assume the risks inherent in both in-house promoted and co-promoted events. Since the success of the PAF hinges on the business and political acumen of its manager, it is imperative for the owner and governing body to employ managerial personnel who possess business skills and political insight. The owner through the governing body must then cultivate and nurture an appropriate entrepreneurial environment that will enable the manager to exercise those business and political skills.

COMPETITION AND FLEXIBILITY

The PAF industry has grown and continues to expand and diversify at a significant rate. A by-product of this growth pattern has been intensified competition. The combination of increased growth and intense competition has heightened the need for prudent financial investments in public assembly facilities and utilization of efficient management practices in order for the facility to serve its constituents in a financially responsible manner. A community's elected or appointed officials and administrators are responsible for the delivery of community services and the use of public tax dollars to pay for them according to prescribed regulations, rules, and policies in order to achieve the vision and to accomplish the mission.

It is unlikely that a PAF can be financially successful if its manager is handicapped by governmental policies and procedures that make it difficult, if not impossible, to conduct the facility's business in a competitive, business-like manner. PAF governing bodies must strive to free their managers from constraints that inhibit the application of sound and reasonable business practices.

SUMMARY

The world has changed. Public assembly facilities are "big business," and they require expert management to not only succeed financially and programmatically but also to protect the lives of the millions of people who attend events at these facilities every day.

This chapter has attempted to demonstrate how complicated it is to blend public ownership with entrepreneurial management. There is, of course, no single answer – except that the owner and manager must know how to effectively deal with each individual situation and make the best of it. More than ever this requires professional development, continuing education, training, and networking with colleagues. While this chapter has offered a number of different ways that a publicly owned facility can be managed, there can be no substitute for quality and knowledgeable management professionals on the front line.

Regardless of type, all facilities have many common operating dynamics. Managers must possess an understanding of these dynamics and how they affect their facility as well as the effect they have on their competitors.

Successful governance requires financial diligence and a good measure of creativity. Some communities create special taxes or taxing districts designed to raise money specifically to subsidize public assembly facility operating budgets. Other communities impose an entertainment district tax or surcharge on ticket sales to accomplish the same financial assistance goal.

Competition within the public assembly facility business is fierce. Success is dependent upon governing boards allowing the facility manager to operate the enterprise in a business-like manner.

Each public assembly facility should have a written statement of purpose or mission statement created and periodically revised by its governing board. This document will clearly identify the purpose of the facility and provide a basis for the governing body when making policy decisions regarding issues of scheduling, booking priorities, tenant oversight, reporting, and budget development.

REFERENCES AND ADDITIONAL READINGS

Drucker, Peter. 1973. *Management: Tasks, Responsibilities, Practices.* New York, Harper & Row, p. 631.

Greenburg, Martin J. 2001. *The Stadium Game*, 2nd ed. Milwaukee, WI: ScheerGame.

IAAM (International Association of Assembly Managers, Inc.). 1994. *1994 IAAM Industry Profile Survey.* Coppell, TX: IAAM.

_____. 2006. *2006 IAAM Industry Profile Survey.* Coppell, TX: IAAM.

Jewell, Don. 1998. *Privatization of Public Assembly Facility Management: A History and Analysis.* Melbourne, FL: Krieger Publishing Company.

Petersen, David C. 2001. *Developing Sports, Convention and Performing Arts Centers*, 3rd ed. Washington, DC: Urban Land Institute.

Russo, Jr., Frank E.. The Case for Private Management, *Public Management Magazine*, Washington, DC: International City Management Association, 1990

Participant's Guide (Performance Through Participation). New York: Van Nostrand Reinhold.

Desseler, Gary. 2002. *Human Resource Management*, 9th ed. Upper Saddle River, NJ: Prentice Hall.

Drucker, Peter F. 1992. *Managing the Non-Profit Organization: Principels and Practices.* New York, Harper Business.

CHAPTER 2

ORGANIZATION
& MANAGEMENT

CHAPTER OUTLINE

CONTROLLING VARIABLES FOR SUCCESS
- DEPARTMENT OF GOVERNMENT
- AUTHORITIES AND COMMISSIONS
- ACADEMIC INSTITUTIONS
- PRIVATE MANAGEMENT

FUNCTIONS COMMON TO PUBLIC ASSEMBLY FACILITIES
ADMINISTRATION
- BOOKING AND SCHEDULING

FINANCIAL CONTROLS
- TICKETING SERVICES

SALES, MARKETING, ADVERTISING, AND PROMOTION
ANCILLARY SERVICES AS REVENUE SOURCES
FACILITY OPERATIONS
NEGOTIATIONS
ETHICS
CREATIVE ENTREPRENEURS
EFFECTIVE COMMUNICATORS
LEADERSHIP AND MANAGEMENT
PROFESSIONAL ASSOCIATIONS AND CONTINUING EDUCATION
SUMMARY
REFERENCES AND ADDITIONAL READINGS

INTRODUCTION

The challenge for all public assembly facilities is to organize for success. While at first glance this may seem simple, it is easier said than done. This challenge is compounded by the fact that most public assembly facility managers are under pressure from a public governing body to maximize both event days and the revenues generated by those events. In order to accomplish these objectives, the public assembly facility manager must juggle and balance variables such as time, space, monetary resources, and staffing, not to mention the demands of the owner and expectations of the general public.

The dynamic nature of the industry makes staffing very difficult because the manager must be able to assemble an "elastic" workforce in order to adjust to the different labor demands associated with each event booked. At the same time, the manager must be able to motivate full-time employees to work extraordinarily long hours that very often fall on evenings, weekends, and holidays. In addition, to assemble an "elastic" workforce, the manager must be able to call upon the services of a large number of part-time and contractual service employees who are available on an "as needed" basis. All employees, full- and part-time alike, must be trained in their specific job responsibilities and must understand the need to be customer service oriented at all times. Although the hiring, training, and retention of such a work force is difficult, it is necessary if the public assembly facility is to operate at peak performance.

CONTROLLING VARIABLES FOR SUCCESS

There are a number of variables that will determine the success or failure of a public assembly facility. Quality management should be rated highest on the list. Aggressive marketing of the facility can influence the number of events that a facility hosts, but it is only through quality management that contracted services with tenants, event producers, and patrons can be delivered in a manner that meets or exceeds each group's expectations. Following the adoption of the public assembly facility's mission statement, it is the governing body's responsibility to create a top management team possessing the insight, intelligence, experience, and energy to bring the public assembly facility's mission and objectives to fruition. Building such a management team may be referred to as "organizing for success." It is accomplished by first hiring a general manager or executive director. Although the title may be different among facilities, the major management functions are quite common.

Later in this chapter we will discuss and illustrate five management functions that are common to all public assembly facilities regardless of their size, type or location. Those five common functions are 1) administration, 2) financial controls, 3) sales, marketing, advertising, and promotion, 4) auxiliary services as revenue sources, and 5) facility operations. Whether the public assembly facility is a massive convention center located in a major metropolitan downtown location or a performing arts center located on a university campus in the Midwestern U.S., management will need to address each of the five aforementioned functions in order to successfully staff and operate their respective public assembly facility.

The type of ownership of a specific public assembly facility will greatly influence the organizational structure of the management team. Publicly owned facilities managed by employees of a public jurisdiction far outweigh any other form of ownership and management. While this form of ownership/management may be more common, there are a number of other organizational structures which are effectively constructed and implemented by the owners of public assembly facilities. Four different organizational models are discussed below. It must be stated that while each of these different forms of organizational structure is successfully employed in different public assembly facilities, the most efficient and effective model for managing a specific facility varies widely. The organizational structure must match the needs of the organization and that of the facility's owner(s).

Regardless of the form of organization, it is necessary that all public assembly facility operations are able to identify the actual costs of running the facility and to ensure that the facility's management personnel abide by the governing body's rules and regulations. In some arrangements, the public assembly facility may be somewhat autonomous with its own dedicated staff and have the ability to outsource a variety of support services.

The lesson is there is no standard, single form of organization within the public assembly facility management industry. What works in one community may not work in another community, just as what works in 2008 may not work for that same facility in 2018. Variables such as market competition, the general economy of the region, and the changing demographics of a community may dictate the need for change from one organizational structure to another.

Figure 2-1 presents a possible organization chart illustrating the relationship of positions and their reporting lines typically found in a public assembly facility. While all of these functions/tasks must be performed, it is not unusual that individuals may be assigned to more than one of these areas. The functions/tasks may be common to all facility types, but the actual organizational structures will vary significantly depending on variables including facility size, location, type of events, form of governance, and the facility's physical aspects. This chart is provided as a sample of how the management team of a public assembly facility may be organized for illustrative and discussion purposes.

Figure 2-1

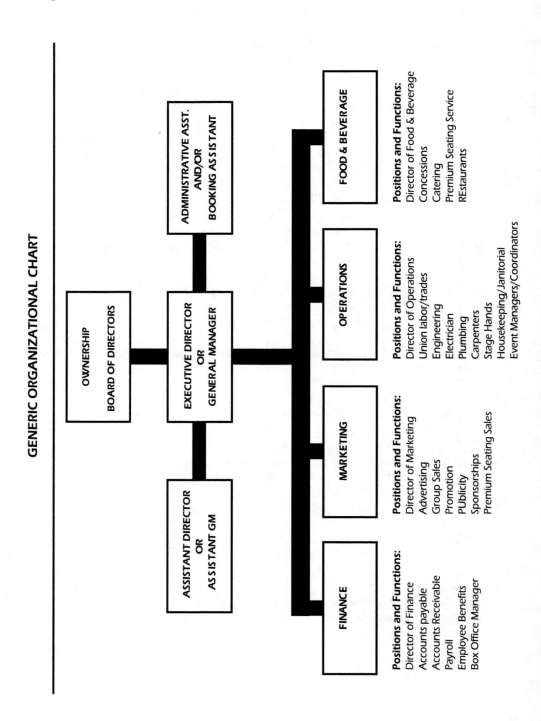

GENERIC ORGANIZATIONAL CHART

OWNERSHIP
BOARD OF DIRECTORS

ADMINISTRATIVE ASST.
AND/OR
BOOKING ASSISTANT

EXECUTIVE DIRECTOR
OR
GENERAL MANAGER

ASSISTANT DIRECTOR
OR
ASSISTANT GM

FINANCE

Positions and Functions:
Director of Finance
Accounts payable
Accounts Receivable
Payroll
Employee Benefits
Box Office Manager

MARKETING

Positions and Functions:
Director of Marketing
Advertising
Group Sales
Promotion
PUblicity
Sponsorships
Premium Seating Sales

OPERATIONS

Positions and Functions:
Director of Operations
Union labor/trades
Engineering
Electrician
Plumbing
Carpenters
Stage Hands
Housekeeping/Janitorial
Event Managers/Coordinators

FOOD & BEVERAGE

Positions and Functions:
Director of Food & Beverage
Concessions
Catering
Premium Seating Service
REstaurants

Department of Government

The setting in which a public assembly facility exists will affect the nature of its organization. A publicly owned facility might be organized as a government department similar to city services departments such as public health, traffic and transportation, or public works. In this organizational context, the facility's general manager might be classified as a public employee who reports directly to another public official. An example is the facility manager being a department head reporting to a city manager or mayor. This reporting structure creates a direct reporting line between the facility manager as a department head and the public official who is either elected by the voters of a civic/municipal jurisdiction or appointed by elected officials. The facility manager often has equal rank with most other department heads such as the chief of police, fire chief, human resources manager, and other department heads. The facility manager must rely on other departments within the governmental structure to provide many of the business and operational functions such as purchasing, payroll, recruitment and hiring, and bill paying. There are also a number of public assembly facilities that operate with this management model on the county level as well.

Support services for a public assembly facility could be provided through various other departments. In such instances, the facility would be subject to the public agency's policies related to human resource management, purchasing, accounting, contracting for outsource services, and other services that often restrict the facility's ability to operate in an entrepreneurial manner. Some municipalities establish departments such as public events, parks and recreation, or facilities administration headed by a general manager and employ civil service personnel to lead the department and operate the public assembly facilities.

Authorities and Commissions

Many facilities are governed directly by an authority or commission which is typically created by a city or county government as a result of state enabling legislation. This allows certain functions of government to operate in a more businesslike manner and without the day-to-day bureaucratic policy and procedure restrictions that restrict typical governmental service departments. Examples of authorities or commissions that operate public assembly facilities include

- Authority: an independent board usually appointed by elected public officials from one or more jurisdictions
- Commission: an independent entity charged with the operation and oversight of a public assembly facility, members of which are appointed by a government official
- Public Facilities District: usually an authority created by state legislation and empowered to plan for and manage public assembly facilities within a specific geographic location

- Not-for-Profit Corporation: an independent authority established to manage a public assembly facility, usually through an operating agreement with the owner or public body

Typical powers of a board or commission include

- Hiring and firing the facility manager
- Annual operating and capital budget approval, although the legislative or elected body often reserves fund appropriation approval for itself
- Adopt booking and usage policies along with rental rates and fee structures
- Approving tenant lease agreements
- Providing direction for overall marketing strategies
- Overseeing risk management programs and insurance coverage
- Approving any interagency or interjurisdictional mutual aid agreements

Many cities and counties view an authority or commission structure as a more comfortable alternative than privatizing the facility in order to remain competitive and financially sound.

Members of the authority or commission are usually then appointed by the governing body. In publicly owned facilities with multiple jurisdictional governing bodies, each constituent jurisdictional governing body will have a pro rata number of appointments to an authority or commission. Generally, the authority or commission form of operation is less politicized and decisions can be achieved in a more expeditious manner than when having to involve other governing councils in the deliberative process.

ACADEMIC INSTITUTIONS

University-owned public assembly facilities are usually operated by the university itself, although there is a growing trend toward privatization in this specialized sector. In the vast majority of cases, the university public assembly facility is organized as a distinct, independent department with its manager enjoying the same rank as other department managers within the institution. The manager will then typically be under the supervision of a Vice President for Administration, a Director of either Auxiliary Services or Business Services, Director of Intercollegiate Athletics or Division of Student Affairs. The general manager will follow university policies and procedures for all business functions, and often other university departments provide services such as accounting, personnel, purchasing, payroll, parking, security, and contracting with outside service providers. In many situations the university's physical plant may provide support services such as maintenance and groundskeeping.

Universities own and operate outdoor stadiums for their intercollegiate athletics department's athletic teams playing football, baseball, soccer and softball; arenas for their basketball, hockey, and volleyball teams; theaters, concert halls, and performing arts centers for their academic departments of music, dance, and theater; and conference centers for the purpose of providing continuing education and training opportunities for their faculty, staff, and guests. The management structure for these facilities varies as widely as the colleges and universities vary themselves. Regardless of the specific management structure, the wide spectrum and variety of public assembly facilities located on college and university campuses serve not only the students, faculty, staff, and alumni of a specific institution, but also the entire population of the communities in which they reside.

A growing number of universities have recently built new arenas on campus that are primarily for university sports teams (basketball or hockey), and are also more "open" in nature and compete directly for a wide array of events with other similar arenas in their markets. The motivation behind university administrators operating their arenas in a more "open" or "public" manner include the following:

- Better facilities enable academic institutions to recruit more and better students, athletes, and alumni support
- More diverse audiences enhance the possibility of increased enrollment and more interaction with the business community that can lead to sponsorships, academic research grants, and student internships and jobs
- Greater likelihood of attracting events that a captive student population can enjoy on campus
- Additional sources of revenue to fund payment of construction costs, bonds, and/or operating expenses to lessen the burden on a university's annual general fund
- Desire for an environment on campus which engages students in on-campus activities that promotes student retention

Private Management

Whether ownership is public or private, privately managed public assembly facilities tend to be organized along the lines of dynamic entrepreneurial operations and are less subject to traditionally restrictive government guidelines. Regardless of ownership, privately managed public assembly facilities tend to encounter less resistance to the implementation of competitive business concepts than their publicly managed counterparts. While private management companies tend to be more bottom-line focused, this is why they are engaged by the facility's ownership or governing body. Private management companies are merely an agent of the owner; however, they are often better equipped to balance the community's needs with improved bottom-line financial results. Finally, private management brings with it a body of intellectual property and combined industry resources that can provide advantages over individually operated facilities.

FUNCTIONS COMMON TO FACILITIES

Exactly how a facility is organized is determined by factors such as ownership, purpose and mission, and facility type. Nonetheless, all general managers face certain common tasks. The core functions evident in each facility are 1) administration (also includes booking and scheduling), 2) financial controls (also includes ticketing services), 3) sales, marketing, advertising, and promotion, 4) ancillary services as revenue sources, and 5) facility operations. While different public assembly venue configurations have special aspects that may make them unique, these five functions are vital to their operation.

The competitive nature of the public assembly facility business mandates that successful managers have the capacity to be strong, deliberate leaders in order to ensure the achievement of established performance objectives and effective management of their facility's most precious commodities: "time and space." Successful managers are leaders who also effectively influence all aspects of the facility.

While these functions exist in all venues, staffing and budget allocations may differ widely depending on the nature of the public assembly facility. Smaller venues in smaller markets have fewer employees, and many of them are responsible for more than one function. In larger facilities, each function may have one or more individuals assigned to it on a full-time basis. Other variables affecting the number of part- or full-time employees assigned to each of these units include the number of events, event types and sizes, and the audience demographic and dynamics.

For example, hosting a Rolling Stones concert in a stadium environment might well require hundreds of staff, including uniformed security officers, peer security staff, first aid staff, concessions workers, box office staff, a media credentialing team, stage crew, plus other personnel such as ticket takers, ushers, custodians, and parking lot attendants. On the other hand, a piano recital held in a smaller performing arts facility or concert hall might only require the services of the stage manager, house manager, front-of-house staff, and a security guard. Nonetheless, the operating dynamics are similar regardless of an event's size. The only difference is found in the scale of application, based on the size and perceived nature of the audience.

Figure 2-2

OUTLINE OF DAILY OPERATIONAL AREAS PERTINENT TO ALL TYPES OF PUBLIC ASSEMBLY FACILITIES

ADMINISTRATION
- Preparing reports and presentations for owners
- Monitoring the operating budget
- Overseeing daily building activities
- Service contracts and tenant leasing issues
- Staff recruitment and training
- Performance evaluations
- Enforcement of employment policies and procedures
- Recordkeeping
- Negotiating labor agreements
- Negotiation and oversight of third party vendor agreements

BOOKING AND SCHEDULING
- Rental rate schedules
- Developing user priorities
- Negotiating tenant leases
- Negotiating individual leases
- Scheduling events
- Promoting and co-promoting events

FINANCIAL CONTROLS
- Prepare and monitor operating and capital budgets
- Financial reporting
- Internal audits
- Inventory control/records
- Bookkeeping, accounts payable, and accounts receivable

- Tax payments/reporting
- Purchasing
- Payroll
- Human resources
- Risk management and insurance
- Cash handling policies/procedures
- Event settlement
- Managing automated teller machines (ATMs)

TICKETING SERVICES
- Ticket inventory and distribution issues
- Occupancy and seating configuration
- Financial accounting and controls
- Staffing, training, and supervision
- Ticketing policies (i.e. refunds)
- Tax collection and remittance
- Secondary market issues

SALES, MARKETING, ADVERTISING AND PROMOTION
- Marketing facility to prospective tenants and shows
- Marketing facility to general public, businesses, etc.
- Marketing of events
- In-house advertising agency
- Advertising signage sales
- Group ticket sales
- Sponsorships
- Promotions
- Public relations
- Media relations

- Web site development and maintenance
- Social networking outreach
- Customer Relation Management (CRM)
- Client surveys/focus groups

ANCILLARY SERVICES AS REVENUE SOURCES
- Food & beverage service/concessions
- Catering sales
- Merchandise sales
- Parking
- In-house business revenue
- Rental of equipment
- Premium services
- Customer service issues
- Inventory controls

OPERATIONS
- Physical plant repair and maintenance
- Facility equipment maintenance
- Housekeeping
- Utility management and control
- Event management
- Safety and security
- Crowd management
- Building safety and security
- Customer/employee safety and security
- Emergency preparedness
- LEED/green initiatives
- Staging, light, and sound
- Information technology
- Capital improvements/upgrades
- Shipping and receiving

ADMINISTRATION

Regardless of facility ownership, the on-site management personnel are typically under the supervision of a general manager who may also be known as executive director, managing director, vice president, or some similar title. This individual must wear a multitude of hats and must be a conduit between the facility and the community; a liaison between the governing body and the facility's staff; and an administrative supervisor, mentor, and leader. Although balancing available resources to achieve the facility's mission is the general manager's primary responsibility, a successful manager must also become the governing body's prime resource, the user's partner, the staff's leader, and the patrons' advocate and sympathetic ear.

A successful general manager not only directs the day-to-day operations of the venue but also can devise a realistic but ambitious goal for the future of the facility and its staff. The manager must have the ability to convey this vision of the future not only to the facility ownership, but also to the entire organization. Without this vision or the skills to communicate it, the facility risks the chance of lagging behind industry trends and losing both its competitive edge in the marketplace and its leaders who depart for opportunities with more progressive organizations.

In most instances, the general manager must ensure that all policies and procedures that govern the business activities of the venue are strictly adhered to. A general knowledge of both state and Federal regulations is very important as is the skill to effectively manage personnel. Knowledge of sound business practices, strong negotiating skills, effective communication abilities, a political acumen, and a thorough working knowledge and passion for the sports, entertainment, arts, travel, tourism, meetings, conventions and tradeshow industries are skills and characteristics that successful public assembly facility managers possess.

BOOKING AND SCHEDULING

The booking and scheduling processes are controls designed to maximize, yet safeguard, the facility's two most important commodities: time and space. Efficient management of these elements is vital to maximizing the number of event bookings and the number of potential revenue streams. Booking and scheduling are the processes that result in the programming of a facility's master calendar and should take into consideration the facility's vision and mission statements along with the needs of its primary tenants and those of the entire community.

When done in a creative yet disciplined manner, the tasks of booking and scheduling will yield a diverse program of events that meets the needs of the entire community which the public assembly facility services as well as all of the stakeholders of the facility itself. This involves managing the facility calendar with uncompromising integrity, establishing scheduling priorities, sequencing events into the calendar to yield the maximum number of event days, working closely with the local convention and visitors bureau, avoiding booking errors or mistakes, and respecting the First Amendment rights (United States Constitution) of artists and event producers.

FINANCIAL CONTROLS

Every facility has a business dynamic that includes budgeting, financial accounting, fiscal management, accounts payable, accounts receivable, payroll, human resources, purchasing, asset management and inventory, and audit control. These functions may be under a department called the business office, finance/accounting department, or some other name. The accounting and auditing aspects of revenue-generating activities normally come under the direct supervision of this business office. Business offices often provide accounting and auditing services to the public assembly facility's ticketing activities, especially if financial transactions with the tenant are tied to ticket sales and event settlements. The fiscal management function of a public assembly facility must focus on the financial performance of the public assembly facility as an organization.

Public assembly facilities, regardless of type, should have a business office, or at least one designated individual, available and prepared to handle large amounts of cash. Collecting and accounting for cash, checks, and credit card receipts from sales transactions involving the facility's revenue sources (e.g., ticket sales, concessions, merchandise and parking), making bank deposits, executing wire transfers, reconciling bank statements, and completing post-event financial settlements with event promoters are typical activities performed by business offices or the facility's designated individual responsible for financial matters. While far from the ideal, the designated individual might be the box office manager, the food and beverage manager, the merchandise manager, or the parking manager whose responsibilities include the financial accounting of each of those respective revenue generating functions. Other business office responsibilities may include the preparation, distribution, collection, and reconciliation of cash boxes used in the concessions and other revenue generating operations, or these tasks may be handled directly by the involved department manager. The ultimate responsibility for implementing financial controls lies with the facility's business manager or finance director who ultimately reports to the owner or governing authority through the general manager or executive director.

Cash has traditionally been the most frequent form of payment for tickets, concessions, parking, and merchandise by patrons at public assembly facilities. Ticket sales, however, are moving toward electronic (Internet) and credit purchases, and the consuming public's prolific use of credit cards to pay for telephone, online, and on-site purchases has resulted in the majority of revenues being generated through credit card transactions in many public assembly facilities. One new trend in ticket sales involving credit card transactions can be described as "up selling" or "bundling" wherein customers are encouraged to pre-pay for parking, concessions, and/or merchandise at the time they order their event tickets either online or over the telephone. This is another form of generating additional ancillary revenues by providing convenience to the customers attending events in public assembly facilities.

TICKETING SERVICES

Ticketing services and box office management have evolved greatly over the twenty centuries of known history of the management of public assembly facilities. This evolution has seen the use of color-coded and/or numbered pottery shards, specially minted coins, pre-written or pre-printed hard tickets, and computerized electronic tickets utilizing barcode technology. Regardless of the phase of evolution, the public assembly facility manager utilizes the ticketing process for financial accounting and inventory control. Issuing tickets helps the public assembly facility manager address issues common to virtually every facility type. These issues include managing and controlling admission to the facility while providing a level of financial accountability for the parties involved with presenting and managing the event.

When used to control access to the public assembly facility, tickets provide for the safe, efficient movement of people while communicating venue and event-specific information directly to the customer and in some cases providing a source of revenue to the public assembly facility through advertising.

When used in connection with the process of financial accounting, ticketing services provide management with an accurate accounting of the revenue generated for each event held in the public assembly facility for which tickets are sold as well as an accounting of all taxes collected on behalf of a local or state authority and any ancillary revenues generated through service charges, facility fees, or surcharges on behalf of the public assembly facility.

Tickets are sold using one of three seating arrangements. Whether tickets are sold for reserved seating, general admission, or festival seating depends upon the seating configuration for that specific event held in each type of public assembly facility. The seating configuration and the corresponding capacity are often determined in coordination with the talent, event producer, and/or promoter of the event. The number of tickets sold or the number of guests admitted into an event is limited to the occupancy limit, usually established by the local fire marshal.

Public assembly facility box office managers work closely with event producers/promoters and tenants to establish the value of the various seating locations within the venue. This is described as valuing a seat location and usually involves a process referred to as "scaling the house." Box office managers also work closely with those same clients and the facility's operations manager to ensure that all seating in the public assembly facility is in compliance with the Americans with Disabilities Act (ADA) in the United States or in other countries with similar laws. Providing appropriate signage, appropriate number of seats in each price category, making seats accessible via elevators and ramps, having hearing assistive devices available, designating seating locations for visually impaired guests, and providing spaces for wheelchairs along with seating for companions of the disabled, and having seats with lifting armrests or no armrests are but some of the accommodations that are required by the ADA and are addressed through effective ticketing services.

The Internet and computerization of ticket distribution are revolutionizing the manner in which ticketing services are provided to customers of public assembly facilities. Today's consumer is looking for direct access to the ticketing system 24 hours a day, seven days a week. This includes shopping for tickets and seating locations on the Internet as well as printing event tickets at home or in the office. The trend of vending tickets at higher than face value through the secondary resale market is becoming more widespread and is forcing facility managers, event producers/promoters, and sports teams to reconsider their ticketing prices as well as their ticket distribution systems. As stated previously, the future of ticketing services involves generating ancillary revenues through the sale of products and services at the time of the ticket transaction. The future of ticketing services will continue to be impacted by advancements in technology and the consuming public's demand for newer, more advanced conveniences.

SALES, MARKETING, ADVERTISING, AND PROMOTION

Regardless of type of public assembly facility, the effective use of marketing, advertising, and promotion is crucial in order to favorably present the venue to potential users, customers, guests, and patrons. Marketing is a term that is often used interchangeably with other related terms such as promotion and advertising. The term marketing has been defined in many ways. However, when used within the context of public assembly facility management, marketing can be interpreted to include the process of searching out and identifying potential business for the facility (see Chapter 4 for the American Marketing Association's definition of "marketing"). Marketing also might include involvement in the process of negotiating an agreement for booking an event. Two primary goals of the sales and marketing function within a public assembly facility are to sell space and time in the facility and to generate event activity.

It can be argued there are two basic areas addressed by marketing in the public assembly facility industry. One is the marketing of the facility to the industry in order to secure a diverse schedule of events. Marketing the facility itself as well as the marketplace it serves is directed at potential users such as event producers, commercial event promoters, non-profit community organizations, and meeting planners who provide the supply of events to the public assembly facility industry.

The second area is the marketing of the events to the community which consists of potential ticket buyers, fans, and event attendees. This latter marketing effort is directed toward target audiences (individuals and/or groups), and advertises specific activity, time, place, date, price, etc. This is where the more typical tasks of advertising and promotion are involved.

In addition, it is very important to market the facility and its programs internally to staff, the governing body, owners, tenants, and other major stakeholders. These various individuals and groups need to understand the vision, mission, goals, and objectives of facility management and how they apply to the specific facility. The operating and event staffs are the individuals on the front line interacting with the patrons. They can "make or break" the facility's image, program, and ultimate success. Successful and prudent facility managers ensure that the facility's staff, governing body, owners, tenants, and major stakeholders clearly understand the overall objectives of the facility's programming and marketing strategies.

ANCILLARY SERVICES AS REVENUE SOURCES

The public assembly facility has a similar challenge that all retail businesses have of attracting customers with discretionary time and income to maximize sales of ancillary services, thus generating revenues. Creating product demand and repetitive sales for the special commodities available at public assembly facilities requires a unique type of salesmanship and entrepreneurship. Meeting and exceeding the customer's expectations whenever possible is one of the goals for every public assembly facility manager in providing ancillary event services. Often these services are delivered through a third party contractor using part-time temporary labor, which adds an additional dimension to the responsibilities of the venue manager. Whether these ancillary services are provided to the venue's customers through in-house staff or through a third party contractor, the goal should be to deliver a "value added" experience through the venue's ancillary services.

The most common ancillary services offered to event attendees include food and beverage services (catering and concessions), merchandise/novelty sales, and parking services. Each of these ancillary services generates high volumes of revenues for many public assembly facilities. Each will be discussed in greater depth in Chapter 7.

Some public assembly facilities may have a wide variety of ancillary services available to their tenants in addition to their event customers. Services such as equipment rental, freight handling (drayage), utility services, telephone and Internet hook-ups, decorating services, and event marketing and advertising are offered to assist the tenant in successfully presenting their event while providing the facility manager an opportunity to generate additional revenue.

The scope and number of possible ancillary services are very broad, and many contribute significantly to the facility's overall revenues. Creative entrepreneurship coupled with consistent quality customer service will ensure that the facility's ancillary revenue sources enhance the guests' and tenants' event experience while enhancing the bottom-line of the public assembly facility's overall budget.

FACILITY OPERATIONS

Along with general maintenance and housekeeping duties of the physical plant, the public assembly facility's operations department is usually responsible for the facility's heating, ventilation, and air conditioning (HVAC); utility management, groundskeeping; security and life safety; and a unique unit often referred to as the event production or stage unit. For most touring attractions, it is not economical to bring their own production personnel such as car loaders, riggers, stagehands, deck hands, and forklift operators. Consequently, public assembly facilities are expected to provide these skilled personnel to meet the production needs of those events requiring such services.

Thus, the facility's operations department is the critical unit that ensures "The Show Must Go On!" In busy facilities with frequent changeovers of multiple types of events (e.g. basketball, hockey, concerts, rodeo, wrestling, motor sports, trade shows, and exhibitions), a skilled and motivated operations department carries enormous responsibilities in meeting the facility's contractual obligations and need for competent, quality customer service in a timely and efficient manner.

For all events involving the general public, life safety is a major responsibility of the public assembly facility manager. Although the guests may appear to be the primary focus of such concern, it is important to understand that the public assembly facility manager must also take appropriate and reasonable measures to ensure the safety of the facility's staff, tenants, vendors, and any other occupants. The local fire department may assign a fire marshal to review and approve all floor plans for shows with exhibits that use an exhibit hall or meeting room or stage events using pyrotechnics. This is done to ensure that the aisles are wide enough to handle the anticipated attendance, that exits are kept unlocked and clear of exhibit materials or other barriers, and that other safety issues of this nature are addressed and satisfied. When a fire marshal is assigned to a public assembly facility, the facility may pay a fee for the service. The facility, in turn, may pass this charge along to the user.

NEGOTIATIONS

One of the more important managerial skills that a manager of a public assembly facility must possess is the ability to be an effective negotiator. Negotiation is a part of everyday life for the manager of a public assembly facility. Whether it is a negotiation with a subordinate on the outcomes of a work project or the artist fee and merchandise commission rate with a talent agent, public assembly facility managers must effectively negotiate with others to achieve results that are in the best interest of the facility and the organization managing the facility.

Every facility manager must be able to skillfully negotiate a variety of contracts. Some of the more common types of contracts that facility managers must negotiate include, but are not limited to: rental/lease agreements, service contracts with third party service providers for services such as ticketing, maintenance and food/beverage, and talent contracts/artist agreements with talent agents/ artist managers. The outcomes of negotiations for most contracts have financial implications for the two or more parties negotiating over the specific terms of a contract. It is very important for the facility manager to understand those financial implications as they relate directly to his/her organization and how the outcome of the negotiation will be viewed by the other parties as well as the facility's governing authority. More and more, public assembly facility managers are being judged and evaluated on the financial success or lack thereof of the facility's bottom line.

It must be noted that different facility managers have different levels of authority to negotiate certain aspects of contracts. Some managers have no real authority to commit the resources of the organization in a negotiation. Some managers have the ability to negotiate terms of an agreement, but must then seek final approval from some form of higher authority. Others have both the ability to negotiate the terms of an agreement and to make the final approval of those terms. In some ways, the effectiveness of some public assembly facility managers is reflective of the amount of authority they have to negotiate contracts.

ETHICS

The successful manager develops and abides by a personal code of ethics and demands the same from all employees. (Figures 2-3 and 2-4 provide examples of codes of ethics applicable to public assembly facility managers).

Venue management is a business like any other that provides many opportunities for ethical lapses in judgment. Most public assembly facility managers see a portion of their work as dealing with the entertainment industry. Venues and promoters have a long history of successful relationships, but also at times of

INTERNATIONAL CITY/COUNTY MANAGEMENT ASSOCIATION CODE OF ETHICS

1. Be dedicated to the concepts of effective and democratic local government by responsible elected officials and believe that professional general management is essential to the achievement of this objective.

2. Affirm the dignity and worth of the services rendered by government and maintain a constructive, creative, and practical attitude toward local government affairs and a deep sense of social responsibility as a trusted public servant.

3. Be dedicated to the highest ideals of honor and integrity in all public and personal relationships in order that the member may merit the respect and confidence of the elected officials, of other officials and employees, and of the public.

4. Recognize that the chief function of local government at all times is to serve the best interests of all of the people.

5. Submit policy proposals to elected officials; provide them with facts and advice on matters of policy as a basis for making decisions and setting community goals; and uphold and implement local government policies adopted by elected officials.

6. Recognize that elected representatives of the people are entitled to the credit for the establishment of local government policies; responsibility for policy execution rests with the members.

7. Refrain from all political activities which undermine public confidence in professional administrators. Refrain from participation in the election of the members of the employing legislative body.

8. Make it a duty continually to improve the member's professional ability and to develop the competence of associates in the use of management techniques.

9. Keep the community informed on local government affairs; encourage communication between the citizens and all local government officers; emphasize friendly and courteous service to the public; and seek to improve the quality and image of public service.

10. Resist any encroachment on professional responsibilities, believing the member should be free to carry out official policies without interference, and handle each problem without discrimination on the basis of principle and justice.

11. Handle all matters of personnel on the basis of merit so that fairness and impartiality govern a member's decisions pertaining to appointments, pay adjustments, promotions, and discipline.

12. Seek no favor; believe that personal aggrandizement or profit secured by confidential information or by misuse of public time is dishonest.

FIGURE 2-3

IAAM CODE OF ETHICS

- Strive for continued improvement in the proficiency and usefulness of service.

- Maintain the highest ideals of honor and integrity in all public and personal relationships.

- Emphasize friendly and courteous service to the public and recognize that the function of the building is at all times to serve the best interest of the public.

- Exercise fair and impartial judgment in all Association and professional business dealings.

- Maintain the principle of fairness to all.

- Have a firm belief in the dignity and worth of service rendered by the building and have a constructive, creative, and practical attitude.

- Refrain from any activity that may be in conflict with the interest of the employer.

FIGURE 2-4

---

strained relationships. Entertainment promoters often are small, entrepreneurial companies and executing profitable events is their sole livelihood. It is extremely important that the venue manager cultivate and maintain a reputation for honesty, forthrightness, and consistency in following standard, acceptable business practices in what can, at times, be a somewhat undefined business environment.

Many venue managers are employees of or contractors for governmental entities such as city government or state colleges or universities. Service in government carries another dimension of ethical obligations – and many legal/criminal liabilities for misconduct. The codes of ethics of the International Association of Assembly Managers (IAAM) and the International City/County Management Association (ICMA) are shown in Figures 2-3 and 2-4. Note that a theme throughout both documents is the duty to refrain from any conflict of interest, i.e., that is, any activity that may be in conflict with the interests of the venue, managers' employer, or owner of the facility.

MANAGERIAL LEADERSHIP

No matter how the facility's management structure is organized, operating a public assembly facility on a daily basis is very demanding and requires a manager who possesses a unique intelligence combination of a strong IQ (traditional intelligence quotient) and an equally strong EQ (emotional intelligence quotient). These combined forms of intelligence provide the ability to acquire the knowledge base from which the manager can draw upon in order to skillfully manage. Public assembly facility managers who are not capable of quickly recognizing and appropriately responding to existing or foreseeable situations, especially when under pressure, will not survive. Good managers tend to be people-oriented, inquisitive, eager to learn and apply new management and business principles, and intensely devoted to fulfilling their job responsibilities. And in today's competitive environment, the successful manager must also be intelligent, responsive, knowledgeable, persistent, flexible, and an excellent motivator and leader of superior staff.

Successful facility managers possess an extensive understanding of each managerial function associated with the operation of a public assembly facility. Very importantly, they also understand how the facility is organized and how that impacts the operational alternatives. Managers of this stature have acquired their knowledge and experience through varying scenarios. In some cases, a manager may have "come up through the ranks," advancing from an entry-level position to higher or different positions within the organizational structure and then eventually being elevated to facility manager. This form of career development generally ensures that the individual has had personal involvement with many of the facility's operational units and, in all probability, has had the opportunity to work with facility contractual agreements and the process of conducting financial settlements.

Other managers may have developed their careers by starting at mid-level management positions such as facility operations, marketing, or promotions and then being promoted to facility manager. Although "on-the-job training" has proven an effective way to gain information, it is neither the only nor perhaps the most efficient method for gaining the requisite knowledge and leadership training. Similar to trial and error, on-the-job training can sometimes be painful and expensive compared to a well-structured training program. It is critical that the facility's management structure be organized in such a way to include strong, consistent, effective training programs. These programs need to be customized to the job functions, education, and experience levels of the employees involved. Cross training by moving personnel around the various departments is an excellent way in which to impart and continue institutional knowledge within the staff. However, even though there is an element of on-the-job training in all management career development routes, other educational opportunities exist that can impart lifelong learning.

CREATIVE ENTREPRENEURS

Even though a facility's mission may not emphasize the creation of new revenue centers or new revenue streams, skilled facility managers will focus energies toward becoming creative and entrepreneurial in seeking opportunities that will serve to maximize the facility's resources and thereby generate additional income. The creative manager knows how to package a public assembly facility in a way that is attractive to businesses, promoters, and patrons. And the entrepreneurial manager knows how to devise and implement marketing and promotional strategies capable of producing favorable financial results. Increasingly, bottom line financial data are used to evaluate both the manager's and the facility's success or failure. Consequently, both the manager and the facility run the risk of elimination if they do not achieve the economic expectation and thus become an economic drain on their funding source(s).

EFFECTIVE COMMUNICATORS

Effective communication is a key element in successful facility management. Public assembly facility managers must be able to effectively communicate with distinct groups: the owner(s) and governing body, staff, tenants, event presenters, the media, attendees, and the community at large. It is the manager's responsibility to develop and maintain direct and efficient two-way lines of verbal and written communication with each of these groups.

The successful manager is a team leader who can work effectively in the present environment while envisioning and preparing for the future; is a consummate advocate of the public assembly facility and its potential; and is aggressive in striving to achieve announced goals. Managers' visions should both inspire and motivate all within the organization. In addition, the successful manager is not only efficient and productive but also skilled in dealing with delegation of responsibilities, discipline, organization, and creativity, and, most importantly, leading by example.

IAAM AND CONTINUING EDUCATION

The International Association of Assembly Managers (IAAM) (www.iaam. org) offers numerous professional development programs designed to create the knowledge and develop the professional skills of both current and aspiring facility managers. Participation in these programs and similar programs of allied industries also assists the participants with developing an expanded network of colleagues. (Appendix D includes contact information for IAAM and related industry groups).

Programs are available for individuals employed in entry-level public assembly facility positions seeking to develop a career path as well as for executive level managers wishing to expand their professional education. The IAAM's Public Assembly Facility Management School (PAFMS) held at Oglebay Resort in Wheeling, West Virginia, is the only program of its type in North America. Its courses focus on providing the participants with information central to the operation and purpose of each function within a public assembly facility. As a testament to the overwhelming success and popularity of PAFMS, the

PAFMS Board of Regents recently created the PAFMS Graduate Institute for graduates of the two-year PAFMS program. The primary focus of the PAFMS Graduate Institute is to develop current managers and to expand their universe of management and leadership skills and understanding through the experience of the PAFMS Graduate School.

IAAM Europe, in conjunction with IAAM World Headquarters and with the generous help of the IAAM Foundation, recently opened the European Academy for Venue Management (EAVM). The EAVM is a two-year course which, upon completion, gives students an internationally recognized certificate of competence. Curriculum at the EAVM is comprehensive and is tailored to European venue management practices and procedures.

The Senior Executive Symposium held at Cornell University in Ithaca, New York, is focused towards the needs of executive managers. The IAAM also presents the Academy for Venue Safety and Security (AVSS) at the American Airlines Training Center in Dallas/Ft. Worth, Texas. The AVSS provides intensive training in security planning and life safety management for the public assembly venue industry. It also offers the most relevant and current safety and security training offered for individuals in facility management. The dynamic nature of the public assembly facility business perpetuates the need for each of these programs in order to disseminate new concepts and practices designed to increase management consistency, effectiveness, and efficiency throughout the industry.

The IAAM also offers a professional certification program. This program involves the study of extensive industry information assembled by the IAAM which serves to expose the manager to core knowledge components instrumental in successfully managing a facility. To attain certification from this program, candidates must complete the core study component and then successfully complete a personal interview and a comprehensive written examination. Successful candidates are accorded the professional status of Certified Facilities Executive (CFE). The CFE designation is intended to say three important things about facility executives: they are skilled managers, are committed to the industry, and are pledged to continued professional growth and development. Managers who have completed the CFE program are recognized by those within and external to the industry as experts in their profession.

Other educational meetings are devised to address specific topics in response to current events. For example, following terrorist attacks of September 11, 2001, on the New York City World Trade Center, the Pentagon in Washington, DC, and the downing of American Airlines flight #93 in Pennsylvania, the IAAM developed several special seminars that focused on security and crowd management. These were a continuation and expansion of IAAM's crowd management programs. It is crucial that public assembly facility managers understand how current events may serve as a catalyst for change, sometimes rapid change, with respect to the principles and practices associated with public assembly facility management. Advanced technology has allowed some of these seminars to be delivered through audio-Internet conferencing, a format that enables the participants to verbally and visually interact with those presenting the seminar. The IAAM Board of Education recently completed the first three-year cycle of the CoreTrack curricula, featured at IAAM district meetings. The CoreTracks are a series of educational sessions that focus on the four core principles of facility management identified by the Body of Knowledge Task Force in the year 2000. The CoreTrack curricula are also now available on-demand through the IAAM E-Learning Center on the IAAM website.

Finally, a host of management conferences dedicated to the various facility types (stadiums, arenas, performing arts venues, convention centers, university venues) concerning specific and timely topics are also presented each year along with the Annual Conference and Trade Show that features internationally recognized speakers, panel discussion sessions, and workshop activities focusing on topics of importance to the public assembly facility industry.

In addition, the IAAM and the IAAM Foundation have fostered a direct relationship with higher education through assistance with the designing of college curricula, development of study materials, and making available financial grants for the conduct of industry specific research. Entry into this realm of education by the IAAM is significant because, in the past, colleges and universities had independently developed facility management courses that were included among required core courses for degree granting curricula such as sport management, sport and entertainment management, sport administration, art administration, performing arts management, and convention and meeting planning.

SUMMARY

The public assembly facility is a complex organization that requires the delicate balancing and leveraging of many relationships. Managers of public assembly facilities must be effective leaders who are self-motivated and focused. They must be well equipped through knowledge, education, and experience to accept the challenges presented by new events, new technology, and changing societal practices and standards and use them as vehicles to enhance both the image and productivity of the facility.

Public assembly facility owners must understand it is neither safe nor productive to subscribe to the "build it and they will come" theory. While the building may serve as the physical site for accommodating events, it is the quality and efficiency of the personnel employed by the facility that determines the satisfaction level perceived by the facility's various users. This team must be carefully developed employing both full-time and part-time personnel possessing varied skill sets and who understand their role in providing a positive experience for all users.

It is extremely important to understand that personnel employed in the lowest level position on the organizational chart typically have the greatest number of personal contacts with the facility's users. And quite often it is these individuals, many of whom may be part-time employees, who establish through their interaction the basis for an event attendee's positive or negative perception of the public assembly facility and the events it presents.

To re-emphasize, the public assembly facility manager is responsible for the organization's five core functions: administration; financial controls; sales; marketing, advertising, and promotion; ancillary services as revenue sources; and facility operations. Additionally, the manager must act as a leader to ensure that each functional area is properly staffed and that it performs at the level necessary for the facility to achieve its performance objectives.

Simply put, organizing for success starts at the top of the organization. Public assembly facility managers committed to this principle are well on the way to developing an efficient team of employees and to establishing a positive relationship with all of the constituents and communities involved.

REFERENCES AND ADDITIONAL READINGS

Allison, Michael and Jude Kaye. 2003. *Strategic Planning for Nonprofit Organizations: A Practical Guide and Workbook*, 2nd ed. Hoboken, NJ: John Wiley & Sons, Inc.

Bryson, John M. and Farnum K. Alston. 2004. *Creating and Implementing Your Strategic Plan: A Workbook for Public and Nonprofit Organizations*, 3rd ed. San Francisco: Jossey-Bass.

Bradford, Robert. 2000. Simplified Strategic Planning: *A No-Nonsense Guide for Busy People Who Want Results Fast!* Worcester, MA: Chandler House Press.

Cohen, Allan R. 2002. *The Portable MBA in Management.* Hoboken, NJ: John Wiley & Sons, Inc.

Condrey, Stephen E. (Editor). 2004. *Handbook of Human Resource Management in Government*, 2nd ed. San Francisco: Jossey-Bass.

Cox, Terry B. 1996. *Managing in a Competitive Environment Participant's Guide (Performance Through Participation)*. New York: Van Nostrand Reinhold.

Desseler, Gary. 2005. *Human Resource Management*, 11th ed. Upper Saddle River, NJ: Prentice Hall.

Drucker, Peter F. 1992. *Managing the Non-Profit Organization: Principles and Practices.* New York: Harper Business.

Ellis, Susan J. 2004. *The Volunteer Recruitment (and Membership Development) Book* 3rd ed. Philadelphia, PA: Energize Books.

Fogg, C. Davis. 1994. *Team-Based Strategic Planning: A Complete Guide to Structuring, Facilitating and Implementing the Process.* New York: AMACOM.

George, Stephen and Arnold Weimerskirch. 1998. *Total Quality Management: Strategies and Techniques.* Hoboken, NJ: John Wiley and Sons, Inc.

Jewell, Don. 2003. *Public Assembly Facilities,* 3rd ed. Coppell, TX: International Association of Assembly Managers, Inc.

Lee, Jarene F., Julia M. Catagnus and Susan J. Ellis (Editors). 2004. *What We Learned (The Hard Way) About Supervising Volunteers.* Collective Wisdom Series. Philadelphia, PA: Energize Books.

Little, Helen. 1999. *Volunteers: How to Get Them, How to Keep Them.* Naperville, IL: Panacea Press.

Robbins, Stephen P. 2009. *Essentials of Organizational Behavior,* 10th ed. Upper Saddle River, NJ: Prentice Hall.

Wilber, Robert H. (Editor). 2009. *The Complete Guide to Nonprofit Management,* 3rd ed. Hoboken, NJ: John Wiley and Sons, Inc.

CHAPTER 3

SCHEDULING FACILITIES AND BOOKING EVENTS

CHAPTER OUTLINE

INTRODUCTION

EVENT BOOKING

THE IMPORTANCE OF BOOKING

BOOKING POLICIES AND PROCEDURES

SCHEDULING

USER PRIORITIES

CONVENTION AND VISITORS BUREAUS

BOOKING

PRIME TENANTS AND MAJOR ANNUAL EVENTS

HOLDING DATES

TIMELY MANAGEMENT INFORMATION

DATE PROTECTION

CHALLENGING HOLD DATES

CONTRACTING

FIRST AMENDMENT ISSUES

SUMMARY

INTRODUCTION

Since time and space are the primary commodities of the public assembly facility, it is essential to understand the value of these assets and their perishable nature. Accordingly, the scheduling calendar which manages the facility's space and time is the most important tool for the booking manager to utilize in controlling and coordinating these assets. This instrument and its inventory of dates must be closely managed with uncompromising integrity and accuracy to maximize profitability and minimize negative client relations.

This chapter examines the principles and practices of scheduling and booking events, industry relationships, and the processes that are required to secure event activity. Discussions include the development and sequencing of the scheduling calendar, fitting events into the calendar, and the involvement of the convention and visitors bureau in sales. Issues related to the establishment of scheduling priorities, the First Amendment rights of the United States Constitution, and the holding and contracting of dates are discussed. Attention is also directed toward booking errors, the potential risks and liabilities associated with scheduling and booking, and other aspects of the scheduling and booking processes.

EVENT BOOKINGS: IT'S WHY YOU ARE IN BUSINESS

One of the greatest challenges of any public assembly facility manager is to book a full and diverse schedule consistent with the mission and public purpose of the facility and the economic expectations that govern its operations. Competition for viable events in publicly managed facilities in most markets is intense as is the competition for audiences among organizations which own their own venue such as theater companies and symphony orchestras. So how does one succeed in this area? A PAF manager must possess certain qualities that are critical to successfully booking events. These qualities include the following:

- Widespread industry presence
- Active and well maintained industry relationships
- Knowing the key contacts
- Honesty and integrity that instill trust on the part of show/event promoters and producers
- Knowing how to negotiate acceptable deals
- Managing the facility in a way that delivers or exceeds expectations and promises
- Having the in-house staff to help advertise and promote events
- Being willing to take some risk as a co-promoter, if permitted

Ultimately, the key to a facility's success will be the ability to effectively compete for events desired by its ownership and the marketplace in general. This is — when all else is said and done—why you are in business. It is your very basic public purpose.

THE IMPORTANCE OF EVENT BOOKING

Event activity is important to the communities served by public assembly facilities for many reasons. Here are some of the most common:

- Quality of life
- Putting the facility "on the map"
- Attracting outside dollars into the community to generate economic impact
- Meeting the demands of the corporate community to help attract and retain the necessary workforce at all levels
- Cultural enhancement
- Helping to fill hotel room nights and attract tourists

Events are the key ingredient that drives all revenue so just for economic viability, events are critical to a facility's success.

BOOKING POLICIES AND PROCEDURES

Most facilities have a set of booking policies and procedures which are approved by the governing body. While the policies and procedures spell out the ideal priority by which dates are assigned, a great deal of flexibility is required in areas such as rental rates and cost reimbursements, set-up and teardown time, and switching dates if necessary to achieve a realistic maximum level of desired event activity.

SCHEDULING

Booking events and scheduling the facility are key responsibilities of a public assembly facility manager. Scheduling may be interpreted in more than one way. From one perspective, scheduling is the process for making all event dates fit with each other. For example, the process is employed when dealing with sports teams and concert productions in order to make sure the event dates are compatible with each other. Put another way, scheduling is, in part, the "strategic planning and decision-making involved in determining the type of events and the timing of their use of the facilities." (Smith, 2008)

Perhaps the key distinctions are that scheduling involves the creation of a strategy to identify desired events and those normally scheduled during the year. Booking is putting the strategy into motion. More generally, however, booking refers to the act of soliciting events to meet the programmatic and financial projections of the facility by providing the best possible mix of events for the community. All facilities book space in some manner, regardless of whether they have the capability to promote or co-promote events.

Achieving a diversified program can only be accomplished through appropriate and proper scheduling. Thus, scheduling is the process of fitting events into the times and spaces available within a facility's calendar. Events must fit the facility physically, its purpose, and the community it serves. Care must be taken at all times to ensure that events are compatible with local, regional, and national holidays; vacation patterns of area residents; or special days celebrated within the community. In addition, all other activities outside the community, but within the region that might impact an event's success must be taken into consideration when developing the public assembly facility's schedule.

For example, scheduling a symphony orchestra performance on the same evening when 80,000 people will be attending a collegiate football game in a nearby stadium may affect either or both events, depending on how many people are loyal fans of both the symphony and the college team. Nonetheless, the core fact is public assembly facilities are in the business of selling the perishable commodity of time and space. All activity by the facility manager and the facility's staff is focused on this singular objective. Nothing else happens if this is not accomplished. Once an opportunity has passed, it's gone forever.

USER PRIORITIES

Scheduling determines the calendar sequencing of events — sequencing designed to provide the best possible mix of events to meet the needs of the community, the user, and the public assembly facility. A diversified event program, properly scheduled and effectively presented, requires a clear understanding of expectations of the events, the events' consumers, and the public assembly facility's governing body coupled with an understanding of the facility's physical plant and/or personnel limitations. Priorities given to prime tenants or facility users can help ensure a high level of event activity without giving such users exclusive rights. In most cases, priority policies and criteria are defined and written to include time-sensitive thresholds.

A number of variables, such as facility ownership and governance, the community's social and economic climate, the community's demographics, and the availability of attractions as well as ancillary support capabilities, can offer direction and guidance concerning an appropriate event mix and schedule. Attempting to host event types considered unsuitable for the facility and community or that may conflict with the facility's prime tenants could produce negative reactions. (Figures 3-1 and 3-2 depict a booking priority for a convention center and performing arts complex).

Understanding a public assembly facility's public purpose can also assist in resolving booking priority conflicts and revenue distribution issues when they arise. A facility manager caught between a popular basketball coach demanding more practice time and a local entertainment promoter with a "hot" concert

---

BOOKING PRIORITIES FOR A CONVENTION CENTER

FIRST scheduling priority is given to conventions, trade shows, corporate meetings and similar activities that use a minimum of 1,500 room nights during the event and that are not normally open to the general public.

SECOND scheduling priority is given to conventions, trade shows, consumer or public exhibitions and corporate meetings using more than 100,000 square feet and less than 1,500 room nights. Second priority will also be given to events which book either the ballroom plus a minimum of 48,000 square feet of exhibit space, or the ballroom when accommodating a minimum of a 600 person banquet function.

THIRD scheduling priority is given to smaller consumer or public exhibitions, local corporate meetings, special events, banquets, and other activities which primarily draw from or appeal to the general public and/or local attendees.

Scheduling for second priority events will not be confirmed more than 18 months in advance; third priority events will not be confirmed more than 12 months in advance. Both second and third priority events are subject to change to accommodate first priority events unless a License Agreement has already been executed by The Center.

FIGURE 3-1

BOOKING PRIORITIES FOR DENVER'S DIVISION OF THEATRES AND ARENAS

GENERAL

The Director reserves the authority to grant reservations at any time but recognizes that certain priorities have been and are created as contractual or historical priorities including but not limited to, the National Western Stock Show, the Colorado High School Activities Association, and certain established annual events. The Colorado Symphony in Boettcher Concert Hall, Denver Center Attractions in the Buell Theatre, Opera Colorado in the Quigg Newton Denver Municipal Auditorium have right of first refusal in their respective venues. Only Opera Colorado may reserve dates up to 5 years in advance.

Scheduling policy is designed to obtain maximum utilization of the facilities and provide fair and equitable availability to a broad spectrum of sports and entertainment presenters. All events are inclusive of load-in, production, rehearsal, performance, and load-out.
a.   Ten (10) weeks each calendar year shall be available for use at the City's discretion in each facility.
b.   Multi-week - multiple performance events have first priority.
c.   Week long multiple performance events, 6 or more, have second priority.
d.   Multiple performance events, 2 or more, have third priority.
e.   Single performance events have fourth priority.

Reprinted with permission by the Theaters and Arenas Division of the City of Denver.

FIGURE 3-2

should be able to rely on the public assembly facility's mission statement for guidance in establishing and adhering to booking priorities. Of course, any existing contracts may determine which party gets the date. A strong mission statement can be used as the foundation to effectively deter those who would seek to use the facility for unsuitable purposes.

The key to setting some type of priority policy lies in the designated use of the facility. For example, if a performing arts facility is built to serve the local arts community (such as the symphony, ballet, theatre groups, and so forth) then those groups should be given certain priority to reserve space. Priority should be given to convention activity in a convention center, particularly if room/bed tax funds are used to retire the construction debt or to pay operating expenses. On the other hand, the university basketball team should be given priority in a campus arena if the construction of that facility was for the team.

Priorities given to primary facility users can help ensure a high level of event activity without giving such users exclusive rights. In most cases, priority policies are defined and written. If not, they should be. Since community needs and tastes are subject to change, a facility manager must continually monitor them and adjust the public assembly facility's programming accordingly. Thus, as a community's programming interests and social standards evolve, the facility's mission statement should be revisited and changed so that it reflects the needs of the contemporary community. By paying close attention to both the community's evolving needs and available business, the facility manager can guide the facility's governing body, clients, and consumers toward the formation of a revised mission. Revitalization often necessitates adopting an entirely redefined focus and mission statement.

CONVENTION AND VISITORS BUREAUS

Scheduling is common to all facility types. Scheduling for convention business is slightly more complex because the decision-maker(s) must take into consideration the event's short-term impact upon the community in order to assess any effect it may have on the community's long-term needs. Strategically, collaboration among the convention center's general manager, the convention and visitors bureau (CVB), representatives from area hotels, and the local hospitality industry is most important. Typically, the CVB, operating as the marketing arm for long-range events, will market the convention center's calendar for scheduling of events eighteen months into the future and beyond while the facility management team will concentrate on short-term bookings "18 months and in." Frequently CVBs and/or hotels will arrange for group housing accommodations. This process ensures the necessary housing for attendees is available for specific dates of scheduled conventions, conferences, multi-day meetings, and trade shows.

It is paramount that public assembly facility managers accept the responsibility for cooperating with other community entities in an effort to coordinate their facility's use with existing community-wide, long-range goals. At the same time the facility manager may be committed to traditional annual events for which the facility was built. In most cases, a priority is given to the scheduling of dates based on the impact the event has on the number of hotel nights that can be guaranteed by the attendees or delegates that accompany a given convention. These major conventions are scheduled with lead times of eighteen months to three years or longer and are actually placed on the facility's calendar before smaller conventions, conferences, multi-day meetings, and trade shows.

THE EVENT BOOKING PROCESS

One of the most critical responsibilities of a management team is the process of booking and scheduling events and negotiating user contracts. Booking is the process of identifying desired events or activities appropriate for the public

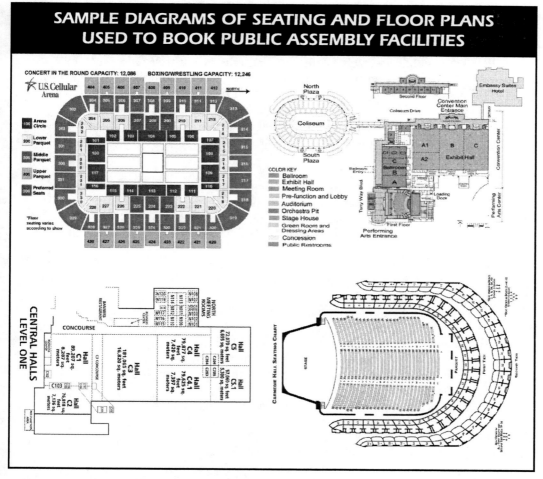

Clockwise from top left: arena, complex with multiple facilities, theater, and exhibit hall.

FIGURE 3-3

assembly facility and the community, contacting owner(s) or promoter(s), and engaging in negotiations leading to a contract with the event or activity to appear in the facility. From the perspective of both the public assembly facility manager and the event or activity's promoter, determining the "when," the "where," and at "what cost" are the prime decisions in the booking process.

A promoter will not contract with a facility for the appearance of an event or activity until first assured the venue is appropriate, available, and economically viable. In similar fashion, a tradeshow promoter is not able to attract exhibitors without knowing the specific date(s), location(s), and costs of the show. Producing an event might include advertising, ticketing, marketing and promoting, staffing, and rentals considerations. All of these are critical to the success of the event and hinge on the booking process. The end of the booking process is the beginning of the production process and the ultimate deliverable outcomes by facility operations. (Figure 3-3 on the previous page illustrates some sample diagrams of seating and floor plans used to book public assembly facilities).

QUALIFYING THE EVENT

Whether the public assembly facility promotes the event itself (contracts for the event to happen and accepts all of the financial risk), co-promotes the event (contracts for the event but shares the financial risk with the promoter or event producer), or leases the facility (rents space to a tenant/client thereby not incurring any direct financial risk), the public assembly facility's booking manager responsible for scheduling and booking must answer several common questions, including:

- Is the event consistent with the facility's mission and expectations?
- Are the date(s), time(s), and space(s) requested available?
- Does the event fit from a scheduling perspective?
- Is the facility large enough (or too large) to accommodate the event's space requirements?
- Can the facility provide specialized support for the event and reconfigure to meet the event's needs (ice for hockey or dirt for a rodeo or acoustics for a symphony)?
- Will the event conflict with a prime tenant or any other activity?
- Are there similar events so close on the calendar that they could cause a conflict, confuse the public or potential exhibitor base, or generally not serve the best business interests of the facility?
- Can the facility meet the demands of the event such as staffing, changeover, etc?
- Does the person seeking to book space in the facility have the necessary experience, authority, and financial resources?

(See Figure 3-4 for a typical booking memo checklist.)

BOOKING MEMO CHECKLIST

- ❏ Date of inquiry
- ❏ Date(s) of event
- ❏ Specific type of event
- ❏ Areas to be used
- ❏ Hold date(s)
- ❏ Hold status
- ❏ Contact's name
- ❏ Contact's address
- ❏ Contact's phone
- ❏ Contact's fax
- ❏ Contact's email address
- ❏ Set up/Take down schedule

- ❏ Rate quotes
- ❏ Showtime
- ❏ Projected attendance
- ❏ Staffing requirements
- ❏ Equipment needs
- ❏ Show running time
- ❏ Name of artist/show
- ❏ Ticket on sale date
- ❏ Ticket prices/house scale
- ❏ Complimentary/trade tickets (tickets provided in return for goods or services)

FIGURE 3-4

It is the booking manager's responsibility to determine if the potential client actually is legitimate and, in fact, can deliver the event in question. In the interest of fairness, consistency, and good business practice, the facility management should have an application process often referred to as a *license application* for qualifying all new promoters or prospective tenants/clients.

There is a correlation between a facility's success and the processes and procedures by which it accepts business. Experienced, reputable, financially sound promoters are essential. Pre-qualifying potential users before negotiating a contract offer helps to minimize the risk of doing business with promoters or events that are highly likely to fail. (See Appendix A, Figure 3-5 for a sample license application designed to acquire the necessary information). It would probably not be used for former users of the facility. It is advisable to verify a repeat user's qualifying information (i.e. address, bank accounts, insurance underwriter, etc.) on an annual basis. The requested date(s) can still be held on a "tentative" basis during this process.

Business statements, bank and financial verifications, agency verification of previously negotiated contracts, past experience, and recommendations from the manager of former contracted venues are several ways to help determine the applicant's qualification to book an event. There are a number of reasons why potential promoters or meeting planners will request a hold on a date(s) even though they may lack the authority to actually deliver the attraction. While most of the reasons are legitimate, the public assembly facility manager needs to be prudent about overcommitting date inventory without establishing control processes that protect from fictitious holds.

Does the person making the inquiry have the experience and resources to produce the event and the ability to contract the talent and book the space? Utilizing the permit application process, the booking manager can shield the public assembly facility from many problems that might typically arise from dealing with an inexperienced or unscrupulous promoter. At the same time, the booking manager should assist, help develop, and encourage new promoters as much as possible.

Booking managers need to evaluate if there are unusual risks and liabilities associated with a proposed event. They must seek as much information as possible about a specific attraction in order to determine its potential risks and legal, social, and physical liabilities. Is the proposed event one that will cause controversy in the community? Potential controversy, however, should not necessarily result in an automatic rejection. Disallowing an event deemed "inappropriate" by the facility's governing body might be illegal based on the laws and statutes of the legal jurisdiction under which the governing body operates. In addition, denying the event may ultimately prove expensive and embarrassing if the promoter seeks relief in the courts.

Refusing to book an event solely based on the management's or governing body's perception of its content might be construed as a violation of the promoter's and the event's right to free speech which in the United States is guaranteed under the First Amendment of the United States Constitution. Court charges, assessed penalties and fines, and a damaged relationship between the facility's manager and the event's promoter frequently result from hasty knee-jerk decisions.

In matters of taste, treading softly is generally the prudent course of action. Three critical issues booking managers must determine about each inquiry received are: Is the proposed event safe? Is it legal? If not, can it be made safe and/or legal? If an attraction can be made safe and legal and is not in direct violation of the public assembly facility's policies and procedures, the booking manager should give the application the same consideration accorded all other inquiries.

Booking the facility actually involves more than simply "answering the telephone." Booking the facility is about relationships, trust, and accountability as partners. Booking begins with an event's promoter contacting the public assembly facility's booking manager for *avails* (available dates). It is the booking manager's responsibility to ensure future business by cultivating potential event owners and promoters. A competent, experienced booking manager will seek to create new and/or alternative opportunities.

The facility should provide an environment that encourages maximum profit with minimum risk to both the promoter and the facility. Essential elements in nurturing the relationship between an artist's or event's promoter and the facility's booking manager include maintaining close contact with these individuals and being constantly aware of available touring attractions and potential convention/conference/multi-day meeting/tradeshow clients. Public assembly facility clientele must experience a sense of trust and partnership if the relationship is to yield productive outcomes.

Ultimately, more events are booked by promoters who trust the facility management team and who believe their best interests and the interests of their event will be best served. In this sense, reputation and personal relationships become paramount to ongoing repeat business.

RESPONSIBILITY FOR BOOKING

The responsibility for booking and scheduling events should be focused on one primary member of the organization who actually controls entries and deletions in "The Book" (actual book or computerized system). This person may be the general manager, a director of event bookings, a director of sales and marketing, or some other similar title. In some cases, an administrative assistant or booking manager will assist in this process by assuming responsibility for the following functions:

- Offering "avails" (i.e., available dates) by phone/email
- Issuing standard license application forms to new (prospective) tenants
- Conducting background reference checks
- Issuing standard rental (license) agreements
- Ensuring that executed agreements along with required deposits and certificates of insurance are received as required and on time
- Answering routine tenant questions

(See Figure 3-6 for a sample booking memo.)

SAMPLE BOOKING MEMO

Show Date(s): _____

Show Time: _____   If event has more than one show time, refer to event data sheet.

Schedule: _____

Music Genre: _____   Plan (Hall Layout):_____   Expected Attendance: _____

TERMS

Lease Start Date: _____   Lease End Date: _____

Rental Rate: _____

Box Office Rate:

Deposit of: _____to be returned by: _____. A second deposit of _____ due by _____.

Additional Deposit Notes:_____

PROMOTER/AGENT   Signator: _____

Company:_ _____

Contact: _____   Address:_____

Phone: _____   _____

Fax: _____   Permit App Received / Approved for Use

EVENT TICKETING   Ticket Header

Pricing Scales: _____

_____

_____

Total Capacity Holds: _____

                                                  Discounts: _____

On Sale Date: _____

FIGURE 3-6

Prime Tenants and Major Annual Events

Many facilities must contract and develop their annual and long-term schedule of events around one or more prime tenants, such as

- Sports franchises
- College/university team(s)
- Symphony orchestra
- Opera Company
- Ballet Company

In what always amounts to a give-and-take process, the prime tenant will typically provide the facility with requested date holds—usually for 30 percent or more than the actual dates they will ultimately require. Once the prime tenant's dates are confirmed (by their league or by confirming the availability of musicians, guest artists, soloists, etc.) the venue can begin scheduling other dates around the confirmed anchor attractions.

For arenas and some stadiums, the process gets tricky and often very frustrating due to the requirement or blocking out a number of "possible" post-season playoff dates. It is often the case that if a team is not eliminated from the playoffs until late in the regular season, there will simply not be enough time to book events much less conduct an adequate promotion and marketing campaign to actually sell tickets.

Still, a prime tenant is very important to the economic viability of most facilities because they offer the following benefits:

- Guaranteed number of events each year
- They significantly enhance the value of certain commercial rights such as
  - Naming and beverage rights
  - Advertising signage
  - Premium seating such as
    - Suites
    - Club seats
    - Loge boxes
    - Party suites
- They generate media coverage and exposure for the facility in its market
- They are the best and most reliable driver of ancillary event revenues such as concessions and parking.

Even in catering to a prime tenant's needs, most arenas block out four or five weekends per year to present long-run family shows or occasionally one-of-a-kind special events. Likewise, performing arts venue managers will reserve prime dates for commercial touring productions while still hosting a non-profit performing arts organization's season events.

HOLDING DATES

A promoter may *reserve* (hold) space in a facility at three distinct levels: *tentative, confirmed* (contract out), or *contracted*. While different facilities or facility types may have different names for these levels (for example firm, pencil in, definite, etc.) and some may have intermediate levels, ultimately there remain only three distinct categories.

The booking agent attempting to *route an event* (booking agent jargon for getting from place to place in the most expeditious manner) will ask the booking manager to place a tentative hold for an open date(s) on the facility's calendar. This tentative hold simply tells the booking manager that the event is interested in appearing in the public assembly facility.

Once the booking manager agrees to hold a specific date, the promoter automatically assumes the event will occur on that date(s), that there are no scheduling conflicts, that the facility will host the event, and that the date(s) will remain on hold for a predetermined period of time and not be reassigned to any other event without agreement with the event's owner or promoter.

The booking manager, by placing this hold on a date(s), signifies the belief that the promoter is serious about producing the attraction and also that the promoter will release the date(s) promptly whenever it is deemed no longer viable. Of course, there is the possibility that a promoter may not release a hold under these circumstances.

Experienced managers have a policy of deadlines whereby holds are automatically released (for example, I'll hold for xx days and then make the date available to others). It is very common for multiple dates to be held by different promoters for the same act. Therefore, it is extremely important that holds are act-specific. If a date is being held by promoter A for act Z and promoter A loses act Z to promoter B, then promoter A also loses control of the date. Whoever gets the act gets the date.

Efficiently routing shows to various non-competitive facilities in various geographical areas is a difficult task. There are many moving parts that must come together. As a result, while it is prudent for a public assembly facility manager to have the automatic cut-off built into the hold date(s), the intelligent manager should be willing to extend that date upon request whenever the event is desired and the booking process is viable and continuing. Granting extensions is also beneficial in maintaining a good relationship with the promoter.

Once routing is completed and the exact date(s) have been negotiated and chosen for the event, the booking manager should be notified so any unused held dates are released and returned to inventory. When a hold is confirmed, a contract is negotiated and issued with a deadline for its return along with a rent deposit and an insurance certificate. When the signed contract and deposit are returned, the event's status becomes "contracted." (See Appendix C, Contract Components.) Any remaining holds for the now confirmed event are released at the point of contracting and the dates are reclassified as open and offered to potential users as the process begins anew.

TIMELY MANAGEMENT OF INFORMATION

Giving specific deadlines for potential users to provide/return information, contracts, deposits, etc., increases the facility manager's abilities to control the dates and the process. If a deadline is missed, the date(s) become available to commit to other potential users. (See Figure 3-7 for the process of holding space/date.)

HOLD IS	PROCESS SEQUENCE	PROCEED OR STOP	
TENTATIVE		YES	NO
	Inquiry - Is date available?	——	——
	Is attraction desired?	——	——
	Potential user qualifies?	——	——
	Basic contract terms agreed?	——	——
		If answers are all YES, proceed. If any answer is NO, stop at that point. No hold is given.	
	Give "tentative hold" for X days (subject to challenges)		
CONFIRMED (Contract Issued)	Promoter qualified. Contract terms agreed. Contract issued. Return required in X days. Deposit required with contract.	Stop process if any deadline is not met unless promoter has requested and manager agrees to an extension of time.	
CONTRACTED	Contract signed & returned. Deposit returned with contract (Subject to bank clearance). Facility signs contract.	Contract follow-up: internal processes to prepare for event and production begins.	

Sample process of holding space/date.   **FIGURE 3-7**

The public assembly facility industry is one of leverage and relationships. The booking process is a prime example because of the level of trust that must exist between booking managers and promoters for the system to work. The importance of clearly defined booking policies and procedures can never be overstated. While no formal agreement may exist that requires booking managers and promoters to abide by the rules, there are definite penalties, in this relatively closed professional area, for those who do not. If a promoter cannot trust a booking manager's word, the promoter has little choice but to bypass the facility. Conversely, booking managers may require a non-refundable deposit for a tentative hold date(s) if they believe a routing agent lacks the proper understanding of and respect for the booking process or is unwilling to abide by the spoken, or unspoken, rules. As within any select community, word "gets around" quickly about who is or is not trustworthy.

One thing is very clear and that is the need to place the responsibility for actually entering and removing events from the official schedule in the hands of one responsible party, if for no other reason than to avoid double bookings or to lose a booking altogether and risk being in contractual violation.

DATE PROTECTION

Facilities are often confronted with multiple requests for proximate dates for shows that appeal to essentially the same audience or exhibitor base. This typically is not in the facility's best business interest, and it also often serves to confuse the public. For example, booking two circuses in the same month or two country concerts in the same week is generally not considered a wise practice except possibly in a unique or the largest of markets. To avoid such conflicts and preserve financial viability, some public assembly facility governing bodies have instituted scheduling criteria requiring a reasonable degree of separation between similar attractions. Policies of this nature are termed *date protection policies* and are designed to facilitate box office success for all parties. Traditional touring family shows commonly request protection from similar events.

Clearly outlined and fairly enforced protection policies tend to be good tools for enhancing the success of an event. (See Figure 3-8 for a sample date protection and event spacing policy.) However, providing protection as a matter of policy can also be the root of problems. For example, a booking manager, working with a policy that provides a two-week window of protection, books a small attendance, local wrestling card. Shortly thereafter the manager discovers an opportunity exists to host a major national professional wrestling show. But, in order to book the major show, the two-week window of protection policy would have to be violated. What should the manager do: abide by the protection policy and lose the bigger production or ignore the policy and schedule both events?

SAMPLE DATE PROTECTION AND EVENT SPACING POLICY

DATE PROTECTION POLICY
When comparable events request the same dates, preference on dates is given in order of requests. The Civic Center will attempt to provide protection before and after events to competitive shows.

EVENT SPACING POLICY
Event spacing shall apply to events which have twenty percent (20%) or more similar exhibitors, as determined by The Center; are charging an admission to gain entry to the show and/or are open to the general public rather than being limited to a well-defined class of persons who normally belong to a trade or professional association.

Similar shows renting the entire ballroom or more than 30,000 gross square feet of exhibit hall space and which are actively competing for specialized and specific local markets shall maintain the following clearance periods prior to the first show day and following the last show day of booked events:

- 45 Days: Public/Consumer shows; e.g., boat shows, RV shows, home shows, car shows, sportsmen shows, nursery/garden shows, business/office/computer shows, etc.
- 30 Days: Hobby/arts and crafts; e.g., antique shows, food shows, collectibles, auctions, bridal shows, career fairs, etc.
- Events not falling into any of these event categories will be spaced at the discretion of The Center.

FIGURE 3-8

A situation of this nature requires a manager to demonstrate a delicate touch and creative flexibility. Possible best solutions include the facility manager offering to reschedule the lesser event for a later date, perhaps at a reduced rental rate. If this approach is not acceptable, the manager might then offer to buy out the lesser act or make some other accommodation.

It is advisable for any protection policy to be reviewed and approved by the facility's legal counsel to ensure against any form of liability or damages.

The open date inventory of a public assembly facility's event calendar is sometimes referred to as avails. These dates are constantly discussed by potential users and booking managers in person or via fax, phone, or e-mail. Computer software programs may allow viewing of the facility's calendar through the public assembly facility's Internet home page. Some of these computer calendar programs also permit prospective users to view the event calendar, initiate reservation inquiries, and gather rental rate information without ever having to talk with the facility's booking manager.

CHALLENGING HOLD DATES

Prospective tenants desiring a date(s) held by another promoter might ask the booking manager for a second hold or issue a challenge for the date(s) sought. (See Figure 3-9 for a tentative hold process). A second hold enables the requesting promoter to immediately gain top priority if the event promoter currently

PROMOTER	REQUEST	ACTION
PROMOTER "A"	Requests tentative hold on date(s).	Grants tentative hold if date is available, attraction desired, user qualifies and basic contract terms agreed. Hold has deadline to go to contract and is subject to challenge.
PROMOTER "B"	Challenges Promoter "A's" hold on date(s). (Assume Promoter "B" meets criteria for contract). Manager may require "B" to provide a non-refundable deposit and understand that s/he will have to go to contract immediately if the date(s) becomes available.	Manager notifies Promoter "A" of challenge and gives a short deadline to receive contract, sign and return with deposit. If "A" cannot, or will not, commit to contract, manager may declare tentative hold is cancelled and available to Promoter "B."

Sample process of a tentative hold   **FIGURE 3-9**

possessing the hold date(s) relinquishes it or doesn't meet the facility's timelines. When a challenge occurs, the facility's booking manager contacts the promoter who has the first hold on the date and announces that another promoter is seeking the same date(s). The tentative hold promoter then must either enter into a contract for the date(s) within 24 (48, 72) hours or remit a non-refundable deposit within 24 hours in order to keep the tentative hold status. If the original promoter does neither, the date(s) are relinquished and awarded to the challenger. The facility may require the challenger to remit a deposit, up to the minimum rental fee, prior to contacting the first hold promoter to ensure the challenge is a legitimate one and not just a means to control dates. The challenging promoter should be required to immediately go to contract if the date(s) becomes available.

It is not unusual for concert promoters, for example, to attempt to tie up facilities with tentative holds. If successful, the promoter is then able to go to the act/artist's agent with that leverage to gain an advantage in competing with other promoters for the act/artist. Facility managers might follow a policy that sets the date aside, for whoever gets the act, when a major act/artist is known to be touring. A key consideration is that facility managers structure the process so that they control the facility's schedule and do not allow others to gain that control.

A challenge may only be issued against a "tentative" hold. If a contract has been sent to a potential user for a date(s), that promoter has until the stated deadline to sign and return the contract along with any required deposit. Of course, if the deadline is missed, the date(s) becomes available for the facility manager to allocate as desired.

NOTE: In Figure 3-9, promoter "A" should be told that if Promoter "B" does not meet his/her deadline, the tentative hold will be reinstated for Promoter "A" with the same original timeline. For example, Promoter "A" is originally given a ten-day hold. The challenge by "B" occurs on day two and the facility cancels "A's" tentative hold on the third day. If "B" fails to perform, "A" should again have the tentative first hold with seven days to perform. Of course, in all instances, the facility manager sets the deadlines. Circumstances will determine how much time and leeway to give to promoters during this process.

CONTRACTING

Once the promoter agrees with the conditions of use for a public assembly facility and the hold is confirmed, the booking manager, using the information previously recorded in the booking memo, will issue a contract. The specific details of the agreement should be itemized succinctly and include, but not be limited to, the name of the event or attraction, the date and times of occupancy, the contracted space or premise, and the financial deal. Additional language should be included stipulating such items as deadline for contract return, expiration dates, lead time for delivery of insurance and performance riders, overtime charges, merchandizing rights and fees, equipment service and labor rate card references, etc., along with applicable boilerplate language that establishes fundamental performance expectations while occupying the facility. This initiative will constitute an offer. Before the agreement becomes legally binding, the recipient must accept the offer and provide consideration in the form of a deposit or collateral.

When the signed contract and deposit are returned, the event's status becomes contracted and the event management process begins. (See Appendix C - Contract Components.) While it may appear the public assembly facility has nothing to lose in a straight rental scenario, it is very important for the commercial promoter to also enjoy success. The long-term success of many public assembly facilities depends upon repeat business, and the only way for that to happen is for the facility owners to adopt operating philosophies that allow both the public assembly facility manager and the event promoter a reasonable chance to succeed. If promoters are successful, they tend to come back. If they're not, they'll go elsewhere or they go out of business. Success breeds success.

Creating the proper business relationship with each of the facility's clients is the responsibility of public assembly facility management. Although there are various types of clients, such as promoters, presenters, vendors, subcontractors, meeting planners, etc., the objective of developing strong and positive relationships remains constant. It is important that the public assembly facility manager create a sense of partnership even though the official working agreement between client and facility may not call for the sharing of revenue, expenses, or risk. This particular type of partnering requires the sharing of information and ultimately a sharing of concern for the welfare and success of each other. It also requires an effort by each party to understand the problems and concerns of the other, to be willing to share energy and resources whenever possible, and to be creative in looking for a win-win solution to any problem that may arise.

FIRST AMENDMENT ISSUES

A manager may be asked to book an event that, although deemed "safe and legal," is so controversial in nature that hosting it would undoubtedly create problems. Public facility managers and their booking personnel must remember, however, that a "controversial" event may have the same legal protection as any other event. For example, in the United States a controversial event might be protected under the provision of free speech afforded by the First Amendment of the Constitution. (See Figure 3-10 for an example of a facility being sued for violation of First Amendment rights).

While a manager, supported by the facility's policies, may reject any event that might distress either the community or the facility's governing body, the prudent

IN THE NEWS

MARILYN MANSON SHOW CANCELED IN SOUTH CAROLINA IN 1997
April 11 – Columbia, South Carolina has told Marilyn Manson they don't want his type of music in their town, forcing cancellation of a concert that had been scheduled for April 20, 1997. The University of South Carolina and the concert promoter, Cellar Door Productions, canceled the show using a buy-out clause in the contract. State Treasurer Richard Eckstrom, who learned about the band at church, led pressure from religious and political groups to force the cancellation. South Carolina's state legislators introduced a bill to ban the use of any state facility for a concert by Marilyn Manson, and shortly afterwards, the cancellation was announced.

MARILYN MANSON GOES TO COURT AND WINS IN NEW JERSEY
April 28 – Marilyn Manson's attorney filed a lawsuit against the New Jersey Sports and Exposition Authority for refusing to sell tickets to the June 15, 1997, Ozzfest at Meadowlands if Manson was a part of the show. Paul Cambria, the band's attorney, said the plaintiffs allege that the New Jersey Meadowlands is violating Manson's First Amendment rights. The ban on Manson was later overruled in court, finding that banning Manson would violate his First Amendment rights, even though concerns over crowd control and "community standards of decency" were made. Ozzfest went on as planned with Manson as a part of the show.

FIGURE 3-10

manager will not refuse to lease the facility to a third party unless the intended activity is patently illegal or the manager believes it presents a clear threat to public safety. A facility with a history of leasing its public space to commercial promoters is obligated by that history to continue this practice, without regard to performance content, so long as the building's protection policies remain inviolate, space is available, the event is properly scheduled and booked, and the activity is both legal and safe.

The operative word here is content. Neither the booking manager, the facility's governing body, the law enforcement authorities, nor the "community fathers" may discriminate against an event or attraction based strictly on its content. For instance, a facility leasing space to traditional religious congregations cannot legally forbid religious cults from use of the same space even though a majority in the community might disapprove. In this instance, the booking manager would be on more solid legal ground by simply denying use of the public assembly facility for all religious activities rather than trying to accept some while rejecting others.

SUMMARY

The booking and scheduling processes are controls designed to maximize, yet safeguard the facility's two most important commodities: time and space. Efficient management of these elements is vital to maximizing the number of event bookings and the number of potential revenue streams. Booking and scheduling are the processes that result in the programming of a facility's master calendar and should take into consideration the facility's vision and mission statements along with the needs of the community. However, these processes are by no means infallible. Careless management may result in unnecessary errors, such as double booking or overlapping of events. Careful consideration must be given to the safety and legality of an event as part of the booking decision.

Although a public assembly facility manager may not agree with or like the content of a prospective event, freedom of speech may well prohibit the manager from barring the event based on content alone. The baseline question is "What is the manager's role in determining what the taste and values of the community ought to be?" Nonetheless, it is understandable that a manager may seek to protect the public assembly facility from any negative publicity that may be generated as a result of a controversial event. It is also important for the facility's event manager to consider the logistical needs and safety concerns of each event and to determine whether the facility is capable of accommodating the requirements.

When governing bodies institute scheduling criteria requiring a reasonable separation between similar types of events, they are establishing policies referred to as "date protection." Such policies should be written and communicated to any event promoter affected by them and should be reviewed and approved by the facility's legal counsel prior to implementation.

Once the terms and conditions for use of the facility are agreed to by both facility management and the promoter or event producer, such details should be committed to writing through a legal and binding contract. All of the specific details of the agreement should be included in the contract, which should take the form of a legally enforceable document. The event contract forms the business relationship between facility management and the event producer and should, therefore, be as specific and detailed as necessary to protect both parties' interests.

REFERENCES AND ADDITIONAL READINGS

Shagan, Rena. 2001. *Booking & Tour Management for the Performing Arts*, 3rd ed. New York: Allworth.

Smith, Rodney. 2008. *Booking and Scheduling,* unpublished manuscript. Coppell, TX: International Association of Assembly Managers, Inc.

Sonder, Mark. 2003. *Event Entertainment and Production*. New York, NY: John Wiley & Sons, Inc.

CHAPTER 4

SALES AND MARKETING

CHAPTER OUTLINE

INTRODUCTION
MARKETING TO OVERCOME COMPETITION
THE BENEFITS OF MARKETING
MARKETING TO SECURE EVENTS
THE SALES AND MARKETING DEPARTMENT
THE MARKETING PLAN
COMPONENTS OF A MARKETING PLAN
INDUSTRY AND COMMUNITY RELATIONSHIPS
- RELATIONSHIPS ARE KEY
- CUSTOMER SERVICE IS KEY
ADVERTISING AND PROMOTIONS
IN-HOUSE AD AGENCIES
SEASON TICKETS AND SUBSCRIPTIONS
MARKETING OF PREMIUM ACCESS
- PREMIUM SEATING AND LUXURY SUITES
- PRIORITY SEATING
THE SALE OF COMMERCIAL RIGHTS
- NAMING RIGHTS
- TERMS AND CONDITIONS
- COMMERCIAL RIGHTS INVENTORY
- RATE CARD
- FULFILLMENT OBLIGATIONS
- POURING/BEVERAGE RIGHTS
- ADVERTISING SIGNAGE
MISCELLANEOUS COMMERCIAL RIGHTS
- SPONSORSHIPS
- MEMORIAL GIFTS
- BRANDING OF FOOD & BEVERAGE PRODUCTS FOR RESALE
SUMMARY
REFERENCES AND ADDITIONAL READINGS

INTRODUCTION

The difference between success and mediocrity is often the ability of a facility to market and promote itself at the expense of less aggressive but nonetheless competitive facilities within a defined market area.

Many agree that a public assembly facility has no inherent right to exist as an institution unto itself. It is meant to present events and in so doing enhance the quality of life in its community, generate direct and indirect economic impact, and allow its citizens to see sports and entertainment in a safe and comfortable gathering place.

Fulfilling this public mandate is no easy task.   It takes daily effort, commitment, and attention to detail.   In an ever increasingly competitive environment, the most desirable events don't just knock on your door and ask for a contract. Successful event programming involves

- Constant salesmanship
- Industry recognition and profile
- A marketplace that buys tickets
- Cooperation of the media in advertising, promoting, and sponsoring events
- Effective ticket sales and distribution systems
- An enabling and supportive governing body
- Excellent facility management

Sales and marketing is what separates the public assembly facility from other public functions or services. Sales and marketing is the common denominator; every phase of a public assembly facility's operation essentially involves some form of sales and marketing.

Admittedly sales and marketing is a broad and very encompassing term. In the context of public assembly facility management and for purposes of this book, our focus in this chapter is on the sales and marketing of the following:

Sales

- Commercial rights to generate long-term, contractually obligated revenue
  - o   Suites and club seats
  - o   Naming and pouring rights
  - o   Advertising signage
  - o   Branding of food and beverage products
  - o   Memorial gifts

- Season tickets to sporting events and theatrical/entertainment series
- Group tickets to major events
- Event sponsorship
  - o Presenting
  - o Associate
  - o Media

Marketing

- Advertising the facility – locally, regionally, nationally, and, in some cases, internationally
- Advertising and promoting events
- Customer service: capturing and acting on the results of surveys
- Public, media, and community relations
- The atmosphere and amenities of the facility as an enjoyable place to be

The purpose of this chapter is to provide industry practitioners and students with the basics of how an effective sales and marketing department should function.

MARKETING TO OVERCOME COMPETITION

Competition is pervasive throughout society. From the boardroom to the classroom to the playing field, the drive to "get ahead" of your competitors is a message that rings true to people of all ages and backgrounds. The old adage "raising your game" refers to the acknowledgement of your opponent's performance level and the need to raise your own to a matching or higher level. Although this phrase is often used in a sports context, it is also applicable to the public assembly facility management profession. People have more choices than ever when it comes to spending their discretionary income. The performing arts, collegiate and professional sporting events, touring attractions, festivals, and concerts are all viable consumer entertainment options. Live entertainment constantly struggles to convince the ticket buying public to leave their homes rather than watch home entertainment devices such as TV and computers.

Most people are no longer restricted to holidays, vacations periods, or weekends to enjoy their choice of entertainment. For example, business travelers may attend a local theatre production as an out-of-town visitor. Conference, convention, and trade show delegates may attend a nearby college or professional sports event. Meeting planners often incorporate available concerts, theatrical productions, and athletic events with meetings, conventions, conferences, and trade shows as a marketing tool designed to make the overall program more appealing to prospective attendees.

Another example of change that has occurred is the scheduling of concerts, many of which appeal to younger audiences, on nights other than the once traditional

Friday/Saturday, holidays, and school vacation periods. This change is significant as it allows the public assembly facility manager much greater flexibility in booking and scheduling acts and events for these market segments and frees up weekend dates for prime tenant sports franchises, thereby generally enhancing attendance at their games.

The examples above demonstrate that entertainment, as well as sports, conventions, and trade shows, enjoy a high priority with large segments of the population. A further analysis of the state of the entertainment industry will help public assembly facility managers better understand how this popularity may affect the overall management strategy for their facility. The tremendous increase in the number of public assembly facilities in the United States beginning in the 1950s was noted earlier. This rapid expansion was largely the result of flourishing suburban communities building their own public assembly facilities coupled with the construction of numerous other facilities as memorials to World War II veterans. Local governmental bodies were eager to invest their financial resources into the development of new public assembly facilities believing they would serve as economic catalysts for their respective communities due to the conventions, conferences, meetings, trade shows, theatrical productions, and sporting events they would bring to the community. So, not only does the public assembly facility manager need to compete for the time and attention of individuals with too many leisure options in today's society, but also with the ever increasing number of competitive facilities within relatively small regional marketing areas. An effective sales and marketing department is a critical tool in this effort.

THE BENEFITS OF MARKETING

What exactly is marketing? Bearden, Ingram, and Laforge assert the most widely accepted generic definition of marketing is that proffered by the American Marketing Association (AMA) which defines marketing as "the process of planning and executing the conception, pricing, promotion and distribution of ideas, goods and services to create exchanges that satisfy individual and organizational goals." (Bearden, 1995)

The expansion of available public assembly facilities along with escalated competition, relatively fewer attractions, shorter concert tours, and the need to generate profits resulted in the implementation of aggressive sales and marketing strategies. Prudent public assembly facility managers know that waiting for business to appear on the facility's doorstep is nothing short of competitive suicide. Consequently, a well thought-out and orchestrated strategic marketing plan becomes an absolute necessity if the public assembly facility manager is to achieve success.

Marketing plans may be developed to acquire specific events, to support promotions by building tenants (such as sport teams, symphony orchestras, dance companies, etc.), and to promote the public assembly facility itself. Marketing techniques should serve to bolster relationships with many parties including guests, promoters, sponsors, teams, resident companies, elected and appointed government officials, and local businesses. They may also help to accomplish business objectives such as increasing the public assembly facility's attendance figures and/or revenues by a defined percentage, or by simply increasing the community's participation in local programs. Business objectives should be written in a manner that facilitates the measurement and evaluation of achievement.

If a manager really wants to increase the community's awareness of the public assembly facility, the first step could be to conduct a study to determine the community's current awareness level. With that measurement in hand, a marketing program designed to raise the community's awareness level could be developed and implemented. A follow-up study would later be conducted to determine the community's awareness level at that point in time. Comparing the pre- and post-awareness levels would then establish whether the marketing program was successful and, if so, to what extent.

It is important to first identify the target audiences and the events or facility spaces to be sold. Most public assembly facilities are concerned with selling facility time and space to promoters for the purpose of producing events. In some instances, the facility sells the tickets to the public in order to "fill seats." Some public assembly facilities are taking over the role of the producer and are assuming the associated risks. In other instances, the facility's role is more that of a landlord. The tenant/promoter, such as a sport team, convention/exhibit firm, resident company, touring show, or concert promoter, etc., is responsible for ticket sales that may be handled in-house or more likely contracted out to a third party ticketing service. Whether the facility actually sells the tickets or not, it still should "sell" the facility and the event so the public will want to buy the tickets.

Thus, when applying the AMA's marketing definition to the public assembly facility industry, the events produced or the facility itself can be identified as the goods and services that the manager must conceptualize, produce, promote, and ultimately sell to the consuming public, to a promoter/presenter, or to both. The exchange may be represented by rental fees, ticket sales, and ancillary revenue from sources such as parking, food and beverage, and merchandise. A marketing plan provides a vehicle for managers to drive sales by balancing the political and economic realities of the owner with competitive demands of the market place.

MARKETING TO SECURE EVENTS

The primary purpose of any public assembly facility is to book viable events that draw high levels of attendees.

Regardless of the facility type, there should be a person(s) that is focused on this responsibility. This could be the general manager, a booking assistant, a director of sales and marketing, or various sales managers at a convention center that focus on national, regional, state and local businesses.

A key to successfully booking events is established industry relationships. The most successful facilities have several common characteristics that include the following:

- A well respected, high industry profile sales/booking team that serves as a magnet for events.
- Solid and continuously reinforced relationships with entities that control event bookings such as artist reps, talent agencies, promoters, show producers, association executives, sports leagues, and many others.
- Effective working relationships with local stakeholders that help make events successful, such as convention and visitor bureaus (CVBs), chambers of commerce, hotel-motel associations, downtown retail accommodations, and the like.
- Pursuing local media relationships that allow for the delivery of effective advertising, marketing, and promotional campaigns that sell tickets and/or deliver to the desired audience.
- Cooperative relationships with local police and fire agencies to ensure easy access to the facility and exiting after the conclusion of an event.
- Great costumer service to the tenants and the audience resulting in high levels of satisfaction and repeat business.

Developing positive relationships requires hard and constant effort. There are so many competitive facilities, of any venue type, in each market that nothing can be taken for granted. You need to ask, negotiate and deliver – again, again, and again!

Event booking is more of an art than a science. Booking a well-rounded schedule of events that attempts to both satisfy the different demands of the market populations while still producing a reasonably positive bottom-line is tricky business. Knowledge of the market's demographics and how to target and reach the right audience for each event is critically important.

The ability to balance the demands of competing event promoters with what is in the best business interest of a facility is also a key to success. Similar shows booked too closely together often cause confusion, lower attendance at each event, and reduced revenue to the facility as a result. Proper spacing and balance give discretionary income a chance to regenerate or it allows exhibits to focus on one show rather than diluting its efforts and presence at multiple shows in the same time period.

The Sales and Marketing Department

A vital part of many public assembly facilities is the sales and marketing department. While job titles may vary by facility type, overall responsibilities include

- Sell advertising signage, sponsorships, premium seating, naming and pouring rights, and other commercial rights.
- Assist with booking of events in some but not all instances.
- Assist in the advertising, marketing, and promotions of events through an in-house ad agency.
- Sell group tickets.
- Place event-related advertising.
- Conduct marketing and customer satisfaction surveys.
- Maintain positive on-going publicity, media, and community relations.
- Arrange for industry-wide publicity of the facility and its events; achieve consistent, positive, and high profile public/industry awareness.
- Place industry advertising for the facility.
- Oversee web site content and design.
- Arrange for the design, printing, and distribution of brochures and other collateral materials.
- Coordinate marketing efforts with local CVB and other appropriate groups.
- Manage and administer any outside advertising agency contract(s).

Ultimately, the job of the sales and marketing department is to induce sales. In other words, their focus should be to sell time and space in every facility, sell every ticket to every event, sell ancillary products, and sell premium access.

The Marketing Plan

Ideally, every public assembly facility, regardless of type, should have a marketing plan and marketing staff in place. The marketing plan presents a strategy for positioning the public assembly facility within the marketplace in order to maximize its business potential and to accomplish its established performance objectives. A sales plan is part of a marketing plan; it's one of the ways the marketing plan is carried out.

While marketing tactics may vary among organizations, the need for effective marketing has taken on a tremendously important role for all public assembly facility organizational formats. Consumers of leisure time activities and events enjoy a continually expanding number of available options for spending their discretionary monies. This escalation in opportunities serves to further increase the level of competition among public assembly facilities for the available events and patrons. Each public assembly facility, as part of its marketing plan, must address several questions that get to the heart of its competitive standing. These include

- What makes this facility different from its competitors?
- Why should event promoters and organizers book this facility rather than a competitor's facility?
- What effective strategies can be employed to maximize ticket sales and attendance?
- What are strengths and weaknesses?
- What competitive threats exist?
- What competitive opportunities are available?

How does a public assembly facility manager construct a marketing plan? First and foremost, the facility manager should remember that the purpose of the marketing plan is to guide the establishment of market position that achieves stated objectives that are in concert with the facility's purpose and mission statements. Stotlar (1993) indicates that all business entities exist to realize such objectives and that the marketing plan is the planning process used to accomplish them.

The manager should examine the facility's mission statement carefully in order to determine what business objectives to pursue consistent with the purpose of the facility. For example, does the mission statement specify that earning a net operating surplus is an objective? And if making a profit is indeed an objective, to what extent or level should it be pursued? Does the mission statement denote a minimum number of event dates that must be booked per year? Are specific events mandated? Information of this nature is extremely useful when determining where marketing energies and resources should be focused.

Numerous books and guides devoted to the process of writing effective marketing plans currently exist. Nevertheless, what the public assembly facility manager needs is a plan that is practical and applicable in a variety of business environments. Most importantly, the plan must be tailored to fit the unique local market condition.

COMPONENTS OF A MARKETING PLAN

Introduction/Executive Summary

- Brief history of the facility
  o When it was built
  o Ownership
  o Management
- Restatement of public purpose and/or mission
  o Events
  o Realistic financial condition
  o Justification of public subsidy
- Review of core business and schedule of events
- Review of "lost business," i.e., desired events that were not booked and why. Some reasons for lost business include
  o Seating capacity
  o Rigging capacity
  o Square footage
  o Need for capital improvements, repairs, maintenance
  o Team/dressing rooms
  o Ceiling height
  o Rental rates
  o Move-in/move-out policy
  o Responsiveness of the marketplace
  o Date availability
  o Local taxes on tickets
- A plan/recommendation on how to specifically overcome each of these problem areas
- Review of marketing staff by function and position responsibilities
- Goals for the coming years, such as
  o Number of events booked
  o Advertising dollars to be placed on behalf of promoters
  o Commissions to be earned on ad placements
  o Square footage to be rented (as a percentage of total)
  o Total commercial rights sales
  o Target dollars for group ticket sales
- Description of industry advertising and marketing campaign to be conducted
  o Placements
  o Publications
  o Frequency
  o Reach
  o Anticipated results
  o Review of marketing message
- Specific strategies to employ against direct competitors
- Entertainment goals

- o   Media
- o   Advertisers and sponsors
- o   Donors (if applicable)
- o   Major group clients
- o   Season ticket holders
- Website enhancements
- Joint marketing plan with CVB
  - o   Sales
  - o   "Fam" tours
  - o   Tradeshow participation
  - o   Facility tours
  - o   Joint advertising
  - o   Joint collateral material
- Any other relevant information that will measure performance and results for the upcoming year.

INDUSTRY AND COMMUNITY RELATIONS

When the terms sales and marketing are mentioned, many individuals immediately think of advertising and promotional efforts. However, it is important not to overlook the need for nurturing personal relationships with guests, teams, resident companies, government officials, business leaders, meeting planners and association executives, and vendors as well as the general ticket-buying public. It is equally important to understand the positive effect these relationships can have on the marketability of public assembly facility managers and their facility. It must be remembered at all times that people do business with people, not just with other businesses. It cannot be stressed too often that the public assembly facility management industry is built on relationships. The personality and management style of the public assembly facility manager is paramount in helping to generate and/or maintain repeat business with promoters and other industry representatives. A public assembly facility may be at the cutting edge in terms of its seating capacity and physical amenities, but generally the most important influence on tenants and promoters to book future dates with the facility is the manager and the facility's staff working diligently to ensure that ticket-buying patrons are attracted to the facility and that all aspects of an event run smoothly.

Yogi Berra once said, "If they don't want to come, nothing on earth can stop them." (Berra). Since public assembly facility managers are generally very knowledgeable about the communities and regional areas in which the majority of potential event attendees reside, it becomes their responsibility to attempt to enhance the public perception of the event-related experience through a strategic marketing program.

RELATIONSHIPS ARE KEY

Creating and maintaining positive relationships with industry colleagues is also very important to the successful public assembly facility manager. Membership and active participation in organizations such as the International Association of Assembly Managers (IAAM) (www.iaam.org) allows the facility manager to interact with colleagues worldwide. The common interests of association members tend to facilitate the creation of friendships and the development of extensive networking. In the process of growing these professional relationships, facility managers have the opportunity to market their facilities, as well as themselves, to a wide cross section of industry members and representatives.

Industry relationships and networking are vital in helping the public assembly facility manager to raise the profile of the facility. While each venue has its own particular characteristics and quirks, most first-time problems encountered by the facility manager are probably not unique and most likely have been experienced by other facility managers. Public assembly facility managers who enjoy strong positive relationships with their colleagues may contact them for assistance or advice when problems arise that others may have already encountered and solved.

CUSTOMER SERVICE IS KEY

In 1979, John Denver addressed IAAM's Annual Conference in Houston, TX. His message is as relevant today, if not more so, than it was then. Essentially he challenged the industry to manage every phase of the customer experience including

- Fair ticket distribution
- Advertising and promotion – a clear and understandable message that results in buying tickets
- Ticket sale lines
- Clear directional signage
- Traffic and parking management
- Admission control
- Food, beverage, and merchandise
- Accessibility and cleanliness of restrooms
- Clear and easy-to-follow seat location graphics
- Cleanliness of seats, floors, etc.
- Crowd management

His goal was for the industry to create a relaxed and enjoyable environment so that when the lights go down and the curtain goes up fans are in a good frame of mind to enjoy the show.

The best marketing plan on earth cannot overcome negative word-of-mouth feedback. Reality is 90 percent perception and facility managers must strive everyday to manage public perceptions – either that or become a victim of it.

Many books have been written on the subject of customer service. One of the first and best was by Karl Albrecht and Ron Zemke entitled *Service America* in which they described their theory of the upside-down pyramid structure for an organization. Basically, senior management's job is to create an organization of empowered front-line staff who come into contact with the organization's customers ("the moment of truth") and the staff treat those customers like senior management would if senior management were there instead.

Customer service starts with commitment, action, and follow-through by senior management. It is a philosophy that is lived, practiced, and improved every day by everyone in the organization.

Call them customers, clients, patrons, guests, or whatever, the people who attend events at the facility can either be so disgusted that it is very unlikely they will return, or they could enjoy the experience so much they will return often. It is hard to quantify (but worth the effort) to determine how much future revenue the facility might lose by just one dissatisfied person.

Customer service is the glue the holds all sales and marketing efforts together. It is the difference between going through the motions and effective action.

ADVERTISING AND PROMOTIONS

As previously stated, marketing can help with the achievement of specific objectives of the public assembly facility. While objectives may differ for each, a commonly shared objective is to increase revenues generated through rent, ticket sales (if the rental fee is based on a percentage of the ticket sales), and income derived through ancillary services. Effective marketing is the key to achieving this and all other objectives.

Advertising campaign strategies are an effective method of planning a multiple attack on the target market. Once an advertising and promotion budget amount is determined, the marketing department will need to assemble the resources available to achieve the promotion objective. This exercise begins with evaluating the market demographics of the event and then determining the various methods, times, frequency, and incentives that will be used to reach the target audience. The campaign can involve a number of different strategies including, but not limited to, multiple pricing scales of tickets, *group ticket sales, cross-bounce coupons*, etc. Additionally, the campaign may employ special sponsored events with local charities as beneficiaries. This tactic might drive consumer sales at area business at the same time.

A media blitz using a myriad of different options, e.g., radio, television, print, and billboards, can be used to achieve saturation levels that reach the target audience in multiple ways. Also, utilizing electronic web sites can be an added asset to the arsenal. The frequency and length of these advertising messages along with the optimum choice of schedules for running the ads is an important ingredient to include in the development of the campaign strategy. For some radio advertising schedules, a *run of schedule* (ROS), i.e., the station selects timing of ads, may be sufficient. (See Appendix A, 4-1.) Using the ROS is often much less expensive per exposure and frequently is tied into promotions sponsored by the radio station or one of the event sponsors. For other advertising and promotion efforts, a prime time segment like drive time, specifying the radio spot to play frequently during times people are driving to and from work, may be the preferred tactic.

If increasing the sales of ancillary products is the objective, group ticket sales and cross-bounce coupon strategies are an effective way to increase attendance. Information about these options is normally displayed in the paid advertising. In these cases, the ticket buyer is getting a value-added benefit by either getting a discount or an opportunity to get a discount at a participatory retail outlet or some other partner. These tactics not only help to grow ancillary receipts but also help build a fan base through exposure to new entertainment and events.

In-House Ad Agency

A clear advantage goes to the facility that can offer the promoter the following services at significantly reduced cost:

- Ad placement in local and regional media
- Ability to involve the media in event sponsorship
- Ability to minimize the expenditure of cash by securing ad and promotional schedules in return for comp tickets
- Generating maximum public relations stories in general news, sports, lifestyle, business, and a variety of other areas that apply to a specific event
- Ability to pre-sell a sizeable number of tickets to the facility's own regular customer base via blast emails
- Ability to receive corporate sponsorships to further reduce the cost of advertising and promotion
- Ability to present the promoter with a clear and well documented media settlement/reconciliation

Marketing departments that have the attitude and enthusiasm to sell every ticket to every event inspire confidence on the part of promoters, and ultimately a promoter's loyalty will rest with the facility at which they "take out" the most money at the least cost.

SEASON TICKETS AND SUBSCRIPTIONS

Packaging or *bundling* is a concept of marketing that often helps to promote events in public assembly facilities. One of the more common practices of this strategy is the season ticketing or subscription price. Whether it is a string of sporting events or a theatre series, the intent is the same, to encourage fans and patrons to make a long-term commitment by purchasing in bulk. To achieve this, the bulk price for the season ticket or subscription is usually less than the combined individual rates of each event. However, if the event being promoted is in high demand, the price does not necessarily have to be less. A season pass to a series may simply guarantee you an exclusive opportunity that individual purchasers may not have, not a less expensive price. Another method of adding value to season subscriptions is to package a specified genre of talent together and schedule the performances over several event dates. Using this tactic, a creative entrepreneur can produce a subscription series by contracting for a well-known and recognized act/talent and then include in the season package some lesser known talent. The (more expensive) loss leader coupled with acts with less or uncertain popularity as a package can be a very marketable series.

In the United States, some Major League Baseball (MLB) and National Basketball Association (NBA) teams have recently begun using this same basic approach, i.e., they are using access to the games with the more attractive opponents to create value. For season tickets, there may be an added cost included in the price for the prime opponents, or there may be no added cost but the fan is induced to buy the season ticket and ensure access to the game(s).

MARKETING OF PREMIUM ACCESS

Regardless of the industry, sales of inventory can very often be enhanced through creative marketing and value-added packaging, and the public assembly facility is no exception. In the sports and entertainment business, exclusive and prestigious commodities that are in limited supply are often more desirable and attractive than the standard fare. Since time and space is the key commodity of value in the public assembly facility, access and especially premium access for clients and patrons alike can garner extraordinary value. These types of sales are an ever-increasing percentage of the facility's revenue pie. Whether it be golden circle front row seating or a captured audience for advertisers, exclusive demand for access is a marketable program. The following segment is devoted to discussions of some of the more prevalent concepts being employed in the public assembly facility industry.

PREMIUM SEATING AND LUXURY SUITES

The sale of premium seating is becoming a financial mainstay of many public assembly facilities. This marketing concept is based on the premise that individual guests and businesses are willing to pay a premium price for seating in areas that offer added amenities. These added amenities might include proximity, front row seats for an opera or basketball game, sightlines, and/or physical comfort. Businesses might purchase these premium seats to entertain clients and others important to their activities.

Luxury suites represent the ultimate in upscale seating. Many businesses lease luxury suites for a specified period. For example, luxury suites at football stadiums are leased on a season or multiple season contract and are available for use during all home games of the prime tenant(s). On the other hand, public assembly facilities that host a variety of events throughout the year generally lease their luxury suites on an annual or multi-year contract. Some public assembly facilities offer leaseholders the opportunity to sublease their suites on a per-event basis. In return for providing this service, the public assembly facility management might collect a commission ranging from 10 to 25 percent of the revenue generated by the sublease.

This service is particularly appealing to suite leaseholders not wishing or unable to attend every event because it allows them the chance to recapture a portion of their leasing costs. It is also appealing to the public assembly facility manager because it provides another revenue stream; it places guests at events who purchase tickets and ancillary products or services (empty seats do not purchase food and beverages); and it provides an opportunity to introduce the suite concept to potential leaseholders.

For sports fans not wishing the luxury of a suite, premium or "club" seats offer an excellent opportunity to enjoy some of the same amenities available to the suiteholder but at a lesser price. Depending on the amenities provided, these premium seats might cost from $500 to $3,500 (US) per seat on a seasonal basis. At the same time, depending on the event and facility, a premium seat may cost a considerable amount for a single event. A courtside seat at an NBA game in a major market might cost $2,500 per game. Premium seating tickets for Las Vegas concerts by Luciano Pavarotti and Barbra Streisand have sold for as much as $1,250 - $1,500 each. Premium seating and luxury suite amenities might include preferential parking, food and beverage delivery service to the customer's seat, access to the facility's restaurants and clubrooms, and admission to the facility through a private entrance.

Premium seating and luxury suites have become such important revenue producers that they can drive the design of new facilities, especially amphitheatres, arenas, and stadiums. The exclusive concept and added amenities of premium seating have long been an element of performing art facilities. A separate organization exists for professionals in this area — the Association of Luxury Suite Directors (www.alsd.com).

Priority Seating

The selling of priority seating or *personal seating licenses* (PSL) represents yet another vehicle for generating additional revenue. In purchasing a PSL, fans pay a one-time fee in order to gain "ownership" of a specified seat and they retain "ownership" with the annual purchase of a season ticket for a specified period of time, up to lifetime. Although not limited to sporting events, the PSL can produce significant amounts of new money in markets with rabid sport fans. However, it must be kept in mind that the sale of a PSL only produces one-time money to help offset construction costs rather than annual operating revenue unless the PSL is for a limited period of time and then must be "re-purchased."

In the collegiate setting, the PSL concept is the same, although applied somewhat differently. Rather than selling a PSL, fans are encouraged to become members of the institution's booster club. Most booster clubs offer a variety of membership levels each requiring a specified minimum financial contribution. Each contribution level provides stated benefits with the number and quality of the benefits increasing as the contribution level increases. In the United States, for most NCAA Division I collegiate institutions, it is virtually impossible to purchase "good" seats for football and men's basketball (and in some instances women's basketball) without being a member of the booster club. Booster clubs are not limited to collegiate institutions. In various places in the world, clubs and even professional teams have booster clubs. Generally, season ticket assignments might be based on a formula that takes into account the number of years the applicant has been a member of the booster club, the total amount of contributions during that membership period, and the current membership level. It is not unusual for an upper tier NCAA Division I institution to generate over $10 million (US) annually from booster donations in addition to the revenue garnered from the sale of season tickets to these members.

THE SALE OF COMMERCIAL RIGHTS

For purposes of this text, *commercial rights* are defined as the following long-term, contractually obligated sources of revenue:

- Naming rights
- Beverage (pouring rights)
- Advertising signage
- Facility sponsorships

- Memorial gifts
- Branding of food & beverage products
- Premium (VIP) seating

This responsibility usually rests with a facility's corporate sales department or it may be a service provided by the marketing department or it may be contracted out to a third party contractor that specializes in the sale of commercial rights.

Regardless of where the responsibility specifically lies, it is critically important to do everything possible to ensure the commercial rights clients are happy, satisfied, and ready and willing to renew their contracts when the time comes.

NAMING RIGHTS

The most significant revenue generator of *commercial rights* is *naming rights*. The sale of naming rights has become almost a necessity in contributing to the capital cost of construction for a new facility. Further, in some cases, naming rights are also a significant part of the economic mix of attracting or retaining a major and minor league sports franchise in a growing number of North American facilities.

Figures 4-2, 4-3, 4-4 and 4-5 below illustrate current examples of various university and major and minor league arenas and stadiums, as well as convention centers which have sold the right to "name" these facilities to a wide variety of sponsors.

UNIVERSITY NAMED FACILITIES

Constant Convocation Center (Old Dominion University)

Save Mart Arena (Fresno State University)

Bank United Center (University of Miami)

United Spirit Arena (Texas Tech)

Jerome Schottenstein (Value City Arena) (Center Ohio State University)

FIGURE 4-2

MAJOR LEAGUE NAMED FACILITIES

Chase Field (Arizona Diamondbacks - MLB)
Lincoln Financial Field (Philadelphia Eagles – NFL)
Wachovia Center (Philadelphia Flyers –NHL / Philadelphia 76ers –NBA)
Staples Center (Los Angeles Kings – NHL / Los Angles Lakers – NBA)
Home Depot Center (Los Angeles Galaxy – MLS)
United Center (Chicago Black Hawks – NHL / Chicago Bulls – NBA)

FIGURE 4-3

MINOR LEAGUE NAMED FACILITIES

Sovereign Bank Arena (Trenton Devils – ECHL)
Blue Cross Blue Shield Arena (Rochester Americans – AHL)
Dunkin Donuts Center (Providence Bruins –AHL)
Comcast Events Center (Everett Silvertips-WHL)
Budweiser Events Center (Colorado Eagles – CHL)
Wells Fargo Arena (Iowa Stars – AHL)

FIGURE 4-4

CONVENTION CENTER NAMED FACILITIES

MassMutual Center (Springfield, MA)
Midwest Airlines Center (Milwaukee, WI)
Duke Energy Center (Cincinnati, OH)

FIGURE 4-5

TERMS AND CONDITIONS

The sale of commercial rights, and especially of naming rights, is a very involved process that requires a great deal of forethought, planning, and preparation.

In many respects a facility's commercial rights package is analogous to a pyramid – the high profile is at the top but the base is where the financial strength and longevity rests.

COMMERCIAL RIGHTS INVENTORY

Ideally, before a facility undertakes any commercial rights sales, an inventory of all rights, sponsorships, advertising signage (electronic and static), media mentions, branding relationships, trade/barter, and the like is prepared. This inventory is intended to help establish:

- Size/dimensions
- Location
- Possible categories of exclusivity
- Contract term
- Value/pricing
- Fulfillment to the buyer, i.e.,
  - o Tickets
  - o Premium seating
  - o Parking
  - o VIP amenities/access

RATE CARD

Once the inventory has been established rates representing a hierarchy of values and fulfillment obligations are established. It is not the purpose of this text to go into the level of detail that shows how various commercial rights opportunities are valued. There are a number of organizations and firms that specialize in this service.

Some, along with appropriate contact information, are listed below:

- Association of Luxury Seat Directors (ALSD) – www.alsd.co
- Front Row Marketing Services – www.frontrow-marketing.com
- Team Marketing Report – www.teammarketing.com
- IEG – www.sponsorship.com

These organizations and firms can also provide guidance on a number of critical legal documents and forms that are necessary in the commercial rights sales process. These would include

- Evaluation criteria
- Comparative pricing
- Sales brochure
- Contract/leases
- Annual reports demonstrating value to the buyer

It is strongly recommended that each facility manager obtain advice on the preparation of all such documents.

Fulfillment Obligations

The term fulfillment obligation refers to the "give back" a facility must provide to a major commercial rights buyer. For example, ABC Corporation purchases the naming rights to an arena for a ten-year period at a cost of $500,000 per year. While this is typically treated as operating income to the facility, it will usually include substantial inventory in the package. Typically, a naming rights sponsor is given a fulfillment package that might include a complimentary suite, four to six club seats and/or a loge box, signage, parking passes, etc. These elements may account for $200,000 of inventory, so the actual incremental revenue to the facility for naming rights is $300,000.

In reality, the give back only represents cash/out-of-pocket expenses when the inventory of whatever is being given back is sold out. So it is wise to establish pricing that takes into account the need for certain fulfillment requirements.

Pouring/Beverage Rights

Beverage pouring rights, as in naming rights, will also include inventory items like signage, premium seating, and promotions, but very often the beverage sponsors will overpay for these elements to gain "exclusive pouring rights" and lock out all competitors. The larger soft drink companies are well versed in this process and often have a revenue formula based on volume sales that they utilize to make a deal. This formula sometimes includes sponsorship fees, commissions, and caseload rebates.

Alcoholic beverages pose a different set of circumstances as it is illegal to tie "pouring rights" and brand exclusivity to any advertising, premium seating, or sponsorship opportunity. Federal and state laws regulate the relationship between alcohol beverage companies and retailers with regard to sponsorships and pouring rights. A retail license holder cannot accept inducements (cash or equipment and sometimes even service) to sell a specific brand of alcohol. Therefore whoever holds the retail liquor license (typically the concessionaire) cannot be the same individual or company that solicits alcoholic beverage companies for sponsorship (typically the venue management). There must be a legal separation between the two parties. The beer companies, in particular, will look for some kind of advertising exclusivity, if available. It is important, as with all exclusives, to define them as narrowly as possible so that revenue can be maximized in the category.

ADVERTISING SIGNAGE

Perhaps the most traditional form of commercial rights sales is advertising signage – both static and electronic, and both interior and exterior. Advertising signage includes

- Scoreboards
- LED's
- Electronic message boards
- Backlit display cases
- Outdoor marquees
- Vomitories
- Concourse TV monitors

Typical business categories targeted for facility advertising include the following:

- Airlines
- Automotive
- Banks
- Communications (wireless)
- Financial
- Liquor
- Insurance
- Media
- Real estate
- Hi-tech

Very often one or more prime tenant teams share advertising inventory. For example, an NHL prime tenant would most likely have the rights to advertising on hockey dashers and the Zamboni (ice resurfacing machine). The team would also most likely have rights to on-ice advertising, although the facility would retain the right to include the logo of the "naming" rights sponsor, or simply the name of the facility.

In some cases, the facility and team cooperate by combining their inventories and selling it through one sales team. This system reduces costs for both entities and offers buyers a much broader package of options tailored to their specific needs.

Some businesses will also pay the public assembly facility for the opportunity to provide event attendees with novelty items such as t-shirts, towels, "thunder sticks," and water bottles, all imprinted with the businesses' name and logo. Baseball teams in both the major and minor leagues are prime examples of sport businesses that capitalize on revenue generation through the distribution of promotional giveaways replete with business advertising.

Scoreboards, announcement boards, and seat cup holders represent additional opportunities for the placement of business advertisements and logos. The possibilities for raising additional monies through marketing/advertising channels are virtually endless, restricted only by the public assembly facility manager's imagination.

With this in mind, the public assembly facility manager must be careful to resist selling too much advertising if clutter is to be avoided. Not only does the presence of too many advertisements produce clutter, it also tends to diminish the facility's attractiveness. In addition, an overload of advertisements makes it very difficult for the facility's guests to recall the names of the advertising partners.

The level to which guests are able to recall advertisers is very important to the advertisers seeking to gain a return on their advertising investment. The guest's level of advertiser recall is also important to the public assembly facility manager seeking to attract new and/or retaining current advertisers. Wise public assembly facility managers will implement periodic research studies to ascertain their guest's recall levels. The resulting data can be very influential when negotiating with current and potential advertisers.

MISCELLANEOUS COMMERCIAL RIGHTS

SPONSORSHIPS

This category could involve *sub-naming* rights which typically involves a major sponsor of a concourse, display column, interactive kiosk, or some interior space or feature even though a title sponsor has its name on the facility as a whole.

Other sponsors also may wish to put their name on a special event. Event sponsorships including the title or presenting sponsor and in many cases one or more media sponsors and often numerous sub-sponsors. A fictitious example might be

Russell Stover Chocolate Presents
John Mathis & The Denver Pops
In a Special
Valentine Day Concert

Sponsored by WHRT Radio
and FTD Florists

Another increasingly common form of sponsorship involves ticketing whereby a commercial sponsor essentially brands the in-house ticketing system. An example would be Comcast Tix at the Budweiser Events Center in Fort Collins, CO, or Dahl's Tickets in Des Moines, IA.

MEMORIAL GIFTS

This aspect of commercial rights refers to the sale of brick walkways, rooms, objects of arts, and the like. Memorial donations are usually one-time gifts that offset the upfront capital cost of construction. They are not generally considered sources of annual operating revenue.

Donor programs are designed to attract individuals or businesses wishing to assist the public assembly facility financially or through the provision of goods and services. The difference between "donors" and "sponsors" is that contributions made by donors are generally altruistic and do not afford the donor any competitive advantage. The return to the donor is more likely to be satisfaction and recognition, such as a plaque at the facility or a room named for the donor. In addition, most donor programs offer donors a tax deduction for their gift. The "buy-a-brick" program used at the Atlanta Olympic Games is an example of a donor program that has been employed to assist many public assembly facilities generate funds for construction projects.

Institutions of higher education have developed excellent donor programs to solicit contributions from their graduates as well as from the business community, philanthropic organizations, and the general public. Public assembly facilities can institute similar donor programs when seeking contributions from foundations, benefactors, and businesses wishing to "give back" to the community. The performing arts represent one segment of the entertainment industry that has benefited greatly from donor programs.

Public assembly facility managers should consider directing their marketing staffs to initiate a donor program, if one is not already in place. Even though donor programs may not seem as profitable as sponsorship agreements, they can create substantial amounts of good will in addition to providing needed revenue or goods and services.

BRANDING OF FOOD & BEVERAGE PRODUCTS FOR RESALE

Many facility food and beverage providers – whether third-party concessionaires or in-house operations – find it advantageous to brand certain food and beverage products with national or in some cases very popular local products. Items typically branded include pizza, coffee, ice cream and yogurt, and hot dogs.

In modern facility management and especially for arenas and stadiums, commercial rights sales have become a vital source of annual operating revenue – in some cases 30 to 40 percent of total. Commercial rights customers therefore deserve very special attention on a regular basis. Regular news blasts via email, access to tickets for special events, especially highly popular concerts where demand for tickets exceeds availability, parking, VIP amenities (lounges, bars, upscale food and beverage, concierge services…) all build loyalty and repeat business.

The re-sale of any commercial rights starts on day one of the relationship and should never be taken for granted. In this case especially great customer service really pays off.

SUMMARY

In many respects, the sales and marketing department is the heart and soul of a facility's organization. This department is responsible for key functions that drive a facility day-to-day as it competes for events and attendees to gain

- Awareness (international, national, regional, and local)
- Event advertising, promotion, and marketing
- Group ticket sales
- Public, community, media, and vendor relations
- Sale of commercial rights

The essence of facility management is booking viable events and then promoting them. Facilities that do this well generate more event activity and more repeat business from event promoters and show organizers. Very often events will schedule one facility over another because of the quality and effectiveness of services they receive from the sales and marketing department.

The sales and marketing plan must focus on the existing and potential marketplace. The demographic and psychographic profiles of both the community and the region in which the public assembly facility exists must be taken into consideration when developing these plans. Research designed to evaluate the success, or lack thereof, of these plans must be ongoing.

Effective sales and marketing is highly correlated with the ability of the public assembly facility manager's ability to create and maintain strong relationships. Effort must be taken to cultivate positive relationships with colleagues, owners, community leaders, promoters, vendors, and all other individuals with whom the manager interacts.

Advertising is an important component of the sales and marketing mix and all appropriate media outlets should be utilized. Every sales and marketing avenue must be explored to assess its potential contribution to the economic success of the public assembly facility.

The possibilities for raising additional monies through marketing/advertising channels are virtually endless, restricted only by the public assembly facility manager's imagination. Yet, diligent attention must be paid to insure the absence of promotion and advertising clutter.

REFERENCES AND ADDITIONAL READINGS

Bearden, W., Ingram, T. and LaForge, R. 2007. *Marketing: Principles and Perspectives*, 5th ed. New York: McGraw-Hill/Irwin.

Berra, Yogi. http://www.yogi-berra.com/yogiisms.htm.

Brooks, Christine M. 1994. *Sports Marketing: Competitive Business Strategies for Sports*. Upper Saddle River, NJ: Prentice Hall.

Burns, Alvin C. and Ronald F. Bush. 2008. *Marketing Research with SPSS 3 CD*, 5th ed. Upper Saddle River, NJ: Prentice Hall.

Bygrave, William D. 2003. *The Portable MBA in Entrepreneurship*. Hoboken, NJ: John Wiley & Sons, Inc.

Cohen, William A. 1987. *Developing a Winning Marketing Plan*. New York: John Wiley & Sons, Inc.

Hall, Doug. 2003. *Meaningful Marketing*. White Hall, VA: Betterway Publishers.

Hiam, Alexander and Charles D. Schewe. 1998. *The Portable MBA in Marketing*. Hoboken, NJ: John Wiley & Sons, Inc.

Hoyle, Leonard H. 2002. *Event Marketing: How to Successfully Promote Events, Festivals, Conventions, and Expositions*. New York, NY: John Wiley & Sons, Inc.

Kerin, Roger A. and Robert A. Peterson. 2006. *Strategic Marketing Problems: Cases and Comments*, 11th ed. Upper Saddle River, NJ: Prentice Hall.

Kotler, Philip. 2008. *Marketing Management*, 13th ed. Upper Saddle River, NJ: Prentice Hall.

Mullin, Bernard J., Stephen Hardy and William A. Sutton. 2007. *Sport Marketing*, 3rd ed. Champaign, IL: Human Kinetics Publishers.

O'Guinn, Thomas C, Chris T. Allen and Richard J. Semenik. 2008. *Advertising and Integrated Brand Promotion*. Mason, OH: South-Western College Publishers.

Perreault, William D. and E. Jerome McCarthy. 2008. *Basic Marketing*, 17th ed. Boston: Richard D. Irwin Publishers.

Ries, Al. 1994. *The 22 Immutable Laws of Marketing: Exposed and Explained by the World's Two.* NY: HarperBusiness.

Sherwood, Dick. Front Row Marketing Services. Private correspondence.

Shimp, Terence A. 2008. *Advertising, Promotion and Supplemental Aspects of Integrated Marketing Communications*, 8th ed. Mason, OH: South-Western College Publishers.

Sleight, Steve. 1989. *Sponsorship: What It Is and How To Use It.* London: McGraw-Hill.

Solomon, Michael R. 2008. *Consumer Behavior*, 9th ed. Upper Saddle River, NJ: Prentice Hall.

Stotler, David K. 2009. *Developing Successful Sport Marketing Plans*, 3rd ed. Morgantown, WV: Fitness Information Technology.

Zaltman, Gerald. 2003. *How Customers Think: Essential Insights into the Mind of the Market.* Cambridge, MA: Harvard Business School.

CHAPTER 5

TICKETING AND ACCESS MANAGEMENT

CHAPTER OUTLINE

INTRODUCTION
HISTORICAL OVERVIEW
WHY TICKETING IS ESSENTIAL
   TO PUBLIC ASSEMBLY
   FACILITY MANAGEMENT
- CONTROLLING CAPACITY
- REVENUE COLLECTION AND CONTROL
- VALUING SEATING LOCATIONS

OCCUPANCY CODES
TICKET SALES POTENTIAL
TICKET DESIGN AND WORDING
- FRONT SIDE OF TICKET
- BACK SIDE OF TICKET

TICKETS AS A LIMITED CONTRACT
/REVOCABLE LICENSE
- SEE AND ENJOY
- LIMITED CONTRACT
- REVOCABLE LICENSE

TICKETS AS A REVENUE SOURCE
TICKETING SYSTEMS PROVIDE
   MARKETING INFORMATION

SELECTING AND DEVELOPING A
   TICKETING SYSTEM
MANAGING THE TICKETPROCESS
E-TICKETS
SECONDARY TICKET MARKET
SCALPING AND COUNTERFEIT
   TICKETS
PREMIUM SEATING AND FAN
   CLUB SEATING
DATA BASE MANAGEMENT AND
   OWNERSHIP
DESIGNING THE BOX
   OFFICE SPACE
STAFFING THE BOX OFFICE
YIELD MANAGEMENT
THE FUTURE OF TICKETING
SUMMARY
REFERENCES AND
   ADDITIONAL READINGS

INTRODUCTION

Ticketing or granting a "right of admission" into an event at a public assembly facility (PAF) has evolved from using hard tickets of one kind or another into a highly sophisticated computerized operation. Box office management, which has the basic responsibility of access control, has transcended from simply selling and taking tickets at the entrance of a facility into a fully integrated access management and information control process that can leverage important information such as direct interaction with patrons, marketing certain events to targeted audiences, and creating a direct dialog with the facility's customers. This process begins when an event is in the conception and negotiation stages and continues through a myriad of steps and processes that culminate with the final financial settlement for an event. This system has two distinctly different processes that can be referred to as ticketing operations and sales.

Ticketing Operations is referred to as the myriad of tasks that need to be completed by the box office manager and their staff, the facility administration, and the *promoter* (which for the purposes of this chapter also includes the event presenter or team) prior to the event having tickets available for sale. These tasks actually begin before the event is booked.

It is the manager's responsibility to develop a ticketing system that accomplishes two essential goals. First, the ticketing system has to be conveniently available to the consumer using four primary sales methods and locations: the box office, retail outlets placed strategically throughout the market, telephone sales, and on the Internet. Second the PAF manager must also be able to explain to the event promoter the demographics of the market and the most efficient and economically effective method to advertise the event using the local media to help the promoter attain the ultimate goal of "sold out." This is a key selling point to promoters and other facility users and a major factor in receiving repeat business in future years, and with some attractions, a second and/or more performances.

The ticketing process begins when the manager receives a call from a presenter/ promoter to book an event. This establishes a process that typically involves the following steps:

The PAF manager and the promoter need to determine the best possible configuration and seating chart with a total number of seats, as well as a ticket price scale to maximize the potential revenue for the event. Once the seating chart has been determined, the box office manager and the operations manager discuss the specific distribution of the seats and desired scale in the public assembly facility to be able to arrive at the total number of seats and gross revenue potential requested by the promoter. This process requires knowledge of all building codes, fire codes, and ADA regulations in order to set the facility up properly.

Next, the box office manager develops a *manifest*, a document which lists the total number of seats to be sold in each section, manages that inventory prior to the ticket sale by allocating seats assigned to be held, and therefore not available to the public, for the promoter, artist, talent agency, ADA, and production issues. These holds are specifically identified by section, row, and seat. This process is usually completed on an electronic ticketing system.

Finally, the box office manager will develop a system to sell the tickets on a "best available" process. This process was developed and is used when tickets are expected to sell out when the show is put on sale. This system needs to be closely monitored by the box office manager and ticketing company to ensure that the integrity of the "best available" system is being protected to be available to customers on a first-come, first-served basis.

Ticket Sales comprises researching, marketing, and advertising ticket sales. It is the process of developing a secure, controlled and comprehensive ticket sales process that begins with selecting an accurate and appropriate seating chart, marketable ticket prices, and a ticket distribution system, and culminates with a box office settlement and the final accounting statements for all revenue. Ticket sales has also become an effective means of pre-event communication as well as a post-event evaluation tool that arms the promoter and facility to more effectively and efficiently reach the ticket-buying population in the future. For many events in public assembly facilities, the use of tickets also serves as a critical tool to control access and therefore capacity. This chapter will highlight the various facets of access management and will discuss the significance for having an accurately managed, time sensitive, ticketing operation and sales process.

HISTORICAL OVERVIEW

In the latter part of the first century, admission into many of the events held at the Roman Colosseum was free to the public. However, social class determined exactly where attendees were allowed to sit and stand. Senators and their families were allowed closest to the action and in front of soldiers and craftsmen/ tradesmen. Women, slaves, and servants, if admitted at all, were usually relegated to the extreme upper level(s) of the facility.

How did the early Colosseum managers communicate the concept of assigned seating to their guests, and how did they avoid exceeding the capacity of the facility when events were presented free to the public? They developed and implemented the first process of access control that we know today as ticketing.

Archeological evidence indicates attendees were issued a predetermined number of colored pottery shards that corresponded to color-coded entrance portals and seating sections in the facility. These pottery shards served as the first control of assigned seating and were the genesis for the evolution that led to today's ticketing process. There is also historical evidence that the early public assembly managers would "barter" with patrons for improved seating locations; thus, an early form to ticket scalping began. A farmer with livestock to offer the public assembly facility manager might be awarded a better location within his social status than a peasant offering fruit or other less valuable commodities.

The issuance of tickets is almost as old as the management of public assembly facilities itself. Whether in the form of pottery shards, specially minted coins (ducats), preprinted hard tickets, or today's computer-generated e-tickets, issuing tickets helps the PAF manager address issues common to virtually every facility type. These issues include

- Controlling the facility's capacity in line with building and fire codes as well as Federal and state codes
- Determining a value of seating locations based on the sightline to the desired entertainment/event
- Communicating with customers prior to the event to establish a safe and efficient flow of people into the facility before, during, and after the event
- Creating a limited contract and revocable license between the facility and the customer
- Serving as a revenue source through advertising on the ticket
- Providing valuable marketing and demographic data on patrons

WHY TICKETING IS ESSENTIAL TO PAF MANAGEMENT

The main purpose of public assembly facilities is to host an event and attract attendees. Ticketing plays a vital role in this regard for the following reasons:

CONTROLLING CAPACITY

Controlling facility capacity is one of the most crucial aspects of public assembly facility management. The capacity of a PAF is dictated by many factors including Federal and state codes, as well as laws and regulations such as

- Building and occupancy codes
- Fire department and exiting capacity codes
- Event seating codes
- The Americans with Disabilities Act

Revenue Collection and Control

Most PAFs and the events that take place in them collect revenue to enable the event to not only offset expenses, but to make a profit as well. Ticketing is a form and method of accountability for facilities and events. It is becoming more and more arduous to account for the ticket revenue due to the numerous ways that tickets are sold. Tickets are now disseminated through four legitimate, primary locations: the facility box office, telephone sales, outlet sales, and Internet sales.

In addition to the numerous locations in which tickets are sold, there also may be multiple ticket prices for each type of event, and there are usually several events on sale at the same time in a PAF. Therefore, the complexity of accounting for each and every ticket, each and every dollar, and for each and every event the box office has on sale is a significant task on a daily basis.

The ticketing process also allows the PAF's management to communicate with customers in a way that contributes to marketing the facility and assisting with crowd management. Yet the ticketing process probably originated as a financial accounting and inventory control tool. Once PAFs began controlling ticket sales and event admissions, promoters and entertainers began to demand a more accurate accounting of gate receipts. Consequently, ticketing, in whatever form it took, quickly became an extremely important facet of the revenue accounting process.

Tickets sold at the box office were presented at the entrance to the PAF. It was a simple process to compare the money collected at the box office with ticket stubs collected at the door. The introduction of turnstiles provided an even more efficient and effective means for managers to reconcile the amount of money collected at the box office against a number of customers passing through the mechanized gate.

Today, due to the advancement of technology, many facilities now print a barcode on their tickets and deploy a barcode reader device to be able to count tickets electronically and in real-time as guests pass through the admissions control turnstile. This gives instant information on the flow and number of people entering the facility. It also gives the facility the ability to prevent attendance from exceeding capacity. Further, it permits facility managers flexibility in monitoring venue access and permits a manager to maximize gross potential value of an event.

The comparison of the ticket sales report with the audit, ticket stub drop count, or bar code reader report and turnstile counts serves as an undisputable comprehensive auditing system. The final ticket sales reconciliation is accomplished through the use of the box office statement that shows the beginning ticket inventory for each price category; the calculated income from the sales for each price category which includes complimentary tickets and unsold tickets *(deadwood)* is calculated and then combined for a total gross sales figure. The resulting number is then compared with the total amount of money collected by the box office, telephone sales, outlet sales, and electronically from the Internet ticket sales. These figures are compared with the drop count or bar code count, referred to as the number of tickets that pass through the turnstiles or get read by the bar code readers.

The information collected on the barcode can also be used in a number of ways other than to verify attendance. A look at the database generated by the barcode information as well as other buyer information can provide critical information related to individual and group attendance and purchasing patterns. Use of this data is important to the development of direct mail and targeted email campaigns, membership club enrollment, and future advertising that may have a direct impact on attendance at upcoming events. This data may also be the catalyst for development of a new or revised marketing plan for the facility.

VALUING SEATING LOCATIONS

As mentioned in the introduction of this chapter, the Romans used colored shards of clay with section designations that enabled the first PAF managers the ability to separate people by their classes in society. In today's culture, most PAFs have multiple ticket prices for multiple seat locations for each event. This enables PAFs and events to charge more for tickets that have the closest proximity and best sightlines to the event, as well as special customer service that we refer to later in this chapter as "premium seating."

Before seats are given a value, the PAF manager, in cooperation with the event promoter and box office manager, must establish the best type of seating configuration for the event. There are many variables that have an impact on which type of seating configuration and subsequent seating chart is used to maximize the revenue of an event and get to the magical two words that every public assembly facility manager and event promoter want to hear: "sold out."

OCCUPANCY CODES

One of the first considerations that needs to be understood when developing a seating chart and manifest is the occupancy codes for the specific PAF and the event that is taking place in it. As discussed previously, the capacity of the facility is one of the most important elements that a PAF manager needs to be aware of and determine depending on the event configuration.

PAFs are given a rating by the fire marshal based on the maximum number of people the space can safely accommodate and also based on a number of other variables. These include primarily square footage, specific activity use, ingress and egress routes, and the availability of multiple exits. Occupancy ratings are calculated and established during the facility's construction phase and prior to management receiving a certificate of occupancy and prior to the public having access to the facility. The PAF manager will find there will be times when promoters and event planners will ask for permission to exceed the maximum occupancy rating of a facility. PAF managers must understand that the only authority that can legally change a facility's occupancy capacity is the fire marshal. Therefore, any change in the occupancy rating must first be reviewed by the fire marshal and subsequently they may issue a variance in writing. PAF history has demonstrated that any attempt to supersede the fire marshal's rating could result in disastrous consequences for both the PAF and the attendees of the event.

Fire and life safety codes vary by state and city or county jurisdiction. Several national standard-setting bodies promulgate fire and life safety codes. The dominant fire code standards in the U.S. are issued by the National Fire Protection Association. States adopt a fire code and cities or counties may further designate codes to be used in their jurisdiction. Therefore, it is important for facility managers to become familiar with the exact codes adopted within the jurisdiction that controls occupancy of their facility.

TICKET SALES POTENTIAL

Once the occupancy rating has been substantiated, PAF managers must understand the legal parameters in which they are allowed to develop the event. The next consideration that the PAF manager must address is the type of event and the ability for that event to achieve desired gross ticket sales. At this stage in event planning, the public assembly facility manager works with the promoter. They review historical information gathered from the box office on similar types of events that took place in that facility recently to determine the capacity that should be established. Every promoter wants to be able to proclaim that their event is sold out. This can be accomplished in many ways by the seating configuration in which the facility is set up. For example, arenas typically have several positions in which to place a stage and accompanying seating locations. Depending on whether the facility is set up in end-stage 360°, end-stage 270°, end-stage 180°, half house, or center stage, all have a bearing on the capacity of an event. Therefore, it can be said that if an event sells all 6,000 seats of a half house seating chart in a 12,000 seat arena, they are for all intents and purposes said to be sold out. The sold-out designation gives a performer and the event credibility as a successful event.

TICKET DESIGN AND WORDING

Tickets are an essential form of communication between the public assembly facility, the promoter of the event, and the consumer. An obvious purpose of a ticket is to notify the user of the event; its time, date, and location; and seating assignment. In addition to event-related information, the ticket is an effective and efficient device for communicating venue specific information directly to the customer, particularly policies relating to carrying prohibited objects into the facility such as guns and knives; food and beverages; backpacks and purses; still and video cameras; banners and signs; and noisemakers and laser lights. For example, baseball parks typically use the ticket to warn customers about foul balls. Arenas use tickets to warn customers about flying pucks and basketballs and to explain the importance of watching the event at all times and to provide the all important disclaimers that protect the venue operators from lawsuit. Performing arts centers benefit by stating their late arrival seating policies on the ticket. When informed in advance, most customers will not hesitate to comply with the public assembly facility's policies and procedures, and they will appreciate the notice and conformity it brings to the event.

Of course, the printing of specific warnings and disclaimers is also very important from a legal perspective. In addition to the ticket itself, signage and other communication should be designed to let patrons know of event policies. Not being informed of entrance restrictions when arriving at the gate generally results in an angry patron and the creation of a negative impression about the public assembly facility's management. Those guests purchasing tickets at the box office should be informed of the restrictions before purchasing a ticket. Posting appropriate language at the location tickets are scanned or torn for gaining entrance into the location can accomplish this important task.

Front Side of Ticket

Usually on the front side of the ticket you will find basic information that communicates the specifics of the event, namely, who, what, where, when, how, or why and includes

- event name
- facility name
- event start time
- event date
- seating location (section, row, and seat)
- face value of ticket

In stadiums, gate location may be provided on the front of the tickets to help the large number of people attending their events find the most expedient way in which to enter the facility from the parking lots. (Figure 5-1 shows a stadium ticket.)

Figure 5-1

Back Side of Ticket

On the back side of the ticket, facilities normally print in very small font information regarding facility and event hold harmless and disclaimer statements that notify the public of their responsibilities and risks when attending an event. A hold harmless statement usually serves to protect the facility and event from issues and situations that arise when a customer is hurt or injured while attending the event in the facility. A disclaimer also serves to protect the facility and event from the inappropriate actions of a customer that result in injury to themselves, other customers and/or interruption of the event. (Figure 5-2 shows sample hold harmless and disclaimer wording.)

The back of a ticket may also have some form of advertising that contributes a source of revenue to either the ticketing company or the facility depending on which entity owns the rights to the ticket stock. In today's e-ticket or paperless ticket marketplace, the back side of the ticket continues to be a place for a facility manager to generate additional revenue streams and provide specific event information, local information about parking, and area amenities. (Figure 5-2 shows advertising on the back of ticket.)

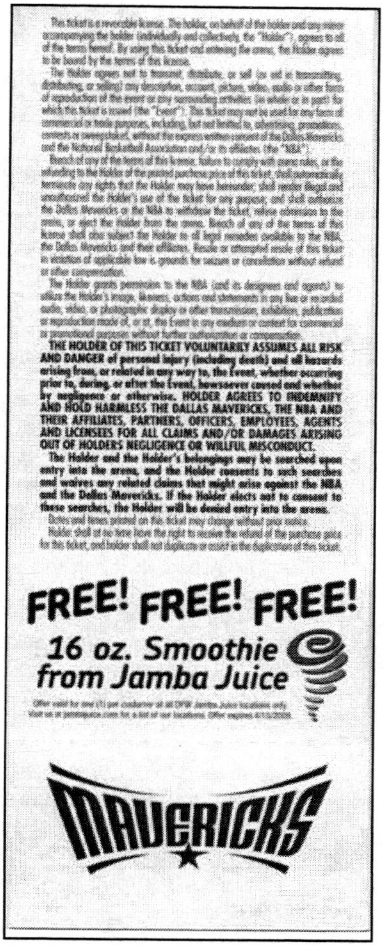

TICKETS AS A LIMITED CONTRACT AND REVOCABLE LICENSE

Figure 5-2

By legal definition, a ticket for admission to a facility and the event is both a limited contract and a revocable permit. For the ticket holder, it provides physical evidence of permission to enter the facility and a guarantee that the presenter will deliver what has been advertised on the ticket face or by prior advertising and promotion. If the guarantee is compromised or not delivered, the ticket then becomes a proof of purchase receipt and can be used in a refund process.

SEE AND ENJOY

In addition to the event presenter being responsible for delivering the advertised product the ticket holder deserves the opportunity to "see and enjoy" the event. Enjoyment in this sense has little to do with approving or liking the performance. It has more to do with being able to see and hear the presentation in an environment free from unreasonable distractions. There are sometimes great disparities between a ticket holder's definition of the phrase "see and enjoy" versus a PAF manager's definition. Therefore, PAF managers and their staffs

TICKETS AS A LIMITED CONTRACT

ATTORNEY GENERAL CUOMO SECURES REFUNDS FOR ROCHESTER CONSUMERS WHO PURCHASED TICKETS TO ANOTHER CANCELED LIL' WAYNE CONCERT

ROCHESTER, N.Y. (January 20, 2009) – Attorney General Andrew M. Cuomo today announced reaching an agreement securing full refunds for consumers holding tickets for the canceled January 21, 2009 Lil' Wayne concert at the Blue Cross Arena.

Tomorrow night's concert marks the third time that Lil' Wayne scheduled a show in the region and the third time that he has pulled out at the last minute. Attorney General Cuomo's Office has obtained refunds for a previously canceled show on October 26 and continued to monitor the situation. Today's agreement with concert promoter RMF Productions ensures that ticket holders will again get their money back.

"Fans who spent their hard-earned money for tickets deserve a prompt refund and my office will continue working to protect their interests," said Attorney General Cuomo.

Consumers seeking a refund must do so by February 6, 2009 and turn in their original concert ticket. Consumers may go directly to the Blue Cross Arena Box Office during normal business hours to obtain a refund. In the event that tickets were purchased through Ticketmaster, consumers must contact Ticketmaster directly, which will issue the refund.

Per an agreement reached in December 2008 with the Attorney General's Office, both RMF Productions and Blue Cross Arena must clearly post the concert refund policy on posters and on the actual tickets at the point of sale.

FIGURE 5-3

must work to create the best patron experience possible for each event, whatever its content or success as entertainment.

LIMITED CONTRACT

If the event and facility as the location hosting the event fail in delivering the advertised event to which the ticket holder has a receipt, the ticket holder may have the right to compensation that can include, but is not limited to, partial or full refund of the ticket price or a ticket to a future performance. In some instances the ticket holder might be relocated to an area within the facility that enables the ticket holder the same or better proximity to the event. (Figure 5-3 provides an example of a ticket refund situation)

For example, customers who buy a ticket to watch a baseball game have the right to complain if they were not informed that their assigned seat location is such that they are unable to see all of the playing field. In this instance, the facility or team representative would either relocate the customer to a seat with an unobstructed view or if none were available refund the price of the ticket.

Often when extremely popular attractions are being promoted, seating that is obstructed or offers a limited view of the event is made available to the public but only once the purchaser has been informed in writing on the ticket that the seats have sightline restrictions. Tickets for these seats should be clearly marked "Limited View" or "Obstructed View." In rare cases, seats that only provide the purchaser with a video screen to view the event rather than a live view or a direct view have been sold and are referred to as "No Direct" or "No Live" seats.

Some PAFs, usually baseball parks and some football and soccer stadiums, especially in Europe, are allowed to sell standing-room-only tickets to otherwise sold-out performances as long as standing-room-only ticket holders do not block exits, entrances, or the view of seated patrons. Since issuing more tickets than the facility has seats might violate the facility's occupancy rating, pre-approval and the issuance of a variance, in writing, from the local fire marshal is usually required before the box office manager can announce the sale of standing-room-only tickets.

REVOCABLE LICENSE

A ticket is a revocable license that the PAF manager, for a number of reasons, may prevent or cancel continued admission to the event by the ticket holder. Typically revoking the ticket (license) will initiate a refund of the ticket price depending on the situation. For instance, if the guest's negative behavior becomes a distraction to others, the facility/event may have their ticket revoked and have them escorted from the facility. A uniformed police officer might give an unruly patron the option of ejection or arrest in cases involving witnessed and documented disorderly behavior. In this case, a refund of the ticket price is usually not a consideration or necessity.

Generally printed on the face of the ticket is the name of the attraction; the date of the performance; the name of the PAF; and the price and service charges paid for the ticket. This information becomes part of the ticket's guarantee obligating the promoter to produce what the ticket promises at the date, time, and place printed on the ticket. Substituting one attraction for another and/or changing the time and place of the performance gives the ticket holder the right to request a refund. If a ticket promises certain entertainers and they do not perform, the ticket holder might have the right to a partial refund, if not a full one. In such cases, promoters typically announce prior to the start of the show which entertainer will not be performing, who the replacement will be, if any, and extend the offer of refunds to dissatisfied patrons. This is a common practice in performing arts centers and theater in which there is a large cast and the cast performs over many nights. Another refund situation might arise when the entertainer delivers an abbreviated performance. Generally, the "headliner" or main attraction is expected to perform for at least 50 minutes. This guideline is not law but has evolved over the years to become an unwritten industry standard. If the entertainer fails to perform for at least 50 minutes, the audience might be due a refund. Performance length minimums are usually contracted and vary by performance discipline.

However, one of the most dangerous situations that can occur is when the main attraction of a high energy event does not appear at all and the show has to be canceled after the audience has been admitted to the facility. This type of situation may even occur after preliminary acts/artists have already performed. A concern facing the PAF manager and a promoter is when to announce the cancellation situation and what to announce. Is this show being postponed (because the artist became ill or was unable to get to the facility due to a transportation issue), or is the show actually being canceled?

If the answer is a postponement, the announcement should include the new show date, if known, and the audience should be told to keep and use their tickets for the new show date and that further information will be available as soon as possible. If the event is canceled, the announcement must be carefully crafted since the possibility of an unruly crowd is significantly increased depending on the demographics. The announcement should include a reason for the cancellation and when and where refunds will be available. Usually customers are asked to return to the point of purchase for a refund.

Whether a postponement or cancellation, the promoter and facility should have in place a prerecorded or predetermined announcement for the existing audience that reinforces the "onstage" announcement. The facility staff needs to have received prior training in assisting the exit of potentially disgruntled fans. The information distribution system used to inform the staff must be quick, precise, and clearly state the major and most critical task is to exit the audience quickly and efficiently from the facility and surrounding area. If at all possible, the box office should be closed and its lights turned off prior to the announcement. This will prevent an attempt by the public to seek refunds for tickets before exiting the facility. If not, this could be a recipe for disaster.

When disagreements between promoters and ticket holders over the substitution of headliners, change in venue, or starting time leads to litigation, the courts tend to side with the ticket holders. Such litigation should be avoided as it is expensive and produces nothing but negative public relations for the public assembly facility and its management.

In cases such as this, the PAF manager becomes the protector of the ticket holder. The facility also has an agreement with the promoter that may stipulate if the event has contracted for certain entertainers to perform, then the facility management has the right to refund ticket revenue to the consumers in the public's best interest. It's important to remember that the promoter is only concerned about the event for that date, but PAF managers are concerned about the ticket purchaser, because they are their customer for the entire year.

As with any contract, either party (in this case the ticket holder or the promoter) may alter the conditions of the contract so long as the permission to do so is granted by the other parties. A promoter may substitute one act for another and/or change the time and place of the event as long as the ticket holder agrees. Tickets to college sporting events, particularly basketball and football games, frequently carry a warning that the "starting time is subject to change." Understanding that many television broadcast decisions, especially televised college events, are made during the course of the season based on records and rivalries, season ticket holders may have to become conditioned to verify the starting time for each event. Some tickets to college sports event carry the statement "Time to be Announced."

In many states, each ticket must show and print the price paid. Printing the paid price protects the box office in case a refund is necessary. Since complimentary and trade tickets may not have a printed price on the ticket, they are not eligible for a refund. If the public assembly facility uses pre-printed tickets that include the printed price, trade and complimentary tickets are usually printed and issued at a $0 value or stamped "complimentary" thereby eliminating them from a potential refund. (Figure 5-4 shows a ticket with face price.)

Figure 5-4

There is also the issue of tickets sold at less than full price. This may occur for several reasons. The ticket may be discounted from full price because it is a child's ticket, a group sale, or as part of an advertising coupon promotion. If it is a traditional hard paper stock ticket, some form of identification is needed on the ticket such as a stamp or punch in instances where there is a discount. For a child's ticket, there might be an additional perforated stub on the ticket that is removed at the time of the sale thus signifying it is a reduced ticket price and inform the ticket taker to admit only a child. The other stub is used as an audit stub—that is, a part of a hard ticket that is retained by the ticket seller which becomes an inventory control device and accounting tool at any given time based on the number of tickets that were sold at what price. Audit stubs provide a basis for estimating expected attendance at the event.

All of the above tasks can be achieved by computerized ticketing when the ticket is printed at the point of sale, and applicable prices, service charges, and taxes are printed on the face of the ticket.

TICKETS AS A REVENUE SOURCE

Tickets can also be used as an ancillary revenue source. Almost all PAFs are now including some type of facility fee or surcharge in the form of a maintenance charge or entertainment tax in addition to the price of the ticket. The governmental bodies that own venues increasingly require these facility usage fees to fund maintenance of the facilities.

In addition, advertising on tickets can become a source of ancillary revenue. If the facility buys its ticket stock for tickets sold at their box office, they have the right to print advertising on the back of the ticket. The value of this advertising is based on the number of tickets distributed from the box office for the term of the advertising contract. The facility can also have advertising printed on e-tickets when they are printed by the consumer.

TICKETING SYSTEMS PROVIDE MARKETING INFORMATION

Computerized ticketing systems today provide venue managers with sophisticated database information about patron buying history and behavior. It is essential, given the increased ways for customers to spend their discretionary dollars in the broad spectrum of live entertainment spending, to know and cater to the likes and dislikes, in general terms, of its unique audiences. Maintaining direct contact with patrons is an important marketing tool for selling tickets to future events at the facility. Many venue managers negotiate rights with artists, team owners, and all presenters to retain access to the customer information collected on an event-by-event basis. By having unlimited access to this information, PAF managers and their staffs may harvest this data to create marketing campaigns for other promoters using the facility. Only then can PAF managers begin to understand the unique demographics of the facility's users. By surveying those engaged fans to learn what other events they are interested in attending, PAF managers can use that data to prove the viability of the venue management and, therefore, strengthen their position with the PAF's governing body with regard to budget requests and resource allocations. Further, customer data serves as a useful tool in working with chambers of commerce, local restaurants, and parking facilities, as well as other organizations such as Rotary clubs to remind residents of the long-lasting, positive value PAFs have on the economic impact of their respective communities.

SELECTING AND DEVELOPING A TICKETING SYSTEM

A PAF manager has the added responsibility to have in place a ticketing system that will enable the promoter to reach every consumer in the demographics that is a potential ticket buyer in the market in which the public assembly facility serves. This is accomplished through creating a system either in-house or through a ticketing subcontractor. Regardless of the type of system the public assembly facility manager selects, it is important that this system is available to all consumers at their most convenient point of sale, i.e., that enables the promoters to theoretically reach every potential ticket buyer in the demographics of the target audience.

It is generally accepted that ticketing systems in PAFs can be developed either in-house, which is common in performing arts centers, or through a subcontractor, which is more common in stadiums and arenas. It is advisable for PAF managers to go through the RFQ and/or RFP process to make sure that the system they are contemplating using is in the best interest of the PAF, the promoter of its events, and the consumers.

Request for Qualifications (RFQ). A request for qualifications is a solicitation process that a public assembly facility uses to seek interested companies that have the capability of providing ticketing services to the facility. This process will only help the PAF manager to determine the capabilities of the companies that are interested in providing ticketing services. The RFQ process generally will not provide a list of resources the company will provide, the service charges they will charge the consumer, and a firm price that companies are willing to pay a facility for the service and equipment they will provide.

Request for Proposal (RFP). A request for proposal is a solicitation process that the PAF uses to seek proposals from companies that are interested in providing ticketing service to the public assembly facility. The RFP process requires a significant amount of information exchange between the public assembly facility and potential ticketing subcontractors. Whatever methods are adopted by the public assembly facility manager, that person or selection committee must consider all opportunities to create revenue streams in all ticketing operations and not simply select a system that is within the venue's budget. The list of information that needs to be provided by the public assembly facility includes, but is not limited to

- Seating capacity of the public assembly facility
- The number and type of events on an annual basis for the past three years
- The range of ticket prices for each type of event for the past three years
- The amount of tickets sold in each price category for each event
- The number of tickets sold at the box office for the past three years
- The number of tickets sold at the outlets for the past three years
- The number of tickets sold on the telephone for the past three years
- The number of tickets sold on the Internet for the past three years
- The number of points of sale at the box office
- The amount of hardware and computers needed to run the box office at the facility
- The type of software needed by the facility to service its tenants, promoters, and presenters
- The type and frequency of training needed by the facility to train the box office employees
- The number of years in which the contract will be in place

Based on this information provided by the box office in the RFP, each potential subcontractor will develop a proposal that will include a list of all of the equipment, hardware, and software as well as training that the subcontractor will provide to the public assembly facility for the duration of the contract. The potential ticketing subcontractors will also provide their ticket sales strategy for the market that should include how they will create a ticket sales network using the box office, outlets, telephone, and the Internet.

For providing this service, the potential subcontractor will include a list of service charges that will be used at the box office, outlets, on the phone, and on the Internet. These service charges will usually vary depending on the base price of the ticket. Additional service charges may include handling charges, special postage charges, and overnight delivery charges.

It is also important to point out at this time that some of these charges are nonrefundable. It is the philosophy of most ticketing companies that when they sell a ticket, they are providing the facility and the consumer the service for which a service charge is levied. Therefore, if an event cancels and a customer goes back to the original point of purchase to receive a refund, generally they will only be refunded the base price or face value of the ticket and the per ticket service charges collected when the ticket(s) were originally sold. Per order fees and electronic delivery fees are sometimes retained by ticketing companies and through the policy of the in-house system due to the fact that there are increased costs associated with reversing the original ticket purchased.

Once the public assembly facility has had the opportunity to review the information in the proposals submitted by the potential ticketing subcontractors, they must make a decision that is in the best interest of the public assembly facility, the promoters, and the consumer.

Sample criteria for the evaluation of an RFP from ticketing subcontractors may include

Public Assembly Facilities
- Quality and quantity of equipment provided/offered
- Training of staff on their system
- Software upgrades (timely and free)
- Length of contract offered
- Commissions offered to PAF

Promoters/Event Presenters
- Ability of system to reach all demographics in the market
- Competitive pricing and fees
- Service quality

Ticket Consumer
- Fair and reasonable service charges
- Convenience of points of sale

Ticketing subcontractors will want to recover the costs of the hardware, software, and training that they provide to the PAF. They will do this through charging service charges to the consumer. The PAF manager's responsibility is to make sure that the service charges that the ticketing subcontractor proposes are not going to be a factor when the consumer is buying tickets for events. If consumers feel that the service charges are exorbitant, it may discourage them from buying tickets to this and future events. If the promoter feels that the service charges are preventing the consumers from buying tickets for their event, they may be reluctant to promote shows in the facility in the future. Service charges, while common, are not a given for all ticketing systems.

Managing the Ticket Process

The ticketing process is a combination of both operational procedures that need to be completed prior to putting an event on sale as well as a system to track tickets when they are on sale to determine if additional advertising and marketing are necessary to get the event to the magical two words "sold out."

It is important to remember that the sports and entertainment business is time sensitive to the extent that once the event happens, it's over and you cannot turn back the clock. Therefore, tickets are considered to be a perishable commodity that must be marketed and sold "before" the start time of the event. Once the event is over, the value of a $100 ticket would become $0. (Figure 5-5 shows a checklist a box office manager might use for planning.)

A.   Determine the Event's Potential to Sell Tickets (Research)
One of the most important parts of the ticket process is to research previous similar events in the market of the facility to see how many tickets they sold as well as what the ticket prices were. Another important piece of research is to determine how many tickets were sold at previous similar events. Also, how many tickets the event is currently selling at other public assembly facilities in other markets? Last but not least, the box office needs to research other shows that are currently on sale in the market that will draw consumers from the same market demographics of the show that is being contemplated. The size of the market and number of ticket buyers in an event's potential market is a finite number. Therefore, if there are other shows in the market that are currently selling tickets to the population base, it may be advisable to either pass on the show or possibly postpone the show to a later date, if possible. It is important that both the PAF manager and the promoter are aware, based on the research, of the event's potential to sell tickets.

B.   Determine the Event's Desired Facility Configuration
Once the number of tickets that can potentially be sold by the event has been agreed on by the PAF manager and the promoter, a next step is to determine the event configuration and seating chart that will be used to maximize ticket sales *(achieving a sell out)*, and to provide the best possible sightlines to the customers.

BOX OFFICE CHECKLIST

Facility Logo Here

Box Office Manager's New Event Checklist

EVENT: _____

EVENT DATE: _____

ON-SALE DATE: _____

PROMOTER CONTACT: _____

ADDRESS: _____

PHONE: _____ FAX: _____

CELL: _____ E MAIL: _____

- ☐ 1. Notify ticketing contractor of event set up specifics on the ticketing system
- ☐ 2. Determine facility configuration and potential capacity
- ☐ 3. Determine event seating chart
- ☐ 4. Develop manifest and discuss with Operations Manager
- ☐ 5. Discuss ADA compliance with Operations Manager
- ☐ 6. Confirm manifest capacity compliance with Operations Manager and Fire Marshal
- ☐ 7. Check potential on-sale dates with Promoter
- ☐ 8. Verify accuracy of ticket text
- ☐ 9. Verify ticket scale and prices
- ☐ 10. Verify ticket contractor service and handling charges
- ☐ 11. Verify mail charges
- ☐ 12. Verify local and/or state taxes
- ☐ 13. Confirm ticket text with Promoter
- ☐ 14. Receive signed booking contract by Promoter
- ☐ 15. Send out booking notice to all facility departments
- ☐ 16. Complete X chart *(best available)*
- ☐ 17. Confirm seating holds and kills in writing with Promoter
- ☐ 18. Confirm ticket transaction limits in writing with Promoter
- ☐ 19. Determine box office on-sale staffing
- ☐ 20. Determine event on sale staff needs with Security
- ☐ 21. Confirm ticket sale information with Contractor for :
  - a. Outlets
  - b. Telephone Operators
  - c. Internet
  - d. Pre-sale holds
- ☐ 22. Pull hard copy of audit prior to on-sale
- ☐ 23. Order cash advance
- ☐ 24. Discuss event day set up with Operations Manager

- ☐ 25. Specials: _____

FIGURE 5-5

Depending on the type of PAF, the manager has several different seating configurations depending on the prerequisites of the event that are typically described in the production rider for the event. Production riders are discussed in greater detail in Chapter 8.

Production Rider. The production rider is the event-specific requirements in terms of stage location and size; sound and lighting equipment; and sound and lighting mix location; and other information that is required for the event set up. In addition, the promoter, as the spokesperson for the agent/talent, will request reserved seating, general admission seating, or festival seating.

Reserved Seating. Reserved seating establishes a separate ticket for every seat, fixed or portable, sold on a section, row, seat basis for an event.

General Admission Seating. General admission seating is the seating format in which all seats are available on a first-come, first-served basis and is generally considered an opposite option to reserved seating. The general admission format can also be used when the house is scaled by identifying individual seating sections that are sold at different prices, but seating within each seating section is still available on a first-come, first-served basis.

Festival Seating. Festival seating is a form of general admission accommodation. Often the area directly in front of the stage or platform has no seating other than a floor or ground surface, which provides the audience/spectators space to gather to observe a performance. Festival seating in an amphitheater is more often at the back of the seating area; the audience is seated on the lawn, often in their own lawn chairs, to observe a performance.

Depending on the type of facility, event configuration and seating chart, the event may have one or a combination of seating types depending on the nature of the event and the production rider. Some facilities are designed to have both reserved and general admission types of seating. One example of this would be an amphitheater, which has both reserved seating underneath the enclosure and festival seating in the grass area behind the fixed seats.

C.   Determine Ticket Pricing Threshold
The next task in the ticket process is to determine the maximum price that can be charged for this type of an event in this market. This can be referred to as the market's *ticket price sensitivity* or *market threshold*. Naturally, promoters will want to maximize their revenue potential without preventing people from purchasing tickets because they don't feel that the price of the entertainment is commensurate with the event. The promoter relies on information gathered about ticket prices of similar types of events that have recently been in the market, as well as the ticket price for that specific event the previous time it was in the market. Once this research has been completed, the promoter can either charge one price for all of the tickets for the event or a second option would be to *scale the house.*

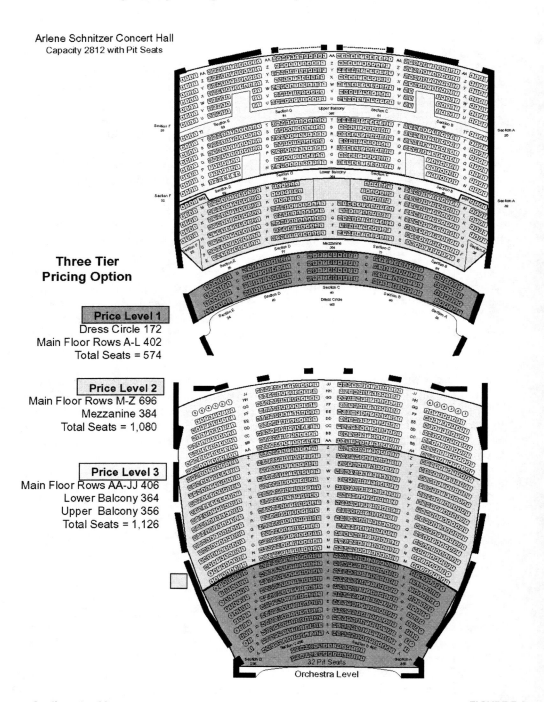

Arlene Schnitzer Concert Hall
Capacity 2812 with Pit Seats

**Three Tier
Pricing Option**

Price Level 1
Dress Circle 172
Main Floor Rows A-L 402
Total Seats = 574

Price Level 2
Main Floor Rows M-Z 696
Mezzanine 384
Total Seats = 1,080

Price Level 3
Main Floor Rows AA-JJ 406
Lower Balcony 364
Upper Balcony 356
Total Seats = 1,126

Scaling the House   **FIGURE 5-6**

D.   Scale the House

When a promoter believes that they may be able to maximize their ticket revenue by pricing the tickets at different values based on the sightlines and proximity to the event, they are said to be *scaling the house*. Larger types of public assembly facilities such as stadiums and arenas generally have the potential for several different ticket prices. In addition, family shows are also known for multiple ticket prices, based not only on sightlines and proximity to the event, but also for specific demographics of the population such as children, senior citizens, military personnel, and large groups.

It is advised that scaling a house should be done along *hard breaks* in the seating setup such as along cross aisles and/or different levels of the facility such as floor, first level, and balcony. Customers who are paying different ticket prices for seating in areas not divided by hard breaks (for example, only one row in front or behind another customer) may become disgruntled and request a refund. In today's pricing schemes, the promoter and others who are "at risk" are speculating that the price points of the tickets will be perceived by customers as reasonable and fair and that all tickets to the event will be purchased. More and more, the public assembly industry is following the well established concept of pricing based on demand or dynamic ticket pricing, similar to airline and hotel pricing. The industry continues to search for the price sensitivity for the entertainment value by giving patrons the opportunity to purchase high quality seat locations through variable or flex pricing methods that include such programs as ticket auctions, added-value ticketing such as buying merchandise or other artist-related items along with entry to an event, an entertainment "experience" such as a meet and greet with artists or team players, etc.

Ultimately, the PAF manager, in consultation with the box office manager and operations manager, should only suggest to the event promoter the scale for the event. The final decision on ticket prices and scale should rest solely with the promoter. (Figure 5-6 provides an example of scaling the house.)

E.   Determine Service Charges and Facility Fees

Ticket service charges are usually specified in the contract between the subcontractor and the PAF. It is important to understand the ranges of ticket service charges based on the price of the tickets for the event. It is also important to make sure that the ticket subcontractor is discharging the appropriate service charges based on the contract for each and every event.

F.   Create Manifest

Creating a ticket manifest is a process by which the box office manager uses a software program to place seats on the seating chart in exactly the location and to scale (price) that they will appear when the event is set up. This manifest will be the document that the ticketing subcontractor will use to create the event on the ticketing system. It will also be the document that the operations manager will use to set up the show.

G.   Determine "Status Seats/Holds" Including ADA Holds

Now that the event configuration, seating chart, and manifest have been established, the event is almost ready to go on sale. One of the last steps before the event goes on sale is to determine a list of seats to put in *"status"* or *"holds."* A seat hold is when the box office manager prevents a seat on the manifest from public sale by putting it in status. When a seat is in a status, it is usually followed by a designation such as promoter hold, building hold, production hold, artist hold, relocation hold, or ADA hold.

In the United States, the Americans with Disabilities Act (ADA) requires facilities to provide reasonable accommodations to customers with disabilities such as appropriate signage, seat armrests that rise or no armrests at all, assistive listening systems, and special platforms. Therefore, before tickets are made available to the general public, the operations manager, event coordinator, and the box office manager must identify seating for customers with disabilities. Most facilities have made modifications resulting in permanent seating locations for the physically challenged. These locations must be scattered or disbursed in both the permanent seating and portable seating areas, so long as they provide the accommodations required by the ADA. Canada as well as many other countries also have laws and regulations similar to the ADA pertaining to the accommodation of individuals with disabilities. It is important to remember that the ADA guidelines impact different types of public assembly facilities and the events which they host differently. Therefore, it is the responsibility of the public assembly facility manager and staff to read and understand how the ADA impacts their facility and its events. In some cases, facilities such as arenas and stadiums have multiple seating configurations and charts. The ADA compliance changes depending on the type of event that the PAF is being set up for.

Once the box office manager has finished putting tickets in status, the list is reviewed by the promoter for final approval. Once the promoter has approved a list of holds, only the box office manager and assistant box office manager should be able to release the holds. When the box office manager releases the holds they should have some type of documentation such as an e-mail or fax that serves as documentation for who the tickets were released to, what price they were sold at, if they were released in a complimentary status, and when the holds were released.

H.   Determine "On Sale" Date

Usually, the on sale date of the event is determined by a consensus of the promoter, PAF general manager, the marketing manager, box office manager, and the ticketing subcontractor depending on the type of event. It is important that the first day of ticket sales is strong in the sense that the show is said to have "momentum." Promoters try to create urgency in the ticket buying population so that shows will sell as many tickets as quickly as possible. Some of the considerations that need to be kept in mind when determining an on sale date are

- The day of the week on which the customer base who are purchasing tickets are most likely to buy tickets
- Other similar events that may be on sale or going on sale in the market
- The day in which the show information "breaks," which means the day the event becomes public information

The box office manager also may manage a number of pre-sales to established constituencies that may include, but not be limited to artist fan clubs, credit card membership groups, and loyalty programs, causing multiple days of pre sales and on sales even prior to going on sale to the general public. The box office manager should work with all parties to ensure that ticket allocations for each of these groups of potential ticket buyers are handled according to the parameters of that focused group. For example, artist holds will typically have general rules of seating placement such as "all of these seats are to be held in the first five rows" and other requirements as stipulated by all the parties.

I.   Confirm and Test All Four Methods of Ticket Sale Distribution
Now that all of the essential information has been determined and confirmed between the PAF manager, a promoter, and their staffs, the box office manager needs to verify the readiness of the system with the ticketing subcontractor to make sure that the correct facility and event information is in place at all points of sale. This is a critical step, because the majority of tickets sold for an event are now purchased at a point of sale outside of the venue box office and the box office manager has very little control over the customer service provided by ticket sellers at the outlets, phones, and on the Internet. The box office manager needs to make sure that the contact persons for the ticketing subcontractor are conveying all the correct information to their staff and that staff is using the highest quality customer service possible to meet the needs of the customers buying tickets for the facility and events.

J.   Put the Event On Sale
The promoter, in coordination with PAF management, may put restrictions on the number of tickets that a person can purchase on the first day of a ticket on sale. These restrictions must be in place so that as many people as possible have an opportunity to purchase tickets to top entertainers and events. When the event goes on sale as scheduled and advertised, the box office manager and the ticketing company carefully watch computer screens and print reports to help identify inconsistencies. It is the facility and ticketing subcontractor's responsibility to guard the integrity of the ticket sale process to every extent they can.

K.   Track Ticket Sales and Reports
Tracking ticket sales from the time the first ticket is sold until the event gets to those magical two words "sold out" is an important role of the box office. Understanding when to add additional dollars to the marketing campaign based on anticipated ticket sales is a function of how many tickets an event has sold in the number of days before the event day.

L.   Will Call/Walk Up

Will call and *walk up* are two terms that deal with tickets sales on the day of the event.

Will call are the tickets that have been purchased and/or assigned prior to the event and are picked up at the box office on the day the event. Will call could also refer to tickets that were purchased online or over the telephone within 48 hours of the event and are sent to the box office to be printed and filed for pickup prior to the event.

Walk up is the term used for the tickets that will be purchased on the day of the event.

It is very important for the facility manager and box office manager to correctly anticipate the potential for walk up and will call of an event. Significant negative customer service issues can develop if the facility has not properly staffed and planned and prepared for an orderly processing of both of these types of ticketing functions.

M.   Box Office Settlements

The box office settlement is the most crucial responsibility of the PAF manager and the box office manager. The settlement identifies how many tickets were sold and at what price they were sold including service charges and taxes that were associated with the sale of those tickets. Today, keeping track of ticket sales has become more complex, because tickets are now sold in four different places including the box office, outlets, on the phone, and on the Internet. Therefore, most of the money for an event comes into the box office electronically, and consequently the box office manager has to be able to account for tickets and the money associated with them in a number of different ways. (Appendix A, Figure 5-7 provides a sample box office statement.)

N.   Event/Promoter Tax Collection

As mentioned in the previous paragraph, the box office is also responsible for collecting all governmental taxes and other fees associated with the sale of tickets at all of the primary ticket sales locations.

O.   Ticket Revenue Distribution

When the box office manager has completed the final box office settlement, the ticket sales information and all of the supporting documents are sent to the finance director to be reviewed and approved. Finally, the box office settlement is included in the overall event settlement and the PAF manager determines, in conjunction with the promoter, any deductions from the final ticket proceeds for facility and marketing expenses relating to the event. The box office manager should not distribute any funds to the promoter until the general manager has signed off on the settlement. Finally, either a check is cut to the promoter or the money is wired into a specific bank account by the finance director and general manager. PAF management must also make the necessary payment in taxes to the appropriate governmental authority on a regular basis.

e-TICKET

Technology continues to change and improve the ticketing industry. One of the most significant technological changes is the ability of the consumer to purchase tickets online through the Internet, download their ticket(s) onto their home computer, and print them on an standard 8½" x 11" piece of plain paper, or to receive that ticket via a personal electronic device. The technology and security feature that allows an e-ticket to be printed at home is the use of a bar code. When consumers download the information for the e-ticket, they also download a corresponding barcode that, to date, has not been widely counterfeited for fraud. Each ticket can be copied and, as with other types of hard tickets, the barcode is the determining factor as to the authenticity of the ticket. Consequently, a duplicated e-ticket can be used for entrance into a facility/event if it is the first

Figure 5-8

time the barcode is read as a person enters a facility. Once the barcode has been read at the entrance, all other copies of the same barcode are null and void, even if the first e-ticket used to gain entry is not the original e-ticket. Although the e-ticket technology is still relatively new, ticketing companies are making great strides in reducing the opportunity for counterfeiters to sell bogus tickets, because an e-ticket can be electronically communicated instantaneously and at no cost, holds unique customer identifiers on the ticket itself, and holds ticket holders accountable for all use of that ticket while in their possession. Further, as the industry becomes digitized, it is engaging in digital marks that will tie a ticket holder to that ticket, virtually eliminating the opportunity to counterfeit those tickets. (Figure 5-8 provides an example of an e-ticket.)

SECONDARY TICKET MARKET

The secondary ticket market gets its name from not being part of the primary ticket market. As discussed previously, the primary ticket market refers to *authorized* ticket points of sale, such as the box office, and the subcontractor's outlets, telephones, and web site. The secondary ticket market is the *unauthorized*

SECONDARY TICKET MARKET

Concert Tickets Get Set Aside, Marked Up by Artists, Managers

By Ethan Smith

Wall Street Journal, Wednesday, March 11, 2009

Less than a minute after tickets for last August's Neil Diamond concerts at New York's Madison Square Garden went on sale, more than 100 seats were available for hundreds of dollars more than their normal face value on premium-ticket site TicketExchange.com. The seller? Neil Diamond.

Ticket reselling -- also known as scalping -- is an estimated $3 billion-a-year business in which professional brokers buy seats with the hope of flipping them to the public at a hefty markup.

In the case of the Neil Diamond concerts, however, the source of the higher-priced tickets was the singer, working with Ticketmaster Entertainment Inc., which owns TicketExchange, and concert promoter AEG Live. Ticketmaster's former and current chief executives, one of whom is Mr. Diamond's personal manager, have acknowledged the arrangement, as has a person familiar with AEG Live, which is owned by Denver-based Anschutz Corp.

Selling premium-priced tickets on TicketExchange, priced and presented as resales by fans, is a practice used by many other top performers, according to people in the industry. Joseph Freeman, Ticketmaster's senior vice president for legal affairs, says that the company's "Marketplace" pages only rarely list tickets offered by fans.

The vast majority of tickets are sold by the artists and their promoters with the cooperation of Ticketmaster. In fact, he says that for any concert to which Ticketmaster carries so-called platinum seats, the Marketplace sells only artist-sanctioned tickets, not those resold by fans.

FIGURE 5-9

points of sale for tickets that have been purchased once and are now being resold for a higher price and with significantly higher service charges and handling fees. The genesis of the secondary market is what is referred to as *ticket brokers* and *scalpers.* Currently there is not a national law that prohibits ticket brokerage or the secondary market. In fact, many state laws are becoming less stringent, making it easier for ticket brokers to exist and flourish, and in many instances the secondary ticket market is becoming authorized.

It should be in the building general manager's primary focus to first get the tickets available for each and every event in their facility sold through the authorized primary ticket system and therefore help the promoter to achieve a sellout. (Figure 5-9 provides an example of the secondary ticket market.)

SCALPING AND COUNTERFEIT TICKETS

Scalping tickets is a process that's been around for a long time, since the early advent of live entertainment in the Roman and Greek PAFs of the day. You could say that scalping was the impetus of the secondary market. Scalping is, simply put, the process of reselling a ticket for more than face value. The beneficiary of the profit usually has no affiliation or responsibility to the building or persons who are at financial risk from the event.

Tickets that are fraudulently duplicated and sold to unsuspecting customers as valid tickets for an event are referred to as counterfeit tickets. With new technology, tickets can be duplicated to look almost better than the original tickets, and the potential to deceive unsuspecting ticket buyers as well as ticket takers at the turnstiles of events remains.

One of the public assembly facility manager's primary defenses against counterfeit tickets has become the barcode. The barcode system currently being used by many PAFs only allows a specific barcode to enter the facility once. Therefore, if someone duplicates a ticket with the barcode, a PAF using a barcode system will prevent the same barcode from being used twice. This enables the box office manager to prevent the facility from going over its capacity for the event. But unfortunately, this does not prevent someone from duplicating the ticket and trying to pass off that duplicate as a valid ticket.

PREMIUM SEATING

In the earliest construction of PAFs, separate locations were designated for distinguished guests and politicians, such as was the case of the Roman Colosseum. In North America, the development of PAFs has also seen the designation of specific areas in facilities for dignitaries and VIPs.

In the mid-1960s, public assembly facilities began to add on locations that could be sold to customers who wanted an exclusive area to discuss business and watch the event of the day in the facility. Those locations were known as *skyboxes* because they were usually constructed above the existing seating areas to avoid major and expensive renovation to the facility.

When this idea began to generate a significant amount of ancillary revenue, the next generations of exclusive seating in stadiums and arenas were designed by architects to optimize the sightlines of these exclusive seating areas so that the marketing staff and teams could maximize the revenue.

This next generation of exclusive seating was referred to as *luxury suites*. The name was appropriate as many of these seating areas began to take on the appearance of "living rooms" and "board rooms" that you would find in the most expensive homes and offices.

Because the connotation luxury was in some respects elitist, the next generation of exclusive seating locations was referred to as *hospitality suites*. In addition to hospitality suites, facilities were able to sell smaller amounts of exclusive seating in the form of *club seats*. Club seats were usually sold in pairs and also gave the ticket holders exclusive access to private clubs within the facility.

Today, PAF managers have developed all types of premium seating to enhance their ancillary revenue. These areas also have a myriad of sizes and shapes; locations and amenities; fees and expenses; contracts and leases; and methods of payment that are tailored to the demographics of the market and based on thorough research. The following list is just a few of the new premium seating concepts available in public assembly facilities

- Party Suites – usually rented on an event-by-event, or one off basis. The price of the suite usually includes tickets and sometimes food and beverage.
- Bunker suites – usually located under the seating area with no direct sightline to the event. Used before, during, and after the event, bunker suites may be decorated like a board room or a suite in a hotel; often they include some individual seats in the event area.
- Founders suites – suites that are sold during construction and have premium amenities.
- Grand suites – very large suites that can accommodate more than 100 people.
- Celebrity suites – similar to party suites. Usually rented for one event and include attendance/hosts such as retired players from the resident teams.

DATABASE MANAGEMENT

Data base management is the collection and use of the information that can be gathered from ticket transactions. This information, which includes credit card information, addresses, and phone numbers, is used to code types of tickets purchased and frequency of tickets purchased. This information can be used in many different ways. This historical data can be used to track the frequency that people attend events, the types of events they attend, and the ticket prices they have paid. This enables the PAF and event the ability to offer those tickets for similar types of events.

Data base management also requires the staff handling such sensitive data to be responsible for the safety and security of the data. Identity theft is a real issue affecting millions, and it is incumbent upon any in-house or contracted ticketing system to make sure personal buyer information is protected from theft or loss. Further, the government requires all companies, including PAF operators, to comply with laws that were enacted to protect consumer information from being used in unlawful or disruptive ways.

Information management laws also require public assembly facility managers to offer each patron the opportunity to "opt-out" from receiving additional information similar to how citizens can state their preferences for "do not call" lists.

Data base management and the gathering of credible, reliable information pertaining to the patrons that visit public venues are essential for that venues success. Moreover, that same data, if used maliciously or with ill-will by careless managers, will dissuade patrons from visiting the venue, regardless of how important the patron wishes to seek the entertainment offered. Powerful information-gathering is an important tool for business growth and a huge liability to growth if used improperly and without rules and without regard for patron privacy.

DESIGNING THE BOX OFFICE SPACE

Due to the increased frequency of tickets being sold online and on the telephone, (in some cases more than 70 percent) the need for large office space for ticketing operations at most PAFs has decreased. An exception to this trend is that some types of public assembly facilities such as theaters feel it is to their advantage to self operate their ticketing system in-house. This decision requires more people and more space to staff a phone room that is large enough to accommodate the needs of that facility. Therefore, when designing a box office in a new facility, the architects need to know whether the program plan is to have a self-operated or sub-contracted box office operation, which in turn will dictate the square footage and facilities to effectively manage a ticketing operation that includes the in-house functions needed to successfully operate a box office.

Staffing the Box Office

Full time staff
Developing a box office staff also has been significantly changed since the majority of tickets are now purchased online. The box office manager will determine staffing levels by the type of facility (stadium, theater, etc), seating capacity of the facility, whether the facility has tenants or not, and whether the facility is a self-operated box office that also staffs its own internal phone room.

Part time staff
In terms of staffing the box office on a non-event day, the box office manager needs to know the number of events on sale. In terms of staffing the box office for an event, the box office manager needs to know the number of tickets that are still available for sale for the event as well as the potential for those tickets to sell. As discussed previously in this chapter, ticket sales that take place on the day of the event are generally referred to as the *walk-up*. In addition, the box office manager also needs to know how many tickets will be picked up at the box office that are already paid for or are complimentary.

Adequate staffing levels are necessary for quality customer service. Understaffing the box office can result in long lines at the box office and may make customers walk away from the event or worse, not return for future events. Overstaffing has similar dire consequences. Too many people in the box office can result in increased and unnecessary labor expenses for the facility and the promoter.

Yield Management

The practice of yield management or revenue management involves the manipulation of prices in order to price event tickets, seating, etc., differently for different customers. Unlike retail goods that are priced the same for all customers, some seat locations and tickets for those seats lend themselves to multiple pricing plans constructed using yield management techniques.

Yield management is a process that encourages facility managers to maximize the potential financial yield on seats they manage by progressively and systematically discounting or increasing the price to the customer based on demand analysis in order to maximize yield.

Five characteristics of products or services that make good markets for using yield management pricing techniques are

- Fixed capacity: the number of seats in a particular configuration is fixed.
- Customer demand can be identified and separated into distinct market segments based on willingness to pay: those willing to pay for better seats, locations, and can be separated from those customers unwilling to pay premium prices for the best seats.

- Product or service is perishable: when the event begins the marketing opportunity is over.
- Product sold in advance of consumption: event has advance ticket sales.
- Consumer demand fluctuates: weekend, mid-week, or seasonal demand for event tickets.

The hotel and airline industries appear to be successfully marketing their inventory by either increasing prices or discounting prices, based on unsold inventory, as the product expiration date draws near. When the expiration date is very close, both airlines and hotels put their product out to bid to other outlets in a belief that getting half the original price is better than nothing at all. Additional benefits to yield management can include a positive impact on ancillary revenue streams (greater ticket sales result in greater concession sales), strengthened consumer buying patterns, and brand loyalty enhancement. Like the hotel and airline industries, the inventory of tickets offered by public assembly facilities is dramatically affected by time. An unsold seat to a performance or event might have a $100 value minutes before the starting time, but actually becomes worthless once the performance or event has commenced.

Public assembly facility managers could benefit from studying the yield management models used for many years by many live theaters and subsequently devise an appropriate application for their various ventures. Located in close proximity to the theatre districts in London, New York City, and other major cities worldwide are ticket outlets that sell day-of-performance tickets at discounted prices. Although the theatre does not gain full ticket value, the discounted revenues are better than none and by filling the seat the probability of gaining additional income from ancillary sales is increased.

One example of how using yield management increased revenue relates to a struggling auditorium housing a summer entertainment series. The facility's manager noticed that ticket demand was highest on weekends and lowest Monday through Thursday. Tickets were priced the same ($30) for all performances. However, demand for weekend tickets was twice that of the facility's seating capacity while only one-fourth of available tickets for the mid-week performances were sold.

Through the use of yield management techniques, the facility manager increased revenues by changing two pricing policies. First, the price for weekend performances was increased to $45 to capture those willing to pay the higher price in order to attend the weekend performances. Second, the price for weekday performances was reduced to $20, thus attracting larger audiences, including those unable to get weekend tickets, but willing to attend a weekday performance rather than not attending at all. In this case, new revenue was generated from the higher prices on weekends without affecting demand, and new revenue was generated from weekday performances due to the reduced price that produced an increase in ticket sales. The new pricing rules evolved from management's ability to divide the total market into segments based on demand and the consumer's willingness to pay.

Many sports teams that use stadiums and arenas are in the early stages of transforming their standard full-price ticket into a higher revenue yielding ticket in two ways. One is to charge a premium price for weekend games, as in baseball and basketball. The second is to charge a premium price for specific games against teams such as current world champions and/or traditional rivals.

It can be argued the concept of yield management is not new, but has simply evolved into its current form. It has long been "usual" for some event types to charge one price for advance sale purchases and a higher price day-of-event sales rather than reducing the prices as expiration time nears. The strategy behind this yield management pricing format is to encourage advance purchase sales.
At times, however, the application of the yield management approach could result in stimulating day-of-event sales as opposed to advance sales. If this were to occur, it might result in making a decision not to book a second show (or third or more) because of the poor advance ticket sales when, in fact, a demand actually exists for additional shows. The end result would be too little supply for the actual demand and the creation of an ideal market for scalpers.

THE FUTURE OF TICKETING

One of the most complex and evolving systems in a PAF is in the area of ticketing and access management. Public assembly facility managers have and will continue to have many ticketing options available to them. It will continue to be their obligation to search for the best possible ticketing system available that most efficiently and effectively meets the needs of their facility, customers, promoters, and tenants. Some of the changes on the horizon include

- *New terminology* – The term ticketing and box office could evolve into a new term *access and data management.*
- *New uses of bar codes* – Bar codes are already being used on cell phones and personal information devices to gain access into facilities for events and eliminate the need for hard tickets.
- *Paperless ticketing* – will also deliver new opportunities for PAFs and box office managers to learn about their patrons buying habits and to thwart counterfeit attempts. A paperless ticket means just that – a ticket delivered exclusively via electronic means with no cost associated by the venue to print, handle, and mail hard tickets out to patrons. Paperless ticketing will also deliver to a venue cost savings in a variety of ways, including labor reductions, delivery, and authentication costs; ticket takers will fall by the wayside of "greeters" and so on.
- *Universal personal identification card* – this card may hold all of your personal identification information much like a driver's license as well as have the capability to be used as a credit card. You may also be able to store information on the card such as tickets purchased. This will enable the consumer to swipe the card and gain entrance to the facility

as well as use the card for the purchase of parking, merchandise, food and beverages

- *The secondary market* – Already changing the face of ticketing, the PAF business will continue to grapple with the ethics and complexities of this growing part of ticketing and access management. Most certainly, however, the nascent idea of retaining and restoring back to the industry the economics that the secondary market offers is drawing huge attention and discussion in the industry. More and more programs and ideas that are aimed at retaining money "in industry" will be of paramount importance to the public assembly manager and his/her employees.

SUMMARY

As complex as ticketing is becoming, it still will continue to have its roots in the fundamentals of access management; the ability to control capacity; the ability to count the revenue based on tickets sold; and the ability to value seating locations based on sightlines and the public's perceived value of the entertainment.

Public assembly managers and box office managers are constantly refining their skill set relative to the changes occurring in the modern ticketing marketplace. Most certainly, the late 1990's into the early years of the 21st century, technological advances have brought more change to the public assembly industry than the previous 50 years combined. Box office managers and by extension, public assembly managers need to be very technology friendly and to be able to leverage the technology in place to maximize ticket sales and ancillary revenue that surround the live entertainment event. It is incumbent in everyone's job description to deliver to the consumer the best in customer service and meet the high expectations of the fickle and demanding wider audience that is available to attend events in a venue. Without superb customer service and therefore the gains won through repeat visits by consumers, venues will suffer and begin to lose audience.

In addition, ticketing and the programs that have developed around the broad based core ticketing component, including self-service ticketing via the web and email campaigns to targeted audiences, have become a significant means of communication between the facility and the consumer; have protected the legal rights of the facility through the use of limited contract and hold harmless language; and have served as an additional revenue stream through the implementation of service fees and advertising.

REFERENCES AND ADDITIONAL READINGS

Baugus, R.V. 2004. "Taking Inventory: Teaming Up to Move Tickets." *Facility Manager* (February/March): 20-23. Coppell, TX: International Association of Assembly Managers, Inc.

Herrick, Julie. 2001. "Selling Tickets at the Speed of Light." *Facility Manager* (July/August): 22-26. Coppell, TX: International Association of Assembly Managers, Inc.

Kramer, Melody. 2008. "That's the Ticket." *Facility Manager* (June/July): 18-21. Coppell, TX: International Association of Assembly Managers, Inc.

CHAPTER 6

BUSINESS AND FINANCIAL MANAGEMENT

CHAPTER OUTLINE

INTRODUCTION
THE BUSINESS MANAGER/FINANCE DIRECTOR
THE OPERATING BUDGET
FINANCIAL STATEMENTS
COST ACCOUNTING
CASH MANAGEMENT
ACCOUNTS PAYABLE AND RECEIVABLE
PURCHASING AND PROCUREMENT
INVENTORY CONTROL
AUDITS
SETTLEMENTS
NEGOTIATING THE CONTRACT
HUMAN RESOURCES
- HUMAN RESOURCE GUIDELINES
- EMPLOYEE ORIENTATION
- COMMUNICATIONS
- MANAGING PART-TIME AND CASUAL LABOR
- SOURCES OF PART-TIME LABOR
RISK MANAGEMENT
SUMMARY
REFERENCES AND ADDITIONAL READINGS

INTRODUCTION

At the very center of each public assembly facility is the pervasive influence of fiscal accountability, without which business as usual would cease to exist. Business and finance are simply the measuring stick that drives decisions and their final outcomes. This chapter will attempt to address the fundamental business and finance concepts and principles that commonly pertain to the public assembly facility management industry. The successful management of public assembly facilities not only hinges upon, but begins with understanding these principles and converting them into sound financial leadership practices.

Irrespective of size, type, mission, or ownership, there are many common business dynamics associated with operating all public assembly facilities. The business and finance activities of a small, university-owned performing arts facility are surprisingly similar to those of a convention center, stadium, or arena. These activities usually involve

- Developing the facility's budget
- Providing information for budget presentations
- Monitoring the facility's operating budget
- Developing the capital expenditure budget
- Developing financial reports
- Developing rate and pricing schedules
- Monitoring, and in some cases managing, the facility's risk management program
- Monitoring and developing contracts
- Monitoring and managing the facility's human resources (HR)
- Debt collection (accounts receivable)
- Payment of bills (accounts payable)
- Payroll, benefits, and retirement
- Monitoring and managing ancillary and non-ancillary revenue streams
- Managing cash flow and investments
- Managing internal audits
- Purchasing
- Event settlement
- Audit controls for cash operations related to parking, concessions, merchandising, and box office operations

It is important to recognize the fact that public assembly facilities are businesses. They may be owned and operated by various types of governmental bodies or non-profit organizations, but if they are not managed and marketed in a business-like fashion they are destined to a life of mediocrity at best.

The business office or finance department, therefore, becomes a critical component of any successful public assembly facility. Unlike traditional governmental accounting practices, public assembly facilities require a more for-profit, business oriented system of controlling revenue and expenses typically known as *cost accounting*.

Also, public assembly facility management requires the unique ability to forecast revenue and to manage expenditures for the purpose of accurately forecasting financial performance. This requires adjusting the budget every month by accounting for any negative variances before they become a major year-end problem.

A major emphasis, therefore, must be placed on event-related budgeting whereby revenues and expenses are budgeted and tracked primarily by events. The typical event-based budget has the following characteristics:

- Estimated number of events by specific event type
- Number of event days for each event type
- Average attendance
- Average ticket price, if applicable
- Estimated gross ticket sales
- Rental income or co-promotion profits
- Estimated revenue based on per capita spending for concessions and merchandise
- Parking fees
- Surcharges on ticket sales, if applicable
- Other revenues based on facility service charges

Logically, full-time and part-time wages, salaries, and benefits as well as basic overhead/operating expenses are forecasted based upon the anticipated annual event activity. Knowing where you stand financially at all times is a critical function of the public assembly facility's business office and requires specialized skills along with specialized accounting procedures that are outlined in this chapter.

The Business Manager/ Finance Director

If the facility has a business manager (by whatever title), that individual usually reports to the facility manager and is responsible for gathering, interpreting, and providing the financial information that enables management to make accurate and timely business and financial decisions. The typical business manager holds at least a bachelor's degree in business administration. Many have more extensive educational backgrounds in accounting, finance, marketing, management, human resources, or similarly related business administration curriculum. However, it is also important for the business manager to be knowledgeable about all financial aspects of public assembly facility management due to the unique manner in which these facilities are funded and managed.

While the skills required to be a successful business manager of a public assembly facility are quite similar to those of similar positions in corporate businesses, there are certain peculiarities practiced by the public assembly facility management industry with respect to the business office. Many of the differences have to do with the nuances of the business functions as they are practiced within the public assembly facility management industry. Regardless of those differences, many of the skills required of a finance director or business manager for a public assembly facility include an individual's ability to manage the following business office functions:

- Accounting procedures and recordkeeping
- Budget preparation and monitoring
- Financial statements - preparation and verification
- Reconciliation of event settlements
- Accounts receivable and accounts payable
- Payroll and benefits
- Purchasing
- Internal audit controls
- Risk management and insurance coverage
- Reconciliation of bank accounts

THE OPERATING BUDGET

The operating budgets (money allocated to cover the operating expenses of the facility) for different facility types are more alike than they are different. Each facility type has similar expenses such as management salaries and benefits, full-time salaries and benefits, part-time wages, utilities, janitorial and maintenance supplies, and a variety of general and administrative expenses. In addition, there may be identifiable expenses associated with the revenue streams noted below. The operating budget identifies these anticipated annual operating expenses, identifies the resources allocated to fund them, and provides the facility's management team with a monthly report and analysis of current and year-to-date (YTD) revenue and expenses as compared to the actual budget. Exactly how a particular operating budget is developed and managed is ultimately the responsibility of the facility manager.

Net income after expenses from food and beverage, parking, and catering operations (whether managed in-house or contracted), along with those generated by facility rental, corporate sponsorships, naming rights payments, specialty seating, suite leases, co-promoted and promoted activities, ticket convenience fees or surcharges, advertising, signage, novelty sales, etc., may contribute to funding the facility's operating expenses. However, in many instances the facility's revenue production is not sufficient to cover its general operating expenses, debt service (interest owed on monies borrowed to construct or refinance the facility), and set-aside cash reserves for future capital improvements. Thus, whenever an income shortfall occurs, some sort of subsidy is required to cover the overall operating deficit.

Publicly owned facilities, especially those constructed with an expectation of increased tourism, usually look toward the hospitality industry (hotels, motels, restaurants, vehicle rentals, etc.) for assistance in covering operating deficits. In most instances, assistance is provided in the form of dedicated taxes. These may be in the form of surcharges placed on general sales, food and beverage sales, lodging, vehicle rentals, amusements admissions, and entertainment charges. University-owned arenas and stadiums generally gain revenue through assessing mandatory student athletic and/or activity fees. Performing arts centers frequently solicit endowments that are invested, and only the interest generated is used to cover operating shortfalls and sometimes physical enhancements. The principal remains intact. Performing art centers might also establish foundations and some or all of the donations may be used to supplement the operating budget. Whatever supplemental funding mechanism is selected, the facility's business manager needs to be involved in the decision-making process.

The operating budget, in addition to providing the basis for the narrative and quantitative financial plan, provides management with a pro-forma for a specified period of time that is expressed in detailed quantitative terms. Calendar year budgets begin on January 1 and run through December 31. Fiscal year (FY) budgets may commence on any date and conclude twelve months later. Many municipal entities operate on a FY budget that commences on July 1 and runs through June 30 the following year. Because FY budgets transcend years, they are commonly referred to by those years. Thus, a FY budget commencing on July 1, 2008, and concluding on June 30, 2009, would be referred to as the FY 2008-2009 budget. There are times when a public assembly facility's budget year may not coincide with that of the owner's budget year. In such cases, appropriate adjustments need to be taken to bring them in line. This process is often referred to as periodicity.

The budgeting process requires facility management personnel to plan in advance and develop and present their recommendations to their governing body. Once the operating budget is completed and approved, it provides management with an ongoing vehicle for communicating their financial plans and objectives to other decision makers within the organization. The development of an operating budget represents one of those unique management processes that allow managers to communicate both up and down the organization's hierarchy.

BUDGET PREPARATION

The budgetary process usually flows through four developmental stages: preparation, presentation, adoption, and execution. Careful preparation and effective presentation of the budget proposal are extremely important to the success of the public assembly facility. The budgeting process can be complicated since it involves accumulating and organizing historical revenue and expense data related to the facility's event activity and operations, assessing and projecting the facility's position in current and future markets, establishing goals and objectives that are consistent with the facility's mission statement, and understanding the overall economic and political environment in which the facility exists.

In most cases, the public assembly facility's operating budget is the result of the budgeting process selected by the governing body. A variety of budgeting formats exist. However, there are five that merit attention: line item budgeting, incremental budgeting, performance-based budgeting, planned program budgeting systems, and zero-based budgeting.

Line Item Budgeting. Probably the most commonly used format, this is a systematic, accounting-oriented method of recording expenditures against various classification categories such as salaries, utilities, supplies, equipment, etc. The line-item budget process allows the business manager detailed control over facility expenses. This process works well for discussions of budgeting control, but not for resolving the broader questions of priorities and effectiveness.

Incremental Budgeting. Sometimes referred to as the fair share approach, this is typically used by organizations employing a top-down style of management. Using this approach, all budget items (occasionally there are exceptions) are either increased or decreased by a prescribed percentage of the previous budget. Positive attributes of this budgeting format are that it is based on a previous year, does allow for line item analysis, and is easy to implement and administer. On the negative side, basic goals are not part of the analysis and the question of program priority is not addressed.

Performance Budgeting. This focuses on efficiency. Performance measures are used as the basis for budgeting and comparison of efficiency in production. Measuring efficiency requires quantitative indicators of both input and output. Since budgets are documents that present inputs in detail, it is a starting place for assessing the efficiency of the facility's operation. In a performance budget, the focus is on activities of the operation rather than objects. The performance approach stresses efficiency through relating money requests to organizational output. However, this format does not encourage discussion of effectiveness. This form of budgeting is based primarily on the input-output concept, and therefore is, generally, not considered an appropriate system for public assembly facilities.

Planned Program Budgeting System (PPBS). This is an attempt to evaluate the programs in which the operation engages so as to choose the programs most appropriate to the facility's goals and objectives. Program budgets are characterized by the following similarities: expenditures are listed and attached to specific programs, a detailed narrative and multi-year timeline exists to explain each program, each program requires annual justification for funding, and quantitative program alternatives are listed. Attempting to institutionalize analysis in the executive decision-making process, PPBS stresses effectiveness through relating expenditures and revenues to goals. This process allows comparison and prioritizing of programs based on the public assembly facility's mission, goals, and objectives, financial realities, and its physical limitations. This system can be effective for public assembly facilities that have two or more prime tenants. For example, the Boston Celtics (NBA) and the Boston Bruins (NHL) are the TD Northbank Garden's prime tenants. Using PPBS, the TD Northbank Garden's management can determine, in a fairly precise manner, the actual amount of time, space (including common space), and resources each tenant consumes. This information will enable the facility's management to include these costs in the lease contract for each entity.

Zero-Based Budgeting (ZBB). This blends concern for both efficiency and improved policy-making by requiring that operations organize current and proposed activities into decision packages and rank the packages according to importance relative to all other decision packages. This process evaluates existing programs alongside new programs and requires yearly funding justification for each. Using zero-based budgeting allows management to deal efficiently with programs that have outlived their usefulness or that are simply not producing the desired results related to program objectives. A down side to this system is the potential for business managers to expend all funds in each budget category based on a fear that failing to do so will result in the next FY budget being reduced accordingly.

FINANCIAL STATEMENTS

A critical aspect of the financial management system is the creation of accurate and timely financial statements necessary for the overall effective management of the facility. Four very useful financial management tools that can be created by the business office are an income statement, a balance sheet, a detailed operating cash flow statement, and a capital expenditures statement. (See Appendix A, Figures 6-1 through 6-3 for sample statements.)

The income statement is designed to report the financial performance of the business entity for a specific period of time such as a month, quarter, or year. Net income represents the difference between operating revenues and operating expenses for the specified period. The income statement presents the results of operations, that is, it reports for a specific period of time those items that provide the total revenue, those items that represent the total expenses, and the resulting net income or loss. Facilities often include this information both on a current basis (such as this month) and year-to-date (YTD).

Whereas the income statement reports financial activity for a specific period of time, the purpose of the balance sheet is to report the public assembly facility's financial status for a particular point in time. The balance sheet specifically addresses the facility's current financial status and provides information relative to the sources and uses of funds statement (cash flow).

The first task in preparing the cash flow statement is to calculate the various changes that have taken place in the asset and liability accounts. The net change in each account is then classified and sorted according to whether it is a source or a use of funds. The sources of funds are assets, liabilities, depreciation, and net income.

The detailed operating statement shows income and expense by category and allows the tracking of each item of revenue and expense to its source. Using the detailed operating statement in tandem with the current budget allows the business manager to determine whether the facility is performing better or worse than expected based on variances from the budgeted figures to the actual figures. The business manager should thoroughly research the causes and be able to explain the variances between budgeted figures and actual figures.

A final important report in facility financial management is the capital expenditures report. Policies vary, but typically capital expenditures are purchases of equipment costing more than $5,000 and with a life of five years or more. Often, facility management will present to owners a five-year capital expenditure forecast, which is updated annually. Each year of the five-year capital improvement budget is included, in sequence, in the annual business plan. Competent capital expenditure forecasting and budgeting is essential to the operation of a well-maintained facility.

Cost Accounting

Since it is the responsibility of the business office, under the direction of the facility's business manager, to determine the financial health of the facility and its various activities, the business manager must have command of a systematic process to make that determination. One of those systems or processes is called *cost accounting*. By identifying and isolating every facility activity and determining the associated costs, the business manager is able to produce a multi-dimensional picture of the facility's financial status.

All financial statements and reports prepared by the facility's business office must be in compliance with Generally Accepted Accounting Principles, more commonly referred to as GAAP. Generally Accepted Accounting Principles (GAAP) is the standard set of guidelines for financial accounting as applied in the United States. It includes the standards and rules that accountants use in recording and summarizing financial transactions and in preparing financial statements.

Effective facility managers need to understand precisely how accountants view and measure costs. Conversely, business managers must be able to look at their facility through the eyes of the public assembly facility manager. The objective of a properly implemented and managed accounting process is to provide management personnel with a valuable tool to assist them in the decision-making process.

Determining the price of a soft drink sold from a concession stand should demand a thorough investigation of its actual cost to the facility, which would include the cost of product, storage/inventory, taxes, labor, housekeeping, paper products, spoilage, capital costs, depreciation, etc. Determining the rent structure for the facility's prime tenant should follow the same process.

The business manager should have the ability to identify costs associated with the tenant and the tenant's activities and arrange that information in such a way that it is understandable to the facility manager. The real object of cost accounting is to create a management tool that will

- Measure the activities of the operation in terms of the local currency
- Assist management in looking at general business decisions
- Justify the need for increased, or decreased, funding or reimbursement

The allocation or distribution of costs is an inescapable challenge in nearly every public assembly facility operation. How the cost of shared services are allocated, how fixed overhead is allocated, and how variable expenses are applied are difficult questions. The answers are not always clearly right or wrong.

Cost allocation, in a general sense, is the assignment of costs to one or more cost objectives. A cost objective is any activity in which a separate measurement of cost is desired. Public assembly facility event management, by its very nature, requires a separate measurement of cost concerning each event activity.

Since the nature of the various costs may differ, they must be defined in a separate manner. Cost allocation encompasses the assignment of expenses incurred from direct and indirect cost categories. Direct costs are expense items that can be identified specifically with a single cost item such as insurance, basic utility charges, and management salaries. Indirect costs are expense items that cannot be identified specifically with a single cost item such as general administration, utility usage, and overtime wages not related to a specific event.

Labor is a common expense for all facilities and all events. Direct labor represents wages paid or owed as a direct consequence of an event or activity. Indirect labor represents wages paid or owed as an indirect consequence of an activity, such as general administration, equipment repairs, specialized employee training, consultant fees, etc. These labor expenses are usually reported as general overhead.

Public assembly facility overhead represents costs not specifically identified that benefit the facility in varying proportions and are allocated in some form of a percentage or specific local currency amount to the facility or specific departments. Overhead is applied to products and services because of management's desire to account for and recover all costs. Overhead is not generally a directly identifiable expense, but it will become a part of the service or product cost and will funnel into the expense stream when the overhead costs are added to the cost of goods or services sold. It is essential to recognize and understand the important role that overhead cost plays in the ultimate cost of goods and services. Each aspect of overhead behaves differently with respect to the level of activity and must be analyzed thoroughly.

Some overhead costs are fixed, some are variable, and some are mixed. Fixed costs such as debt service, service contracts, and professional services are constant. Variable costs, such as indirect labor and supplies, change in proportion to the activity. Mixed costs or semi-variable costs contain both fixed and variable elements such as an employee who is paid for a 40-hour work week and then earns overtime pay for additional hours. Calculating a facility's overhead ratios typically includes associating a common denominator to factor each result; fixed overhead totals use a factor of operating event days or operating hours, while variable overhead totals use a factor of occupancy loads to determine the cost per patron.

In addition to implementing and managing the processes that allow for the monitoring of facility costs and revenue streams, the facility's business manager might be responsible for a number of day-to-day financial activities such as cash management, inventory control, fixed assets, labor, utilities, contracts, and risk management.

CASH MANAGEMENT

Common to almost every public assembly facility is the issue of dealing with an accumulation of cash, whether it is derived from box office ticket sales, rent deposits, parking collections, concession sales, catering sales or novelty sales. Cash-on-hand is an ever-present issue in the public assembly facility management industry. Presented below are some of the generally accepted principles concerning the handling of cash.

- Bond all employees who have access to cash. Bonding is a type of insurance that protects the facility from loss brought about by employee theft. The bond premium becomes a cost to the facility. Typically, business managers, box office managers, accountants, concession managers, and those employees whose everyday work involves the handling of cash are bonded. The premium for this protection is so expensive that it usually requires the acceptance of a very high deductible in order to make the premium affordable. For this reason, many municipalities forgo bonding and simply accept the risk (self insuring).

- Where the process allows, the use of cash registers and/or point-of-sale systems are advised. This can improve the efficiency of the reconciliation of cash draws and cash on hand at the end of every shift. Having a cash-out cashier on hand to reconcile cash drawers and sales in the presence of the seller is desired. Leaving large amounts of cash in the building overnight presents serious risks that must be addressed with personnel and physical/equipment solutions. These might include a night watchman, controlled access, and a substantial fireproof vault. When possible, routine bank deposits with a security escort are desirable.

- Unannounced cash audits are strongly recommended. Periodic, but formal, cash audits create a healthy tension in cash management. Cash audits of the box office, or any cash operation, should include validating the amount due against ticket/product sales. In the box office, this is determined by tickets originally available, less tickets on hand (deadwood) equals tickets distributed. A break down of how distributed tickets were sold will result in the amount of cash required to balance. For purposes of the sold number, this would include tickets sold at full price, discounted prices, traded, and complimentary. This format is valid for both hard tickets and those sold from a computer. While not physically present, tickets remaining in the computer's inventory would be classified as "available" and thus considered as unsold or deadwood.

- The facility's checking account must be safeguarded. All checks should be preprinted and consecutively numbered. Checks in excess of a specific dollar amount should require two authorized signatures. The facility's bank accounts must be reconciled monthly in order to verify deposits, balances, and withdrawals.

- A facet of the business finance function often abused is petty cash. The facility should not maintain a petty cash fund larger than needed. Strict procedures should be established concerning the use of the petty cash account and it should be reconciled regularly. It should be firmly established that without prior authorization and the presentation of purchase receipts, petty cash should not be part of the purchasing process.

- If the facility has a history of generating excess cash, even short-term excesses, investment of that cash in interest-bearing accounts or certificates of deposit might be in order. Significant interest income can be earned through careful management of cash from the time of collection until the time of payout to promoters by placing it into short-term sweep accounts. In many instances, owners (such as other municipal departments) will manage and monitor the investment of excess cash. When this occurs, the public assembly facility manager should lobby to credit the facility's operating account with a portion, if not all, of the interest income generated from the facility's excess cash.

ACCOUNTS PAYABLE AND RECEIVABLE

Two additional common financial functions are the billing and collecting for products and/or services and making payments for services and products received. A procedure for dealing with accounts receivable should be established and strictly followed. All receivable accounts should be frequently reviewed to verify payment. Delinquent accounts should be notified. Registered letters should be sent to non-responding delinquent accounts. If the debt is still not paid, the debt should be removed from the facility's accounts receivable and the burden assumed by the owner or a collection agency. If the debt continues to remain unpaid, it should be declared uncollectible and written off. Each step in this process should be undertaken in a timely manner and documented.

Accounts payable (accounts to which the facility owes payment) should be managed as diligently as accounts receivable. However, given the fact that the public assembly facility gains by keeping its money in interest-bearing investments for as long as possible, it is prudent for the facility to delay making payments for as long as good business practices will permit. This can be called "aging" the bill.

PURCHASING AND PROCUREMENT

Many public assembly facilities are governed by public jurisdictions which have very restrictive policies and procedures for purchasing goods and procuring services. In many cases, public assembly facility managers must adhere strictly to those restrictive policies or face severe sanctions. Some facility managers describe their governing body's purchasing procedures as unduly cumbersome and time consuming.

Policies that limit the facility manager's purchasing authority along with policies that require a minimum number of quotations or lengthy bids on items priced above a predetermined price threshold often inhibit the facility manager's ability to provide the kind of customer service that promoters and event producers demand. In such circumstances, it becomes extremely important for the facility manager and the facility's business manager to plan ahead and know all of the purchases that need to be made on behalf of a specific event well in advance.

The use of procurement cards has increased dramatically in recent years. Similar to a personal/business credit card, some facility employees or department heads may use these procurement cards to purchase goods on behalf of the facility or an event. These cards are issued through the municipal or university's purchasing department along with specific guidelines for their use. The use of procurement cards facilitates purchasing transactions and is a great benefit to the public assembly facility staff, as long as the policies that govern their use are followed by the individual employees of the public assembly facility.

The public assembly facility's business office should verify that all purchases are made in accordance with the purchasing policies that management and the governing authority have in place, regardless of the method used to complete the transaction. Most public assembly facilities spend hundreds of thousands of dollars in purchasing goods and services both locally and nationally each year. The facility's business manager should know those vendors with whom the facility spends large sums of monies each year and should share that information with the sales and marketing staff as potential sources for sponsorships, signage sales, and sale of luxury suites and/or club seats.

Inventory Control

The public assembly facility's business office will be involved in the managing of the facility's inventory of supplies and equipment. Insisting that supplies be stored in a secure area and that a check-in/check-out system be in place and enforced will lessen the potential for supplies being misappropriated. Unscheduled audits of stored inventory and holding supervisors responsible for maintaining and accounting for these items will help reduce shrinkage, especially with respect to consumable products such as housekeeping and general maintenance supplies.

Timely submission of supply orders prevents the need to deal with rush orders which tend to be much more expensive. When needed products/services must go to bid, adherence to the established bid process will speed the process and reduce administrative costs. All received purchases should be recorded and the specifics of the order verified to ensure that the correct items have been delivered and in the quantity ordered. Generally, supplies should be inventoried and stored in a manner that allows for the issuance of items on a last-in, last-out basis. This is especially true for perishable items and those with a short shelf life.

Audits

Unscheduled internal and external audits that focus on the handling of the facility's finances coupled with audits that focus on the facility's adherence to policies and procedures are necessary in maintaining a healthy business environment. In applying the audit process, generally, one of the public assembly facility's events, such as a concert, trade show, exhibition, etc, will be randomly selected. The various transactions associated with that event will be reviewed from the start of the event until its conclusion. The audit process might include a review of contracts, advertising agreements, box office receipts, settlement document, payments to vendors, clients and customers, and payroll documents. Special attention must be given to those charged with conducting the internal audits to ensure that no favoritism or collusion occurs. And although departments may be selected for audit by random, a mechanism must be in place to ensure that all departments are audited within a specified timeframe.

A thorough investigation of a randomly selected business activity should give the auditor a sense of how the facility is being managed. Without some sort of "annual physical," facility managers might grow myopic and lose focus on the overall goals and objectives. The audit process can provide an unbiased observation of the facility's finances and the way the facility is operated and managed. In most instances, the public assembly facility manager is provided a draft of the audit report and given a period of time to deal with or at least debate any negative issues brought to light by the audit before the report is released to the governing body. Although the audit process may at times be stressful for the facility's management and may require significant demands upon their time, the audit process and the subsequent report should be viewed by the facility's management team and its governing body as an excellent opportunity to evaluate performance.

SETTLEMENTS

The settlement process which represents the formal accounting and distribution of funds related to facility events is a somewhat unique activity associated with the public assembly facility. The process itself is not as unique as is the timing of the activity. In most businesses, billing and collection activities occur "after the fact" or after the transactions have taken place. Bills are issued and payments are normally made at the end of the month or within thirty days. The settlement process in a public assembly facility, however, usually takes place the same day or night of the event and occasionally while the event is literally taking place. For example, a stadium concert that has generated a million dollars in ticket sales might be settled while the headliner is still on stage. This may include presentation and payment of bills for labor, transportation, rent, and catering; reconciliation of tickets and ticket receipts; and writing checks and/or making bank wire transfers. The settlement process has evolved as a way for the event promoter to receive money collected through box office ticket sales in order to pay accumulated bills for their engagement prior to moving on to their next engagement. The process also allows/provides the public assembly facility manager an additional way to monitor box office receipts. (See Appendix A, Figure 6-4 for a sample event settlement statement.)

Representation at settlement depends on the structure of the event. For example, a settlement for a traveling theatrical event promoted or presented by the performing arts center will require a representative from the facility who is authorized to issue checks and a representative from the theatre company who is often the tour's accountant. Present at the settlement for a commercially presented concert will usually be a representative from the public assembly facility's management, the tour's accountant, and a representative from the promoter's operation. Typical documents needed at the settlement include

- A box office statement detailing tickets distributed, sold, and not sold
- Invoices from the facility documenting production, security, and contracted or in-house labor required by the event and provided by the facility
- Invoices concerning equipment owned or secured by the facility but used by the event
- Catering bills
- Advertising bills with back-up materials such as notarized affidavits
- Invoices for anything else asked for by the event and provided by the facility

It is essential for the facility manager to have a copy of the artist's contract available if the public assembly facility is the promoter or a copy of the facility's lease agreement if a commercial promoter is simply renting the facility. The terms of those contracts which specifically define the financial relationships between the parties and/or the details of "the deal" must be strictly adhered to during the event financial settlement.

The settlement process has evolved to allow the public assembly facility to withhold from box office receipts an amount equal to the promoter's or the attraction's financial obligation to the facility and for the facility's representative to ask the promoter or the tour's accountant how the remaining revenue should be distributed. Promoters who need cash on the night of the show are obligated to inform the facility in advance so the correct amount of cash is available. At one point in time, most events were settled in cash but that's no longer the case. Today, most settlements are concluded through the issuance of a check by the public assembly facility or by remitted funds using a bank wire transfer.

NEGOTIATING THE CONTRACT

The negotiating phase of the contracting process in most facilities is conducted by the facility manager. In facilities with a business manager, that individual might also be involved in implementing and monitoring the financial terms of the contract; a sales and marketing manager also may have responsibility for contract negotiations, especially in convention centers. Contracts exist between artist agencies and acts, artist agencies and promoters, promoters or artist agencies and facilities, and facilities and contractors/service providers.

A contract is an agreement between two or more parties based upon sufficient consideration to do or to refrain from doing some lawful activity. A contract must create an obligation. In addition, a contract must have the following four aspects:

- Mutual assent
- Legal right and capacity to make the contract

- Fair consideration
- Terms

A common contract is the lease agreement that allows the public assembly facility, or a portion of it, to be rented for a specific period of time for some specific lawful activity. The facility usually receives an agreed upon amount of money (rent) from the promoter or event producer for the use of the facility. The rental payment may be either a flat fee or a percentage of the total ticket sales revenue.

If the public assembly facility's management acts as the promoter, as is often the case with performing arts centers, the management contracts directly with the artist's agency. Much of stadium, convention center, exhibit hall, and arena business is rental business whereby management allows the facility to be leased by a promoter in consideration for rent. In the case of lease/rental arrangements, the promoter usually reimburses the venue for expenses such as front-of-house staffing, security, stagehands, and ticket expenses in addition to paying rent. Sometimes the estimated cost of all these items is combined with the rental fee in an all-inclusive flat payment for rent and services.

Due to the large number of contracts used in most public assembly facilities, it is very important for the manager to understand negotiating philosophies, strategies, tactics, and techniques. Unlike with some contract negotiations, facility managers frequently negotiate a series of contracts with the same party. Consequently, the astute facility manager will keep in mind the need to develop and nurture relationships along with trying to negotiate a satisfactory deal. Many successful facility managers ascribe to the "win-win" school of negotiating philosophy, understanding that the deal has to be good for both parties if a long and mutually beneficial relationship is to occur.

HUMAN RESOURCES

Since one of the largest expenses for any facility is labor, direct and indirect, public assembly facility management should be skilled in identifying, recruiting, hiring, training, and paying employees. An effective manager will mandate the development of procedures for the hiring of full- and part-time employees. In addition, management should normally specify procurement procedures concerning subcontracted labor. The facility's responsibilities include

- Being aware of and understanding the laws concerning Immigration and Naturalization Service (INS) documentation in hiring or the appropriate agency in other countries. In the U.S. the INS is part of the U.S. Department of Homeland Security.

- Monitoring facility hiring and firing activities in light of employee rights and responsibilities.

- Managing the payroll process and being knowledgeable about rates of pay, payroll dates, workers' compensation insurance, withholding taxes, and overtime compensation.

The typical public assembly facility employs a relatively small staff of full-time employees while maintaining a large pool of workers willing and able to work on a part-time, event-related basis.

Its type, volume, and kind of business it attracts generally dictate the size of the public assembly facility's full-time staff. Small facilities might have a general manager, a business manager, an operations manager, and/or building superintendent/engineer. On the other hand, a large facility might also employ managers and support staff for security, advertising and marketing, catering, concessions, box office, event coordination, housekeeping, etc. Full-time hourly employees might work 37.5-40 hours a week and may be eligible for overtime pay for any additional hours worked. However, it should be noted some jurisdictions allow for the employment of hourly employees who are not eligible for overtime compensation. Management will specify which job categories qualify for overtime payment and those that do not. Management will also decide whether to use time cards and/or an electronic time-keeping system, and they may dictate the guidelines used to determine under what circumstances employees are eligible to work overtime.

Human Resources Guidelines

Normally, a public assembly facility develops and implements human resource guidelines that mirror those of other agencies under management's supervision. Although the public assembly facility management business can be very different from other "public works" activities, the organization of human resources services information is quite similar. Typically, most facilities/agencies under a municipal or public university ownership will use similar processes in developing job descriptions, announcements and applications, advertising openings, collecting and processing applications, interviewing and selecting employees, and evaluating performance. Agencies and/or facilities generally follow common guidelines for employee promotions and dismissals.

A carefully constructed and accurate job description should be established for each job title. The job description should include at least

- A title that accurately describes the job
- Description of the nature of the work
- Examples of work assignments
- Supervision received and provided
- Skill-level and physical requirements associated with the job
- Required experience
- Minimum educational requirements

The job description is crucial to the human resources process because it provides the basis for the formal relationship between employee and employer. The objective of those responsible for recruiting and hiring employees is basically twofold: to attract applicants who meet established job qualifications and to identify and hire people who will perform their assignments at the level and in an appropriate manner required by the position.

The first part of the recruitment process involves announcing position openings and then identifying and hiring people with adequate skills, training, and abilities to do the job described. A careful assessment of the job applications which evaluates the merits and qualifications of each candidate can accomplish most of this process. Education levels, accumulated skills, work history, etc., can and should be verified. Depending on the position, credit checks and security background checks may also be required.

The second part of the recruitment process involves screening the applicants. Identifying and hiring employees whose personalities and work habits mesh with the existing employees in the work group and whose personalities and work ethics contribute to, rather than detract from, the facility's ability to achieve its goals and objectives can prove much more difficult. The key to successful hiring is having an individual responsible for the human resources process who completely understands the job position to be filled, knows the necessary interactions required with other facility employees, and is cognizant of the facility's mission statement. Employing a carefully structured interview for all candidates, requiring candidates to provide writing samples and to demonstrate computer skills when appropriate, and including current employees on the interview team will generally provide important insights relative to the compatibility of the candidate.

If the initial applications are thoroughly screened in order to identify candidates to interview, then each candidate interviewed should have the necessary skills and abilities to perform the job. Thus the ultimate goal of the interview process is to identify whether the candidate possesses the personality, temperament, and work ethic that should enable him/her to work in harmony and be productive with other members of the workforce.

The "matching game," placing employees in positions in which the employee's qualifications and the position's requirements best fit, is more art than science. Generally, facility managers in the United States may hire whomever they desire as long as positions are properly posted and advertised; the candidate meets the qualifications stated in the job description; the decision to hire is in accord with the requirements of the Equal Employment Opportunity Commission and the Americans with Disabilities Act; and there has been no discrimination on the basis of certain protected characteristics such as age, national origin, gender, sexual orientation, race, color, qualified disabilities, or religion.

EMPLOYEE ORIENTATION

Orientation is the process of introducing new employees to the workplace. The orientation program should also be structured to assist the new employee in understanding the facility's overall goals and objectives and the employee's role in that process. Training is the process of instructing and guiding the development of the new employee in the workplace. To be successful, the training program should guide the employee through a series of exercises or experiences that teach how to respond to specific requirements of the job. While orientation is normally a one-time activity, training should be an ongoing part of the employee development process.

The public assembly facility's manager is responsible for determining the most effective and efficient employee training programs for the operation, and these programs should be aligned with the facility's overall goals and objectives. The public assembly facility's manager should document and keep verifying records for each employee who successfully completes the orientation program and all other successfully completed training programs.

COMMUNICATIONS

Communication is another critical element in human resources management. In addition to the employee policy and procedures manual that outlines the rights and responsibilities of each employee, there are other excellent communication vehicles available such as

- Written materials provided during orientation and training sessions
- Bulletin boards
- Employee newsletters
- Scheduled staff meetings
- Job specific employee manuals

Employee evaluation is another important communication tool for supervisors to communicate job performance expectations. All employees deserve to hear how they are doing. Formal annual reviews of all employees are typical, though continuous coaching and evaluation is advisable in many supervisory situations. Although this process can be an arduous one, it is a desired practice that benefits management and employees alike. An employee evaluation and development plan can contribute equally to the professional and personal goals mutually shared by the employer and employee.

MANAGING PART-TIME AND CASUAL LABOR

One major difference in public assembly facilities from most other businesses is the large number of part-time or casual employees that are hired to work events. Consequently, a very important task of the facility's HR is the orderly recordkeeping of this segment of the labor force.

Many public assembly facility managers use the terms part-time and casual labor interchangeably or use casual labor to encompass both. However, it must be noted that a difference may exist between casual and part-time labor, even though casual labor works only part-time. The difference may be how the employee's schedule is driven/determined. A casual employee's schedule can be one that is, most always, event driven; no event, no work.

An employee who is considered part-time is more likely to be scheduled to work a specific number of hours on a continuing basis. This might include a position such as a clerk-receptionist who works four hours for a number of days each week. Some public bodies term this "regular part-time" to differentiate from individuals who are hired for part-time tasks, not event driven, but for a short-period of time (e.g., an annual maintenance function requiring extra hands).

The distinction between these part-time and casual employees is murky. The distinction of regular part-time individuals is more clearly recognized.

An ironic situation exists in that a regular part-time employee may not be scheduled to work enough hours in a year to receive fringe benefits while casual employees may. For example, in California the number of hours required to receive fringe benefits in jurisdictions that are part of the Public Employees Retirement System (PERS) is 1,000. Employees reaching that level then receive the fringe benefits retroactive to their first hour of employment. At the same time, casual employees such as ushers, ticket takers, and other "event" personnel may qualify for fringe benefits through a union contract, on a monthly basis, simply by working a certain number of hours, such as eighty.

SOURCES OF PART-TIME LABOR

Few if any public assembly facilities, regardless of size, type, or business volume, can afford to maintain a full-time event staff such as ushers, ticket takers, ticket sellers, security guards, peer security, runners, etc. Nonetheless, these personnel are essential for the proper operation of facility events and activities. Traveling attractions, concerts, trade shows, performing artists, meetings, assemblies, and conventions pay for casual labor, but they depend on the public assembly facility to supply and manage these employees.

There are a couple of ways that a facility can accomplish the task of providing this workforce. Under an in-house operation, the facility may assume the responsibility for identifying potential employees; recruiting, hiring, and organizing their paperwork; and training, managing, insuring, and paying them. Another way would be for the facility to subcontract the labor, turn the process over to local unions, or use a combination of in-house and subcontracted labor or local unions. Each procedure has its advantages and disadvantages and each decision should be based on the availability of the labor pool, payroll, skill requirement, available training programs, employment statutes and regulations, the political climate, and other related factors. Traveling theatrical productions and musical attractions often have a union stage crew with the show.

As mentioned earlier, many public assembly facilities depend on subcontracted labor to staff housekeeping and some front-of-house positions. Labor positions requiring only minimal training and experience but direct and sometimes intense supervision might also be subcontracted to labor providers. Some labor providers specialize in certain areas such as housekeeping personnel, general construction workers, general uniformed security guards, peer (T-shirt) security guards, ushers, and supervisors. They also may be able to provide experienced and well-trained first-aid personnel.

In many publicly owned facilities, contracting for these services must go through a bid process. Once the bid is awarded, a single provider usually supplies all the required casual labor called for in the contract. When labor is subcontracted, the public assembly facility typically initiates the labor call, the provider supplies the labor, and the facility is then billed for the personnel and the provider's administrative expenses. In some instances these expenses may be recharged to facility users. Allowing a subcontracted provider to supply casual labor not only eliminates the expense of recruiting, training, and insurance, it also eliminates the cost of producing and managing the payroll.

Another potential source of labor is the independent contractor. Independent contractors are individuals hired to do specific tasks such as repair telescopic risers, dismantle and repair message and scoreboards, etc. By definition, independent contractors are unsupervised, set their own work hours, are paid at the completion of the task, and are self-insured. Before independent contractors are allowed to work, depending upon the job, they should be required to provide their certificate of insurance and endorsement naming the facility, its officers, employees, and agents as additional insured. Some public facility managers believe part-time labor associated with events meet the definition of an independent contractor thus excusing the facility from wage and hour considerations and insurance. However, most event personnel must perform tasks in ways specified by the hiring body/facility, during specified hours and specified locations. Consequently, they do not meet the United States Internal Revenue Service's criteria as independent contractors.

Volunteers are unpaid employees who represent yet another labor category. It's not unusual for most, if not all, of the entire front-of-house staff at performing arts centers to be volunteers. Many universities use students as ushers and find the practice both efficient and effective. If the public assembly facility were situated in an environment where ready and able volunteers are available from colleges and universities, senior citizen centers, civic and fraternal organizations, and booster clubs, it would benefit the public assembly facility financially, politically, and from a public relations standpoint to utilize their services. The facility manager must keep in mind that although volunteers are unpaid, their personal safety is still the responsibility of the facility; therefore, they need to be protected by the facility's general liability insurance policy and/or worker's compensation program. The facility manager must also remember that volunteers require training and work incentives to motivate them just like paid workers.

RISK MANAGEMENT

In every activity in which the public assembly facility participates, there is an element of risk (potential for harm) and liability (responsibility). Typically, the public assembly facility's management is involved in monitoring, if not directly managing, the facility's activities concerning risk management. The facility management team must understand that risk is omnipresent and that potential individual and/or facility liability exists at all times. Thus, it becomes the responsibility of the public assembly facility's management to design a plan for dealing with risk management and the attendant liability issues.

The public assembly facility manager is responsible for communicating to all full- and part-time employees the importance of understanding that potential risks are associated with every activity held in the facility and on its grounds. They need to understand the concept that every employee is a member of the risk management team and that they must be constantly vigilant in recognizing, reporting, and eliminating all potential risks. The team must understand that any risk left unmanaged may become a threat to the facility as well as to their jobs. Potential risks must be identified and either isolated, repaired, replaced, or completely eliminated.

Whether dealing with a common attendee slip-and-fall or a catastrophic structural failure, risk and liability are the two most important considerations. For virtually every accident that ends up in litigation, the common questions that will certainly be asked of the facility management are: "Should you have anticipated the accident? If so, what was done to prevent it?" An appropriate risk management program will provide the facility's management with the information required to properly respond to these critical questions.

Regardless of the risk management philosophy, the public assembly facility's plan should direct the facility manager to seek and implement ways of reducing and managing anticipated risk. This may be accomplished by understanding the nature of the event, its anticipated audience, and the facility itself relative to potential accidents. Armed with this knowledge, the facility's risk management team may be able to identify and isolate potential accidents and implement measures that may totally eliminate them or at least minimize the possibility of occurrence.

There are five basic ways for dealing with risk: avoid, assume, prevent, reduce, and transfer.

Risk avoidance. Sometimes the very best method of dealing with an exposure to loss is to try to avoid all possibility of the loss occurring. Some risks are not avoidable and, in such case, the exposure to loss for this type or risk can often be reduced but not entirely eliminated. For other exposures, avoidance is the only reasonable alternative, especially for those risks when the chance of loss is high and loss severity is also high.

There may be times when the facility's booking manager will be requested to book an activity for which the potential for accidents is so great that it would not be in the facility's best interest to enter into a contract. As noted in Chapter 3 - Scheduling Facilities and Booking Events, one reason not to book an event is when it is apparent "based on historical data" that the event poses a danger to those in attendance. In such cases, the facility's response to the booking request would be one of avoidance. It is not uncommon for facilities to avoid activities that have both a high frequency of risk as well as a high potential for risk. But, in all instances, the practice of avoidance must be justified.

Risk assumption. Risk assumption means assuming the consequence of a loss will be borne by the party exposed to the chance of loss. Often risk assumption is a deliberated, planned risk management decision. This is, the assumption of the risk is undertaken with the full understanding of the consequence of a potential loss, and with the full understanding the consequences will be borne by the one assuming the risk. Many risks are assumed because the consequences of a specific loss would not be costly enough to justify using any other risk management tool. Sometimes risks must be assumed such as deductible provisions in an insurance policy. In summary, deliberate risk assumption is a desirable alternative when the maximum severity of loss is relatively low and the chance of loss is also low.

Just as some events justify avoidance, there are also events and activities with such a low risk factor that the facility itself may be willing to assume the associated risk. For example, the facility manager may be willing to rent the space for a small meeting without requiring the planner to purchase additional insurance. However, public assembly facilities are less likely to take on the assumption of risk due to the extremely high number of suits arising out of basically insignificant incidents. The litigious nature of society has forced public assembly facility managers to protect their facilities and their employees at all times.

Loss prevention. Loss prevention activities are utilized to lower the chance of loss and to make the occurrence of loss less frequent. There is a close connection between loss prevention activities and insurance premiums. The more effective the loss prevention, the lower the insurance premiums should be. Whenever the frequency of loss is high, loss prevention activities should be applied. However, loss prevention is feasible only if the benefits realized from few occurrences of loss are greater than the cost of the loss prevention measures.

An example of a loss prevention program would be the installation of reflective, skid resistant materials and handrails on the steps and stair risers of the steep upper tier seating sections of a stadium or arena.

Loss reduction. Loss reduction activities are designed to reduce the severity of losses that do occur. Regardless of all the preventive steps taken, some losses will and do occur. Loss reduction activities aim at minimizing the impact of the losses. In general, when the severity of the loss is great and when the loss cannot be avoided or transferred, loss reduction activities are appropriate - provided the cost of said activities does not exceed the benefits gained.

Examples would be the installation of an automatic fire sprinkler system which is not designed to prevent fires but to stop the fire from spreading, fire walls, or silent alarms.

Risk transfer. Risk transfer means the original party exposed to a loss is able to obtain another party to bear the risk. The usual way to transfer risk is to obtain insurance coverage whereby contractually the element of risk is given to the insurance provider. Insurance is an especially appropriate risk management tool when the chance of loss is low and the severity of a potential loss is high. Beyond the usual way of transferring risk through the use of insurance, there are non-insurance risk transfer methods that can be utilized as well. The hold harmless and indemnification clauses in facility user contracts have been an effective method of public assembly facility managers in transferring risk to the facility users. In addition, when managers contract out services (e.g., security, guest services, concessions, etc.), they also transfer the risks associated with those specific areas of operations to the contractor.

Another common method for dealing with risk is simply to transfer it to someone else. The transference process involves "holding harmless" the public assembly facility and its employees. When this occurs, the facility and its employees are sheltered from any liability or financial responsibility associated with injury or loss of property due to negligence. Facility managers who elect to deal with risk by transference will require clients leasing the facility to include indemnification clauses in their contracts that hold the facility and its employees harmless. In essence, the client assumes responsibility for any and all negative occurrences during the rental period.

The most common method for transferring risk, however, is through the purchase of insurance. Requiring both insurance and a hold harmless clause is also a possibility. Public assembly facilities normally have a general liability insurance umbrella policy that protects its property, employees, guests, and invitees. It is normal procedure for a public assembly facility manager to require event promoters to properly insure themselves as well as their attraction, agents, and all employees associated with the event. Further, the promoter will be required to name the public assembly facility and its owner as an additional insured for a pre-determined amount of coverage and provide both a certificate of insurance and a valid endorsement. The purpose of this process is to give the public assembly facility two layers of coverage - its own general umbrella policy and the additional coverage provided by the promoter.

Some facilities use what is called a Tenant Users Liability Insurance Policy (TULIP) which is a blanket insurance policy held by the facility wherein the facility obtains coverage for the tenant in the case that the tenant should fail to obtain coverage on time or the tenant is unable to otherwise obtain the required insurance coverage. This approach allows the user to have the required coverage under the umbrella of the facility's TULIP policy. There is often a charge to the tenant/user for this coverage.

The cost of insurance premiums for public assembly facilities and attractions has escalated to the point where insurance coverage is sometimes simply not affordable. The reasons for the escalation include the frequency of accidents and the severity of injuries, the number of suits and high cost of defending and paying judgments, and a general increase in crowd misbehavior. At one time, concert promoters could insure themselves, the attraction and its employees, and the facility and its guests and employees with a million dollars in coverage at a cost of less than twenty-five cents (US) per person attending the event. Unfortunately, current insurance costs have significantly impacted the total operating expenses of attractions and facilities alike.

SUMMARY

There are many similar business operating dynamics associated with all public assembly facilities. Each facility has its own operating budget. However, for some facilities the cost of operating is greater than the income they can generate. Consequently, these facilities must seek supplemental funding in order to cover their operating deficits in the form of subsidies.

Fiscal year budgets are more common than calendar year budgets. There are several budgeting systems from which public assembly facility governing bodies may select. The more commonly used systems include line item budgeting, incremental budgeting, performance budgeting, and zero-based budgeting. The budgeting process usually flows through four developmental stages: preparation, presentation, adoption, and execution.

The issuance of financial statements is critical to any financial management system. Income statements are designed to report the financial performance for a specific period of time such as a month, quarter, or year. Balance sheets report the financial status for a particular point in time and provide essential cash flow information. Operating statements show income and expenses by category and allow the tracing of each item of revenue and expense to its source. Cost allocation, in a general sense, is the assignment of costs to one or more cost objectives. A cost objective is any activity in which a separate measurement of cost is desired. Public assembly facility management, by its very nature, requires a separate measurement of cost concerning each event activity.

Direct and indirect labor costs are common expenses for all facilities and all events. Direct labor represents wages paid or owed as a direct consequence of an event or activity. Indirect labor represents wages paid or owed as an indirect consequence of an activity or event such as equipment repairs, consultant fees, etc.

Public assembly facility overhead represents variable costs or those not specifically identified that benefit the facility in varying proportions and are allocated in some form of a percentage or specific local currency amount to the facility or specific department. Overhead costs might be re-charged to users based on a formula included in the contract.

The public assembly facility business manager might also be responsible for day-to-day activities such as cash management, inventory control, fixed assets, labor, utilities, contracts, and risk management. Safeguards must be implemented to protect the facility's checking account. Preprinted and consecutively numbered checks should always be used, and checks above a specified amount should require two authorized signatures. All bank accounts should be reconciled monthly, and strict policies regarding the use of petty cash should be adopted in an effort to avoid abuse. Unscheduled internal and external audits focusing on the handling of petty cash should occur.

Managing accounts receivable and accounts payable are two additional responsibilities of the business manager. When practical, public assembly facilities should follow the practice of maximizing the time funds are in an interest bearing account by "aging" the bills.

The settlement process employed by public assembly facilities is not in and of itself unique, but it is unique with respect to the timing of the activity because it typically occurs the same day or night of the event. In fact, it sometimes occurs while the event is taking place.

Labor, both full- and part-time, is a major expense for public assembly facilities.

Managers must be knowledgeable of laws and regulations related to the recruitment, hiring, and termination of employees as well as those related to the payroll process. Carefully constructed and accurate job descriptions should be established for each job title. Depending on the position, credit checks and security background checks may be necessary prior to hiring an applicant.

The key to successful hiring is having an individual responsible for the human resources process who understands the job position to be filled, knows the necessary interactions required with other facility employees, and is cognizant of the facility's mission statement.

Some public assembly facilities subcontract for their part-time event staff and thereby eliminate the expense of recruiting, training, insuring, and managing the payroll for these employees. For certain tasks, the services of an independent contractor may be engaged. Before commencing any work, depending on the job, the independent contractor should be required to present a certificate of insurance that names the public assembly facility, its officers, employees and agents as additional insured. In turn, the public assembly facility should add the independent contractor's name to its "named additional insured" section within the facility's umbrella policy.

Volunteers represent another labor category. Although not paid, their safety becomes the responsibility of the public assembly facility. Facility managers must remember that volunteers, just like paid workers, require training, supervision, and work incentives to motivate them.

Basically, there are five ways to deal with risk: avoidance, assumption, prevention, reduction, and transference. Risk management must be stressed with all employees because of the many factors that may potentially threaten the facility, its patrons, and its employees.

REFERENCES AND ADDITIONAL READINGS

Cotts, David G. and Edmund P. Rondeau. 2007. *The Facility Manager's Guide to Finance and Budgeting.* New York: AMACOM.

Dropkin, Murray and Bill LaTouche. 2007. *The Budget-Building Book for Nonprofits: A Step-by-Step Guide for Managers and Boards,* 2nd ed. San Francisco: Jossey-Bass.

Dropkin, Murray and Allyson Hayden. 2001. *The Cash Flow Management Book for Nonprofits: A Step-by-Step Guide for Managers and Boards.* San Francisco: Jossey-Bass.

Fried, Gil, Steven Shapiro, and Timothy DeSchriver. 2007. *Sport Finance,* 2nd ed. Champaign, IL: Human Kinetics.

Livingston, John Leslie. 2001. *The Portable MBA in Finance and Accounting.* Hoboken, NJ: John Wiley & Sons, Inc

Madden, Turner D. 1998. *Public Assembly Facility Law: A Guide for Managers of Arenas, Auditoriums, Convention Centers, Performing Arts Centers, Race Tracks and Stadiums.* Coppell, TX: International Association of Assembly Managers, Inc.

Ruppel, Warren. 2007. *Not-for-Profit Accounting Made Easy,* 2nd ed. Hoboken, NJ: John Wiley & Sons, Inc.

Skinner, Bruce E. and Vladimir Rukavina. 2002. *Event Sponsorship.* Hoboken, NJ: John Wiley & Sons, Inc.

CHAPTER 7

EVENT AND ANCILLARY REVENUE SOURCES

CHAPTER OUTLINE

INTRODUCTION
FACILITY RENT
PROMOTER-RELATED ANCILLARY REVENUE
- IN-HOUSE MARKETING AND ADVERTISING AGENCY FEES
- TELEVISION, RADIO, CLOSED CIRCUIT SERVICES AND FEES
- UTILITY FEES
- LABOR CHARGE BACK FEES
- SPACE RENTAL
- EQUIPMENT FEES

CUSTOMER-RELATED ANCILLARY REVENUE
- TICKETING ANCILLARY REVENUE
  - Facility Fees
  - Ticket Surcharge Rebates
  - VIP Order Fees
  - Interest Income from Ticket Sales Escrow Accounts
  - Reimbursable Expenses From Promoters
- FOOD AND BEVERAGE SERVICES: WHY IT IS SO IMPORTANT!
  - In-House vs. Contract Food and Beverage Service
  - Food and Beverage Contractor Compensation
  - Physical Layout and Design of Food and Beverage Service
  - Food and Beverage Merchandising
  - Foodservice as A Marketing Tool
  - Wait Service and Hawking (In-Seat) Sales
  - Beer and Alcohol Sales
  - Trends in Foodservice
- MERCHANDISING
  - Types of Merchandising Contracts
  - Permanent Tenant Merchandise Stores
- PARKING, TRAFFIC AND TRANSPORTATION SERVICES
  - Limo, Bus, and RV Parking
  - Valet Service
  - Parking Lot Only Events and Services

SUMMARY
REFERENCES AND ADDITIONAL READINGS

INTRODUCTION

First impressions are powerful and lasting impressions. They influence human behavior and impact our experience, whether good or bad, and will shape the frame of reference someone has, now and in the future, of a given environment. The public assembly facility (PAF) has the same challenge that all retail businesses have–attracting customers with discretionary time and income and maximizing the opportunity to sell "an experience" to them. Creating product demand and repetitive patronage for entertainment-based, niche event experiences requires an uncanny ability to focus on establishing a trust relationship with the customers. Ultimately, the target audience must get more than they bargained for, i.e., "good value for money" by meeting and exceeding expectations whenever and wherever possible. To accomplish this, each customer should be afforded a "value added" experience.

A PAF manager has two customers–the customer who rents a PAF, referred to as the promoter, producer, presenter and/or the team, and the customer who attends events in a PAF, referred to as the guest, consumer, client, or attendee. For the purposes of this chapter, we will use the term "promoter" to refer to and include producer, presenter, show organizer, and/or the team. In turn, we will use the term "customer" to refer to and include guests, consumers, clients, or attendees.

When we refer to the promoter that rents the facility, we usually refer to the revenue derived from this relationship as *primary revenue*. In addition to the rent, there are also additional revenue streams associated with the production of the event that can be referred to as *secondary revenue* or what the industry refers to as *ancillary revenue*.

This chapter will focus on both promoter primary and secondary revenue as well as the lucrative customer ancillary revenue programs that help PAF managers create an inviting environment embedded with positive experiences that tend to draw guests and generate additional revenue.

All PAFs share a common thread in their mission or public purpose statement: "to fill, not necessarily sell, all available seats" (or floor space for convention centers and trade shows) as frequently as possible and for every event. Why not sell all the seats or floor space? Some public assembly facilities may have financial profit as their primary focus while others may concentrate more on providing programming that best serves the community's needs. Regardless of the mission statement's emphasis, the success of any PAF is contingent on its ability to attract promoters and customers.

The concept of selling every seat may be literally applied to arenas, stadiums, performing arts theatres, and amphitheatres. With respect to convention centers that normally do not have traditional seating, the goal may be to attract conventions, multi-day meetings, trade shows, and conferences that bring large numbers of out-of-town attendees who spend "new" money in the community, thereby stimulating the local economy. Of course it must be recognized that other types of PAFs also attract out-of-town audiences from outside the taxing jurisdiction who also spend "new" money.

One challenge may be filling every seat while a greater challenge is providing a level of customer service that will leave the event promoter and customer with a very satisfied feeling as a result of having produced or attended an event in the PAF. This satisfaction will, in turn, create repeat business, which is one of the main objectives of a successful PAF. The experience of attending an event is much more than buying a ticket and sitting in a seat. There are a host of other variables associated with attendance. For example,

- Did attendees experience any traffic problems while traveling to the facility?
- Was parking available, easily accessible, and reasonably priced?
- Were the parking areas and walkways to the facility viewed as a safe environment?

The experience continues when the guest enters the PAF:

- Were the box office staff, ticket takers, ushers and security courteous and helpful?
- Did the quality of the food and beverage service meet or exceed expectations?
- Was the price for food and beverages reasonable?
- Was the merchandise quality and price reasonable?
- Were the restrooms clean, stocked with supplies, and quickly accessible?
- Was the event or activity entertaining and professionally produced?

There are a myriad of dimensions to the promoter's and customer's experience, and each aspect must be delivered both in a timely manner and professionally.

The wide variety of PAFs in terms of size/capacity, design, and purpose results in differences in their interest or ability to offer some events and programs. Consequently, it is important for the management of PAFs to set expectations and educate event promoters and prospective customers prior to the event. For example, many small theatres, auditoriums, arenas, and/or civic/community centers present events without issuing/selling tickets and without food and beverage service or merchandising.

Well organized and delivered event parking, food and beverage service, and merchandising not only serve to enhance the customer's experience, but provide crucial and significant additional income streams for the PAF's operating budget.

The PAF manager needs to constantly think entrepreneurially. Every possible ancillary revenue service needs to be considered for its potential to generate additional revenue through purchases, fees, and surcharges.

In most PAFs, the number of seats and attendance capacity are regulated by codes and are a fixed number. The revenue from ticket sales or space rental sales is usually the property of the promoter or team with the exception of facility fees and ticket service charges. The PAF will collect rent in the form of a flat fee or possibly a fee based on ticket sales. Facility rental potential is, however, limited, especially in competitive markets. For many facilities, the opportunities for increasing total overall revenue are largely from ancillary services, particularly those that are creative and new to the facility.

To achieve these goals, the PAF manager needs to be certain the highest standards of quality are maintained with respect to service, product, and presentation. Constant feedback from users of the services, and/or purchasers of products, is essential. Focus groups of attendees such as season ticket holders, random customer interviews, and questionnaires distributed to attendees and event producers are all possible evaluation approaches to soliciting feedback.

The scope and number of possible ancillary services, and consequently, revenue generators, are very broad. For clarity and definition, this chapter will separate the ancillary services and their related revenues into two categories:

Promoter-related ancillary revenues

- In-house marketing and advertising agency fees
- Television, radio and closed circuit services and fees
- Utility fees
- Labor charge-back fees
- Space rental
- Equipment and utility fees

Customer-related ancillary revenues

- Ticketing fees
- Food and beverage service
- Merchandise and novelties
- Parking, traffic, and transportation services
- Business service centers
- Telephone, network, and Internet connections

Many of these areas are significant revenue generators. The basic issues and requirements for success in these areas are applicable to other possible ancillary areas in a PAF as well. Several additional revenue generating activities are also discussed in Chapter 4 Sales and Marketing.

Before we begin the extensive description of ancillary revenue, it is important to define what it is not.

FACILITY RENT

Facility rent is considered primary revenue, as opposed to ancillary revenue, and is usually income derived from event rent. Facility rent can be calculated and collected by several methods. Some of the more traditional methods include:

Rent as a percentage of gross ticket sales:
Facility gross ticket sales x Percentage = Facility Rent

Rent as a percentage of net ticket sales:
Facility gross ticket sales – ticket expenses – promoter expenses – admissions taxes x Percentage = Facility Rent

Rent as determined by the number of people in attendance:
Facility drop count x predetermined dollar amount per person = Facility Rent

Flat rent:
A predetermined amount of money regardless of attendance and expenses

Rent caps:
Often when using a percentage of gross or net ticket sales to determine rent, the calculation could generate a significant amount of money. Depending on the event and the promoter, a cap (or maximum) is usually negotiated and placed on the amount of money the PAF can collect as facility rent.

Rental structure = $3,500 vs. 12% with a cap of $50,000 plus expenses. If the gross or net revenue from an event was $500,000 and applied to the above formula, the promoter would save $10,000 with a rent cap at $50,000.

Co-Promotions:
Rent equals the percentage split of the net revenue after both facility and promoter expenses are deducted. The PAF and promoter either split the net revenue equally or on a predetermined percentage basis.

Rent plus expenses:
As discussed in the above rental structure, most often a PAF will charge several expenses in addition to the rent. These expenses may include

- Set-up, tear-down, clean-up labor
- Stagehands labor
- Event labor (police, fire, ushers, security)
- Utilities (electricity, gas, oil, telecommunications, Internet)
- Equipment rental (forklifts, spotlights, tables, chairs)
- Advertising
- Catering

All-in: In this situation, the promoter and the PAF manager negotiate and determine the amount of rent and expenses that the promoter will pay for both rent and expenses. The Promoter then pays the PAF a lump sum of money.

As discussed in the introduction of this chapter, ancillary revenue can be divided into two separate categories: promoter-related ancillary revenue and customer-related ancillary revenue.

PROMOTER-RELATED ANCILLARY REVENUE

IN-HOUSE MARKETING AND ADVERTISING AGENCY FEES

Although explained in depth in Chapter 4, creating an in-house marketing and advertising agency is another potential ancillary revenue source. Many one-time event promoters and producers looking to stretch their event advertising resources effectively and efficiently often enlist the PAF marketing and advertising staff to purchase and place their ads under the umbrella of the PAF. This significantly increases the amount of advertising that the PAF places in the local media and therefore decreases the expense to the promoter.

This savings is passed onto the promoter, and, in turn, the promoter pays a portion of the savings to the PAF through a straight fee or a percentage fee.

TELEVISION, RADIO, CLOSED CIRCUIT SERVICES, AND FEES

With growth of the cable channels, more and more independent networks are looking for programs and events to telecast to their audiences. These broadcasts from the PAF can be great for the public image of the facility as well as the city it is located in. They can also be a source of ancillary revenue. Some of the areas and categories may include

- Origination Fees – These fees are charged to the promoter of the event and/or the telecast producer as well. This is usually a negotiated fee that can range from several hundred to several thousand dollars. These fees are generally pure revenue, meaning that they usually are not offset by an expense.
- Connection Fees – These fees are charged by the facility to the telecast producer to pay technicians to make connections for TV and radio trucks used for remote location broadcasts.
- Equipment Fees – Several items can be charged to the networks under this category such as sound systems, scoreboard rental, and specialized lighting used to enhance broadcasts.

- Production Fees – Production fees are usually charged by facilities that have in-house production capability to produce closed circuit feeds to TVs in the premium seating areas, concession stands for viewing while customers are standing in line and/or for in-house security.
- Internet Fees – A charge to promoters that take advantage of the facility's Internet connection.
- Cyber Café Fees – A charge usually assessed to conferences and conventions that use the PAFs computers and access to the web and Internet for attendees usually clustered in the entrance to the PAF.

UTILITY FEES

Utility expenses are hard costs. These expenses are real and need to be paid to the utility provider by someone using the facility for every event. The PAF also has utility expenses on dark days that are an expense of the operating budget. For the facility to charge promoters/producers for event utility expenses, the facility must be able to accurately separate normal dark day utility expenses from increased utility expenses due to events. This can be accomplished by the PAF's engineers using the building's automated monitoring systems (BAS) or other computer software programs. A list of the utilities that can be negotiated into the event contract as a fee are

- Natural gas
- Electricity
- Water
- Heating/ventilation/air conditioning (HVAC)
- Pressurized air
- Refrigeration
- Cable TV

LABOR CHARGE-BACK FEES

Most PAFs have a system to charge back the event for personnel that the facility hires for the safe and secure operation of the facility during an event. Personnel numbers and labor rates are usually established in a rate sheet that lists the labor rates for all front- and back-of-the- house personnel, including union and non-union personnel. The rate card also covers policies and rates for straight time, time and a half and double time rates and the regulations which determine those increased personnel pay rates. Included in these rates are the base rate, benefits, processing percentage, and a mark-up which is usually profit per hour/per employee. The labor categories can include

- Police
- House security
- Fire personnel

- Ushers
- Box office personnel
- Load-in/load-out personnel
- Stagehands
- Decorating
- Service desk staff
- Drayage
- Freight handling and storage

(Figure 7-1 provides a sample rate card.)

SAMPLE EXPLODED RATE CARD

Title	Base Rate	Medi(1.45%)	FICA(6.25%)	H/W(5.0%)	PP(6.25%)	SDI(.01%)	UE/WC(3%)	Overhead(10%)	Billed Rate
Supr.	20.00	.29	1.25	1.00	1.25	.20	.60	2.00	26.59

Supr. = Supervisor
Medi = Medicare
PP = Pension Plan
UE/WC = Unemployment Insurance and Workmen's Compensation Insurance.

Positions may not have numbers in every column, e.g., FICA and PP (Pension Plan) columns.
H/W column may be union plans.
State may not have SDI (State Disability Insurance) or it may be an employee paid plan.

FINALLY - Facility may decide to absorb any or all of the add-ons to the base rate.

FIGURE 7-1

Space Rental

In addition to the standard facility rental, some PAFs such as convention and conference centers rent additional space. These charges are usually a one-time base rate that may include phone connections and computer connections as well as other amenities such as a coffee service. Some of these areas include:

- Production office
- Conference room space
- Hall rental

EQUIPMENT FEES

In addition to all of the previous ancillary revenue categories, PAFs may also rent numerous types of equipment on either an hourly rate, daily rate, or an event rate to the promoter. Sometimes equipment may be rented in bulk or other times by the piece. Some types of equipment in a PAF that may be rented include

- Stages
- Tables
- Chairs
- Linen
- Pipe and drape
- Crowd control barriers
- Spotlights
- Forklifts
- Scissor lifts
- Risers
- Carpet
- Cable trays

CUSTOMER-RELATED ANCILLARY REVENUE

TICKETING ANCILLARY REVENUE

As discussed in Chapter 5, ticketing services can be an additional revenue resource for a PAF manager to add to the bottom line. Fees can be generated in-house, in cooperation with the event promoters, and/or as part of a ticketing sub-contract. These fees may be generated through the methods such as facility fees, ticket service charge rebates, VIP ticket order fees, and interest income collected from ticket revenue being held in escrow accounts until the event has been successfully completed.

In most states, the government requires that all fees, services charges, and taxes are fully disclosed on the face of the ticket. These can include

- **Facility Fees.** A facility fee is usually a small base charge between $ .25 and $3.00 that is added on to the base ticket price. This fee is sometimes called a restoration fee or capital improvement fee and is generally used for facility maintenance, repairs, renovations, and/or capital improvements.

- **Ticket Service Charge Rebates.** Service charges on tickets vary based on the type of ticket service (in-house or sub-contracted), the type of facility (arena or theater, etc.), the base price of the ticket, and the relationship (third party agreement) between the PAF, promoter, and ticketing sub-contractor. This ticket surcharge can range from pennies per ticket to several dollars per ticket. The PAF usually receives an additional percentage of the ticket surcharge from the ticketing sub-contractor.

- **VIP Order Fees.** PAF management usually has many business and political relationships that necessitate the need to fill ticket orders without the purchaser going through normal ticket-buying location options. Managers usually handle these customer relationships through their administrative assistants who, in turn, place the order through a special allotment of premium ticket holds in the box office. These fees can range from a few dollars to several dollars per ticket and may also include a handling fee for this privilege.

- **Interest Income From Ticket Sales Escrow Accounts.** In many cases, ticket revenue is collected by the facility on behalf of the promoter. These dollars are not the property of the promoter until they have produced the event that the consumer paid for. Consequently, the facility will hold the revenue in an escrow account until the promoter has fulfilled their obligations to the consumer and facility. Once these stipulations have been met, the PAF manager will disburse the funds to the promoter at the settlement following the event.

  If a PAF has several events on sale at the same time, there could be thousands and potentially millions of dollars, depending on the capacity of the facility, in escrow accounts for months. A diligent manager and finance director can work with local banks to sweep these funds into short-term, no risk financial instruments that can net the PAF significant additional ancillary revenue from interest.

- **Reimbursable Expenses From Promoters.** Providing ticketing services is also a form of ancillary revenue for the PAF. These forms of revenue can be derived from charging back the cost of box office staff, group sales staffs, and the associated material costs.

Food and Beverage Services: Why Is It So Important!

Throughout history, one of the greatest pastimes when members of almost every society gather is eating and drinking. There is something special about the dynamics of "breaking bread together" that people in most cultures enjoy. When you add this commonality to the combination of sport and entertainment, you have a significant, enjoyable, and potentially revenue-producing experience. For many PAFs, especially stadiums and arenas with large capacities, greater numbers of seats/space, and presenting more commercial programs than a community center, small theatre, or auditorium, the food and beverage service may represent one of the most important revenue-producing ancillary services provided. In today's society, many business days stretch into evenings and weekends, and the traditional times when families sit down together for dinner has all but gone. Customers now expect to have their evening meal served in the same place they enjoy their leisure entertainment and sports. Such expectations represent an opportunity to generate substantial ancillary revenue. Scheduling events during these times also enhances the value of meeting rooms and premium seating areas in which food and beverages are available. The presence of these facilities can be used as an "added value" in attracting consumers willing to spend significant amounts of their discretionary income. Convention centers without food and beverage service and dining facilities may have a more difficult task in attracting multi-day meetings, conventions, conferences, or trade shows.

While individual tastes may vary by demographics, food and beverage operations seek to provide an array of universally popular items as well as those popular within the geographic region. Having these items available tends to enhance the customer's overall event experience as well as increased *per caps* (a term used to define the average amount of revenue derived per person for the event).

Over the past 20 years, the number of touring and available events/acts/shows has declined whereas the number of facilities has increased. The net result is a much more competitive PAF business. Managers must employ aggressive and strategic sales and marketing techniques to attract more events to their facility in an effort to generate essential operating revenues. Once an event is booked, providing food and beverage service and concession choices appropriate to the event can create significant ancillary revenue streams.

In-House vs. Contract Food and Beverage Service
Food and beverage service operations have grown exponentially over that of the past several years in terms of sales and profits. The food and beverage service operation may range from the traditional concession stand and basic catering to fine dining and banquet facilities.

Older public assembly facilities may still only offer the traditional concession stand operations. However, new and refurbished food and beverage service facilities are designed to enable the food and beverage manager to offer an expanded menu, one that frequently includes items from well-known restaurants and brands. Customer's demands for these offerings are generally accompanied by higher customer service expectation levels.

Some of the newer public assembly facilities also feature fine dining restaurants located on the premises which are open to the general public as well as facility guests. The presence of premium seating areas, such as hospitality suites, club seats, and exclusive gathering areas, provides another avenue for providing upscale/fine dining food and beverage service. Depending upon the event, an increase in the availability of specialized services, such as pre-event hospitality areas, meet and greets, and VIP areas, may be warranted.

With the demonstrated and proven potential for gaining significant profits from a properly managed food and beverage operation, prudent managers must give this operation a significant amount of attention. This then gives rise to the question of who should be managing the facility's food and beverage operation. A PAF manager has the option of managing the food and beverage service in-house or awarding a sub-contract to a private company to operate all or part of their food and beverage business. Numerous public assembly facilities have privatized their food and beverage service operations. (See Figure 7-2 for advantages of both in-house and private contractor.)

IN-HOUSE -VS- CONTRACT

SELF OPERATION	**PRIVATE CONTRACTOR**
■ Ability to retain control	■ Capital investment management
■ Ability to retain flexibility	■ Use of proven systems
■ Ability to retain all financial control	■ Provides liability protection from operations, especially alcohol

FIGURE 7-2

How does a PAF manager decide whether or not to privatize the facility's food and beverage service? The manager should assess the infrastructure of the facility to determine whether self-operation or sub-contractor (also referred to as *privatization*) would be most lucrative to the facility on a net income basis as well as meeting the needs of the customers they serve. Included in these considerations would be

- an analysis of the available labor pool
- the level of staff skills
- staff training requirements
- labor laws
- financial resources
- capital equipment
- and the manager's time and ability to effectively oversee such an operation

While each public assembly facility exists in a different ownership and governance structure, there are distinct advantages to both self-operated and privatized food and beverage service management.

Simply stated, if the food and beverage service is self-operated, the PAF management maintains total control of labor, products, services, and profits. When allowed to function in a for-profit mode, some facilities, both large and small, have generated substantial profits from their self-operated food and beverage service. However, the PAF must also assume all, and in most cases, significant risks associated with the operation. This operating format works best when the principles and policies governing the PAF facility allow the manager to function in a for-profit mode. Unfortunately, restrictive bureaucratic measures can, at times, complicate this structure and could potentially have an effect on customer service and product quality.

If sub-contracting, the management will want to use the *request for qualifications* (RFQ) and/or *request for proposal* (RFP) in a systematic effort to select the best overall sub-contractor. There is an important distinction between the RFQ and the RFP.

The purpose of the RFQ is to pre-qualify firms by determining if they have the experience, financial ability, and knowledge to provide the type, level of service, and quality of products desired and identified by the facility.

An RFP is usually sent to only those firms that have been deemed qualified. An RFP is also used to collect the best financial proposal in a competitive submission process.

In any case, however, it is important that the selection process be a proposal for professional services rather than a bid; otherwise some municipalities may require you to only select the company proposing the highest commission without regard to the equally important issues of management ability, quality of investment, company's financial standing, as well as their operational experience and reputation in comparable venues.

When a PAF contracts its food and beverage operations to a private company, the facility's manager is able to spend more time overseeing other aspects of the facility's operation. Depending on the type of contract, the private food service company might assume the responsibility for labor expenses such as hiring and training; health department permits and compliance; alcohol licensing, liability, and compliance; food product costs and storage; and often the cost of providing and amortizing the fixtures, furnishings, and equipment (FF&E) as well as the food and beverage physical build-out costs.

Food and Beverage Contractor Compensation
The most common form of food and beverage contract compensation is a commission agreement whereby the concessionaire pays the facility a percentage of gross sales. If it is a management-fee-based contract, the concessionaire receives its management fee and likely an incentive bonus. The bonus can be based on various combinations of achieving pre-determined goals. These can include a percentage of gross revenue, a percentage of net revenue, or a reduction in cost or owner subsidy.

When a PAF is constructed utilizing tax exempt bonds, more and more venues are required, under Internal Revenue Service (IRS) rules, to have management fee contracts structured with the concessionaire earning a lump sum fee and incentives based on any criteria other than profits. There are many technicalities to this type of agreement and the facility manager should seek legal advice from a bond counsel for a complete interpretation of the rules.

There can be other variations of these basic formulas. There also may be a penalty clause in the contract that requires a rebate of a part of the base fee if certain targets are not met. If it is a profit-percentage-based contract, the concessionaire simply receives an agreed upon percentage of the profits. Incentive bonuses may be included in the contract whereby the concessionaire's percentage of the profit increases once established amounts of profit are achieved.

In instances when a private company manages the food and beverage operation, tensions may build between the facility manager and the concessionaire over issues such as event bookings and staffing requirements. Prudent facility managers will learn to document their efforts to book as many events as possible to demonstrate their tenacity on behalf of all sub-contractors.

Whether concessions are operated in-house or through a private contractor, the facility manager is still responsible for ensuring that the food and beverage service operation functions in the most efficient and customer service oriented manner as possible. Regardless of the type of food and beverage contract, the PAF manager must reserve the right to approve product quality, menu selections, and product pricing. It is also critical that facility management retain the right to approve the hiring and/or removal of the food/beverage manager.

Chris Bigelow, a noted food and beverage consultant, of The Bigelow Companies, Kansas City, MO, points out that too many PAF managers believe that when a private contractor is involved, there is little they can do to enhance the food and beverage service operation (Bigelow 2008). Yet, just because the contractor appears to be performing effectively does not relieve facility managers of their responsibility to regularly assess the quality of service being delivered to ensure it meets or exceeds agreed upon standards and objectives. In the same manner, managers operating in-house food and beverage service should be constantly examining their operations to maintain the highest standards possible while maximizing efficiency. Given the importance of food and beverage service as a significant ancillary revenue and the role it plays in producing customer service and therefore repeat business, the manager has a responsibility to professionally manage and promote exemplary food service to all guests.

Physical Design of Food and Beverage Service
When new PAFs are being planned and designed, from a day-to-day operating perspective, careful consideration must be given to food and beverage service operations including the location of the commissary, permanent concession stands, portable concession kiosks, restaurants, premium seating food service support stations, and the overall presentation quality of the food service

operations in the PAF. Of particular concern are the size, design, and location of food and beverage service areas.

In all cases, the owner, architect, food service consultant, and builder should examine the PAF's purpose carefully along with the functions and events the facility is expected to accommodate. This form of examination will help determine the type of food and beverage areas required and their number, location, layout, and size. Financial and capital resources also must be taken into consideration when shaping this determination. The elimination of potential flaws during the design stage will serve to minimize operational problems and allow for maximizing revenue once the facility is in operation.

Commissary. An important consideration is the availability of support facilities such as commissaries that are ample in size and convenient in location. This is of particular importance to convention centers because they rely heavily on their ability to cater large meals and other social functions. Adequate refrigeration and dry storage space are necessary for a kitchen to properly function. The location of shipping and receiving areas and the proper location of service elevators in multi-level facilities can further maximize the productivity of food and beverage service employees.

Concession stands. The proper placement of concession stands requires careful planning. It should always be remembered that concession stands generate significant revenues if positioned in optimal locations. Products will be more easily marketed when traffic flow, ingress and egress, and the positioning of concession stands are planned as a package. (See Figure 7-3 for some design flaws within concession operations).

SOME DESIGN FLAWS WITHIN CONCESSION OPERATIONS

DESIGN FLAWS WITHIN CONCESSION OPERATIONS:

- Inadequate number of concession stands relative to seating capacity.
- Inadequate kitchen location and space.
- No installation of floor drains in kitchen and stand areas.
- No provision for hawking (selling food, beverage, or novelty products in the audience area) or vending operation (selling food, beverage, or novelty products from stands or kiosks.)
- Service elevators inadequately located relative to storage facilities.
- Inadequate size and location of loading docks and storerooms.
- Inadequate ventilation for cooking capabilities.
- Insufficient water and energy availability.
- Insufficient concourse areas to accommodate traffic flow.
- Access and location of support services.

Courtesy of Russo (1980)[2]

Design flaws within concession operations   **FIGURE 7-3**

Some PAFs use staging or prep areas in a commissary to accommodate vendors and hawkers and to provide security for stored products. Hawking items in the seating areas is often very effective because many people are reluctant to leave their seats during a close contest or an entertaining performance. Others may not be physically able get to concession stands or wait in the lines that generally form at intermission and/or during sporting event breaks. Thus, making products available to these guests while they remain in their seats produces sales that otherwise might not occur. Failing to provide an area to accommodate the needs of these vendors and hawkers is poor design and planning. Management must overcome these shortcomings.

Managers of existing PAFs who do not have the financial resources to create an optimal environment for their food and beverage service operation should still evaluate potential improvements that might assist in maximizing their operation's success. Questions to be asked include

- Using a typical return on investment (ROI) analysis, would the improvement costs be justified when compared to the additional revenues that might be generated?
- Are the areas in which the food and beverage service operation function attractive to guests?
- If not, what would be the cost of making them more attractive?
- Would the makeover result in the generation of additional revenues?
- Of equal importance, would the physical improvements increase the ability to serve the event's guests and improve the quality of the experience in attending the event?

In essence, managers should be aware of and ready to deal with the need to make changes on a continual basis.

Food and Beverage Merchandising

Food and beverage sales are enhanced through the implementation of strategic and timely marketing and merchandising techniques. To effectively motivate customers, attention should be given to creating appeal by stimulating the customers' senses, both sight and smell, based upon determination of guests' needs and appetites.

Food and beverage operators should make sure that menus listing available items and their prices are prominently posted. Providing potential purchasers with a view of food in preparation, such as hamburgers and hot dogs on the grill, may also stimulate their sense of smell and sight in a way that might persuade them to make a purchase. The same is true for displaying the various sizes of beverages, French fries, popcorn, and other products. It has also become a trend to offer children's sizes at lower prices when the demographics of an event are predominantly under the age of 12. Managers constantly must be aware of changing demographics of the facility's events and be prepared to make appropriate adjustments to their menus. (See Figure 7-4 for food service per capita spending).

FOODSERVICE PER CAPITA SPENDING

EVENT	LOW	HIGH
High School Sports	$0.25	$2.00
College Basketball	$1.25	$7.00
College Football	$2.50	$10.00
Minor League Baseball	$4.00	$12.00
NBA Basketball	$5.50	$15.00
NHL Hockey	$6.50	$15.00
MLB Baseball	$7.00	$18.00
NFL Football	$8.00	$20.00
Championship/Super Bowl	$10.00	$40.00
Concerts	$1.25	$25.00
Family Shows	$2.50	$5.50
MLS	$5.00	$11.00

(Bigelow 2009)

FIGURE 7-4

To assist in the marketing of menu items, the PAF manager in cooperation with the food service manager should strive to have adequate signage present throughout the facility, but especially in close proximity to the concession stands, that depict the various menu items in a stimulating and graphic manner. In the same vein, many public assembly facilities contract with regional and national brand name companies to sell their products on an exclusive basis. When this occurs, the names of these products should be included in all product-related signage. Seeing the name of the known product may provide additional brand recognition, thereby further inducing the guest to purchase that item. In many cases, such as selecting an exclusive beverage provider like Coke or Pepsi, the manager may be able to negotiate menu signs with the name brand provider.

Purchases from concession stands and kiosks as well as visits to on-premise restaurants are often spontaneous decisions. Food and beverage managers seeking to create and maintain a successful operation must present and package their offerings in an enticing manner. They must create an appropriate menu and price each item reasonably based on attendee expectations and industry standards for their geographic region. It is very important that all personnel are properly trained to provide clean, efficient, and courteous customer service to every customer. In many aspects, food and beverage presentation is as important to the customer as the cost and quality of the products being served.

The creative use of lighting technology contributes to the presentation of food and beverage items. In addition, giving customers the ability to view the event via strategically located closed circuit television screens located in view of the concession queue will attract the customers to the concession stands. They can watch the event while it is in progress therefore preventing the customer from missing portions of the event and increasing food and beverage per caps.

Foodservice as a Marketing Tool

Although food and beverage is considered an ancillary service, it also has the potential to significantly enhance the PAFs image. As an increasing number of facilities seek to generate additional revenues by renting space for private events, the availability and quality of the facility's food and beverage service operation become paramount.

For instance, stadiums, arenas, and performing arts facilities with on-premise restaurants and premium seating locations may rent these areas on days when the facility does not have a scheduled event for private parties, weddings, and banquets. It is important to market the availability of facility space and ancillary services jointly, including back-stage services, to potential clients in order to take full advantage of additional revenue-generating opportunities. Of course, this type of activity is common for convention and community centers as well.

Convention centers generally depend upon their in-house food service operation or concessionaire to provide for the food and beverage needs of groups meeting in its facility. Convention centers must strive to keep their costs in line with competitors, such as hotels and other banquet facilities, in order to successfully compete for meeting and convention business and accompanying food and beverage service. When convention centers host international, national, regional, and local meetings and conventions, the food and beverage service should be marketed in a manner that targets each of these diverse guest segments. In every instance, the same rules apply with respect to the high quality of the food and beverage service, its efficient and convenient delivery, and its appearance at presentation.

The ability of the convention center to attract international, national, and regional conventions and meetings is very important because their presence helps to fill hotel rooms, and the attendees generate additional business for area restaurants and retail stores. Hosting local meetings and conferences may not generate substantial new revenues but does allow the convention center to provide for community needs. At the same time, existing money in a community that is circulating has a positive impact on the economic vitality of that community.

Wait Service and Hawking (In-Seat) Sales

Depending on the type of event, many guests will make purchase decisions based upon the convenience of having merchandise, food, and drink brought to their seats. *Hawking* or *in seat sales* (i.e., selling concessions and novelties in the venue seating areas by mobile vending staff) is a typical way additional sales are created in many events that have applicable formats such as arena and stadium sporting events and family shows. Some of the more creative ways to enhance hawking sales include utilizing local dignitaries or media personalities to participate, usually pushing a special cause or promoting endorsements. Suffice it to say, the entertainment value of an animated peanut salesman or program vendor in the stands can provide an exceptional experience to a baseball game audience while increasing the sales per caps.

In some facilities, especially those with suites or club seats, wait service may be provided to enhance the guest experience. This service may include menu cards at each seat and an individual that periodically comes by, sometimes with an electronic recorder, to receive any orders. Also, in many of the new, technologically advanced facilities, small computers are placed by the PAF or food service contractor in the premium seating areas to allow the consumers to order food, beverage, and merchandise throughout the game or event. This exclusive service tends to be found in newer sports complexes, but can be retrofitted into most any facility that desires to raise the level of guest satisfaction. In so doing, management is enhancing convenience and is providing the guest with value-added service.

Beer and Alcohol Sales. Beer and alcohol sales have become a significant ancillary revenue source and a staple product that enhances the customer's experience while attending sports and entertainment events. The ability to purchase beer and alcohol at a facility and its events has become such an established customer expectation that its availability can be the deciding factor for customers when making a decision to attend an event. If multiple venues are competing for the same demographics within the same market, the most often attended facility will most likely be the one serving alcohol.

Accompanying the consumption of beer and alcohol is the PAF manager's responsibility for safe and effective alcohol management. Training of servers and attendants in most U.S. states is a required part of managing the alcohol service environment. Due to increasing fan violence and liability issues, concession and event managers are using techniques to pre-qualify servers and to set service standards prior to events. (See Figure 7-5 for guidelines from TEAM).

A risk analysis using any variety of criteria can assist PAF management in evaluating the potential risks and implementation of alcohol management techniques, such as limiting size of containers, number of cups that can be sold per person, and early cutoff of sales. Age demographics, seating configurations, and guest service ratios may be applied to determine whether the event will have full service, limited availability or a no alcohol environment. (See Appendix A, Figure 7-6, for sample documents on determining the sale of alcohol.)

Beer and alcohol companies enjoy the benefits of a captured audience and often are great advertisers and sponsors of sporting and public events. This provides a unique opportunity for the public assembly facility in several ways. Although all related elements are usually wrapped together, spin-off revenue benefits usually include, but are not limited to, product prices, promotional products, prominent advertising exposure, and presenting sponsorships.

Unfortunately, unlike soft drink purveyors such as Coke or Pepsi, PAFs are not permitted, under Federal law, to negotiate an exclusive vending agreement with alcoholic beverage manufacturers and distributors such as Anheuser-Busch or MillerCoors. Therefore, a PAF needs to investigate creative ways to negotiate and display vendor advertising and marketing funds within the facility's design.

ALCOHOL SELLER/SERVER INFORMATION

ID GUIDELINES

Serving alcohol to underage people is illegal in every state. Use the three ID Guidelines to help avoid problems.

1. Ask for positive ID - don't guess.
2. Ask for more proof if you have any doubts.
3. Know where the alcohol is going.

CUT OFF GUIDELINES

Sometimes it becomes necessary to refuse a sale and inform a guest that he or she will not be given any more alcohol. Follow these guidelines to help diffuse the situation.

1. Say "No" and move on. Keep the line moving.
2. Give clear reasons and don't judge the guest. Never say "You're drunk."
3. Call for backup if the guest makes trouble.

SAFE-DRINKING GUIDELINES

Keep your guests safe and having a good time while they're drinking by following these guidelines.

1. Buy time. At an outlet, limit the number of drinks a guest can buy. In the stands, limit the number of times you walk by people who may be misusing alcohol.
2. Offer alternatives to alcohol. Suggest food and non-alcohol beverages to impaired guests.
3. Use the personal touch. Make eye contact and some friendly conversation with every customer as often as you can.

This information was excerpted from the TEAMS Training Manual. TEAM (Techniques for Effective Alcohol Management) Coalition is a non profit organization promoting responsible drinking and positive fan behavior at sports and entertainment facilities.

FIGURE 7-5

Trends in Foodservice

To remain financially successful in a competitive environment, food and beverage service operations have experienced dramatic changes during recent years. In addition to the traditional concession stands, many public assembly facilities boast dining service with some featuring on-premise fine dining restaurants. PAFs that offer premium seating are afforded an excellent opportunity to generate additional revenue by providing catering to the occupants during scheduled events and by providing for the catering needs when the suites are used for private parties, receptions, etc. PAF managers are also leasing facility space to local and/ or national companies so they can sell their products at the facility's events. For example, one company might lease space to sell beverages while a second might sell specialty sandwiches and a third may provide the on-site catering.

Some trends in food and beverage service operations include

- Food courts taken from the shopping mall concept where a variety of short order foods are available in a common seating area.
- Specialty carts strategically placed in high traffic areas selling such items as Espresso coffee, ice cream bars, gourmet hot dogs, etc.
- Internet ordering for suite holders.
- Decreased price sensitivity for quality product.
- Licensing agreements with brand name pizza chains, fast food restaurants, and local ethnic restaurants.
- Increased use of brand name products. Studies show sales increase 10-300 percent with brand name products because guests relate to quality and familiarity.
- Destination restaurants and lounges.
- Performing arts theatres' club seating.
- Use of charitable organizations to operate concessions booths, reducing labor costs and maintaining quality service.
- Credit, debit, ATM, and smart cards used for foodservice.
- In-seat ordering from a cellular phone.
- Exhibition cooking. Guests buy with their eyes, and seeing something cooking proves freshness.
- Increased cooking capabilities for concessions. Charbroiling, grilling, and deep frying are replacing the boiled hot dog. New induction heat speeds cooking.
- Local, regional and ethnic foods - Italian, Mexican, barbecue, and Asian are all very popular.
- Celebrity chefs.
- Locally made/micro brewed beers.
- Brand extension (not just adding new items but improving and adding variety to core items).
- Fast pour beer taps and bottles replacing draft.

Many food and beverage service options are available to the PAF manager with respect to menu items, management alternatives, and branding opportunities. Prudent public assembly facility managers realize the impact the food and beverage service can have (both positive and negative) upon the satisfaction level experienced by their guests, their operating revenues, and the marketing potential for their facility. Wise managers will take appropriate action to maximize each of these opportunities. Appropriate use of logos and signage associated with the various products available for sale will not only assist in stimulating guest purchases, it also provides an opportunity to charge the product producers/ distributors with a fee for their placement within the venue.

Merchandising

Selling event merchandise and novelty items are another ancillary service that has proven popular with guests and lucrative to teams and events. The terms merchandise and novelty items refers to tangible non-perishable souvenir products. These souvenirs are also referred to as "product."

Some of the earliest novelty items such as pennants, programs, and buttons were sold at carnivals, circuses, and sporting events. In later years, popular music concerts, aimed at increasing the sale of favorite artist records, introduced new types of novelty items, especially recordings of the artist. Elvis Presley was one of the original musical artists to produce a full-line of merchandise and novelty items for fan purchase. Today, it is sometimes possible, depending on the event ticket prices/sales that the merchandise gross sales can exceed ticket sales.

The sale of event merchandise and novelty items has in the past been a major income source for PAFs. While facility profits from merchandise have been shrinking over the last several years, it is still a viable source for ancillary income. These opportunities come from tenant sport teams and artists who perform concerts in the facility. Touring events such as professional wrestling, ice-skating shows, and even Broadway productions also represent excellent opportunities for the sale of merchandise and novelty items. "Branded" items, with the team or touring show's logo, are extremely popular items as are event-specific items memorializing the fact that the purchaser was there.

Known by some in the merchandise sales business as the *blowout* (the moment when everyone in attendance leaves the premise), it is very often one of the best times to sell merchandise. Capturing the moment of elation from a grand finale or the exuberant high of a competitive victory can extend the sales market exponentially. Special attention and emphasis should be given to capture this unique opportunity by predicting the staffing needs to adequately handle the consumers in a timely manner.

PAF managers have several merchandise operating formats from which to choose. Similar to the food and beverage service, PAF managers may elect to operate their merchandising in-house or to contract the operation to a private company. In most instances, the event itself travels with its own novelty and merchandise operation including product and staff. Determining which sales system to employ should be preceded by conducting an analysis of the local/regional business climate and taking into consideration factors such as the PAF's type and mission; the size, training, skill level, and availability of its staff; and its event schedule. What might be the correct decision for one public assembly facility might not be appropriate for another. Important decisions of this nature should be made only after all facets of the issue have been thoroughly considered. It must be understood at all times that the potential to generate large revenues also generally carries with it the necessity to accept significant risks. These risks include, but are not limited to, consumer and employee theft of merchandise and cash, credit card fraud, overstocking, and overpriced merchandise that goes unsold and is printed with a specific date These determinations should be part and parcel of the booking, scheduling, and contracting process.

Types of Merchandising Contracts

Basically three kinds of merchandising contracts are used by PAF managers. They are, flat-rate fee, per-person fee, and percentage-of-sales fee. Chris Bigelow offers the following descriptions of these arrangements:

- **The flat-rate fee** - a one time fixed rate dollar amount. However, it usually does not produce maximum revenue results for a facility, and the facility has little control over what or how much is sold at the event. This is often used in smaller buildings and markets or for performing arts events that produce historically low merchandise sales. This system is also used at convention centers when a show promoter wishes to sell ancillary products such as tapes, books or other souvenirs.

- **The per-person fee** - based on a predetermined amount to be charged for each person attending the event including both complimentary and paid admissions (turnstile count). This, too, is a simple approach. It can be an effective approach if the historical per capita sales for the event are researched. However, if this information cannot be obtained, then this fee base will be ineffective as a maximum revenue producer.

- **The percentage-of-sales fee** - is probably the most common and accepted fee arrangement for the right to sell novelties at events. Under this arrangement, the authorized retailer of the facility splits a percentage of the sale of novelty and merchandise items with the merchandiser. While this fee arrangement is more common, it requires additional supervision, control systems, and marketing knowledge by the facility and retailer. The retailer's role under this fee arrangement is to provide personnel to inventory, display, sell, and account for the novelty and merchandise sales. (Bigelow, 2008)

Both the flat-rate fee and the per-person fee provide income to the facility with little or no involvement for equipment or labor. The facility also has no reporting requirements for payment of wages, product, etc. The percentage-of-sales approach is more labor intensive on the part of the facility management, especially in exercising inventory controls of the products being sold. The prime issue in collecting a percentage of sales is "what is the total sales figure?" Because merchandise sales are more often cash sales at multiple locations, the financial/audit controls are more likely to be a result of inventory controls at a central location.

The facility's financial arrangement with its retailer has many variables, such as investment, advanced commissions, signing bonuses, etc. However, the following structures are fairly representative of the major facilities that host traveling shows and concerts:

Payee	Percentage
State Sales Tax	X %
Gross Sales	100 %
Merchandiser	70 – 80 %
Remainder	30 – 20 %
Vendors	5 – 7 %
Retailer	3 – 7 %
Facility	10 – 25 %

(Bigelow, 2008)

The final amount the facility receives from any of the contract arrangements can also be impacted if a middle-man/concessionaire has been given the rights to the merchandise operation. In that instance, the concessionaire would contract with the event promoter, provide the services involved, and pay the facility an amount of the concession contract. It is likely this would be less than had the facility directly handled the merchandise operation but the facility has transferred risk and responsibility to a third party. Bigelow notes a declining supply of available events has resulted in some PAF managers lowering their percentage take of the merchandising profits in an effort to attract events to their facility.

While merchandise per capita spending varies greatly due to a team's or musical group's popularity, color and style fads, geography (coast versus heartland, North versus South), event types and the resulting customer demographics, the following are representative of industry ranges:

Event	Low	High
Major League Sports	$ .75	$ 4.00
World Series/Super Bowl	15.00	30.00
College Sports	.25	3.00
Family Shows	1.00	4.00
Country Concerts	2.00	*15.00
R & B Concerts	2.00	*10.00
Rock Concerts	3.50	*15.00
Performing Arts	.15	2.00
Professional Wrestling	3.00	20.00

*Exceptional shows may generate as much as a $25.00 per capita.

(Bigelow, 2008)

In all financial arrangements, the division of the revenue/cost of merchandise business is ultimately determined by the risks, responsibilities, and contributions (labor, product, equipment, selling rights, etc.) each party assumes or brings to the table. The more a party is involved and at risk, the greater its expectations when sharing revenue.

As with other facility functions, the PAF manager should be knowledgeable of the current merchandising environment in order to maximize profit regardless of the fee structure negotiated. Although fans and guests may request a myriad of novelty and merchandise products, items offered for sale at a particular event should be selected based on the anticipated audience demographics, their historical purchasing data, and the profit margin the item offers. An attractive and clearly visible display of available merchandise and novelty items combined with an efficient sales system and staff will produce the most successful financial results. Merchandise and novelty points-of-sale should be adequately staffed to assist guests in making their purchases. Forms of payment including cash, credit, debit, and smart cards should be accepted. Sales personnel should be uniformly dressed, knowledgeable about each item offered, and trained to be courteous and professional at all times.

Merchandising can be an added income source if properly managed. As with other PAF functions, the manager must be aware of the various sales alternatives in addition to being familiar with the current status of the merchandising business. To protect the interests of the PAF, the manager must take the required steps to ensure that all parties to the merchandising operation are held accountable for fulfilling their responsibilities and obligations.

Precautions must also be taken to prevent the sale of stolen products, non-licensed products, and any item that infringes on copyrighted logos or marks. Security personnel, under the direction and supervision of local law enforcement officials, should be responsible for the protection of all money in addition to ensuring only authorized persons sell merchandise and novelty items on the facility's premises. Enforcement of security measures may include the seizure of "bootlegged" merchandise. It is very important that the facility obtain legal advice in setting its rules and regulations and enact procedures consistent with laws pertaining to these issues. Local authorities should be hired and retained to enforce laws and regulations governing unlicensed vendors selling food and beverages or merchandise and novelty items on public or private property in proximity to the PAF.

Permanent Tenant Merchandise Stores
PAF managers are also being asked in tenant negotiations to provide permanent space for merchandise space. This is usually negotiated as part of the overall tenant contract and it may be either a square foot charge and/or a percentage of business fees.

PARKING, TRAFFIC, AND TRANSPORTATION SERVICES

One of the first impressions a customer arriving at a PAF for an event will be derived from the efficiency and effectiveness of the parking, traffic, and transportation plan that has been developed and implemented. The customers desire to return to a facility for an event will be significantly impacted by the delivery of these critical, initial customer services.

Parking

Parking and parking lots are another ancillary service revenue source that is often not maximized. Although most parking operations charge guests a flat fee to park while attending an event, people are willing to pay additional sums for added conveniences. Depending on the number and location of available parking spaces, the PAF manager may construct a variable fee schedule charging higher prices for parking located in closer proximity or more convenient to the PAF.

Selling parking passes to season ticket holders and frequent users of the PAF; making day-time parking available to the general public during non-event days; leasing parking spaces on a monthly or annual basis to individuals who work in close proximity to the facility; and making valet parking service available during scheduled events are examples of how a parking operation might generate additional profits. The facility manager should carefully assess the parking inventory (parking locations and spaces available); staff available for assignment to the parking operation, and the facility's event schedule in order to determine what types of parking services might be appropriate and profitable. The service might vary from event to event.

Most guests are accustomed to paying for their parking in cash when they arrive at the PAF or adjacent PAF-controlled and managed lots for an event. Therefore, an accounting system with appropriate audit controls must be adopted and implemented to discourage employee theft. Employees allowing guests to park for free or who pocket a portion of the collected fees represent two forms of theft that may occur if proper supervisory and accountability measures are not continuously monitored and enforced. Some PAF managers separate their cashiers from other parking employees in an effort to reduce the number of individuals handling the money. Other theft deterrent measures include the issuance of numbered tickets that must be displayed on the front windshield of each vehicle entering the parking area, physically counting the number of parked vehicles shortly after the event has commenced, and using advanced technology by installing electronic devices (often buried) that provide a count of the vehicles passing through the parking entrance.

Whenever a public assembly facility provides parking for its guests, the facility must be prepared to assume the liability and risk involved in this operation. It does not matter whether a fee is charged or the parking is free; the facility must provide a safe environment for both the guests and their vehicles. To accomplish this, the parking areas should:

- Have adequate lighting.
- Surfaces must be free from debris, snow, ice, and other hazards.
- The surface must be kept in good repair.
- Parking personnel should be present in the parking areas before, during, and after the event in an effort to deter potential property thefts or physical assaults.
- Parking lots and garages must provide for the safety of pedestrians leaving and returning to their vehicles.
- Guests also expect assistance will be available in the event problems are encountered with starting a vehicle and when requesting directions about exit routes to particular areas. Parking personnel need to be trained and properly equipped to meet these expectations.

Traffic

Parking for many PAFs can be a very complex issue. For both new facility development and planning and existing facilities alike, parking has become a critical issue with respect to the location and design of parking lots/garages, allocation and location of sufficient identified "handicapped" parking spaces in order to comply with ADA's handicapped parking requirements, and providing for the safety of pedestrians within the parking lot or garage. In planning for parking, traffic surveys should be designed and conducted. Planners should work in close consort with the various community services departments, especially the police traffic control department.

Parking lots/garages should be designed to allow for controlled and efficient entry and rapid exit of the vehicles. Sufficient personnel should be available to collect parking fees or check pre-paid tags. Entering vehicles should be directed to park in specific areas based on a parking plan. At the conclusion of an event, parking personnel should be available to direct vehicles out of the lot/garage. As many exits as possible should be opened to facilitate the surge of vehicles departing at the same time. Local police departments should be consulted and advised of anticipated event attendance. The police should be requested to provide appropriate personnel to direct traffic to and from the facility. Usually, requesting a police detail for parking supervision is a cost that will have to be calculated into the expenses that are charged against the overall parking revenue. Based on previous knowledge, all "choke points," "bottlenecks," or "gridlock" areas should receive special attention by traffic personnel. Depending on the size of the anticipated crowd, some streets might be restricted to one-way traffic both before and after the event, in order to better move the volume of vehicles.

Transportation

Often sufficient parking may not be available in close proximity to the public assembly facility. Available resolutions generally require the assistance of other agencies. One method is for the public facility manager and the director of public transportation to develop a plan that expands the number of buses or other modes of transportation that service the facility prior to and following a scheduled event. Another is to establish one or more remote parking areas within the community and to provide either municipal or private contracted bus service from those sites to the facility. The cost of this bus service might be borne by the user or billed to the event.

Limo, Bus, and RV Parking

Other periodic opportunities exist whenever attendees demonstrate an interest in congregating in advance at the site of an event. One tradition at many sporting events is the tailgating party. Facility management may provide logistical support for these events but must also exercise control. Parking lots, especially those with parking spaces designed to accommodate RV's and motor homes, can capitalize on this demand and the additional profit it will generate. In the same vein, other formats exist for large expanses of parking lots with concepts for use such as flea markets, outdoor trade shows, etc. Some public facilities have installed water/waste, shore power (electricity), and even data connections in some lots in order to attract touring RV caravans and/or their convention, fair or exhibition business.

Valet Service

Another potential source of ancillary revenue related to parking is valet service. As mentioned in the preface of this chapter, there are also expenses that are associated with the liabilities and responsibilities that come from putting an employee behind the wheel of a customer's vehicle. Because of these issues, it is common for a PAF to sub-contract out this service to a third party contractor. Even if the revenue derived from this added value is equal to the expense for providing this service, it may be worth the effort to add another value-added service that keeps consumers returning to your facility and events.

Parking Lot Only Events and Services

There are two basic types of parking lots, surface lots and parking spaces that are constructed in a facility with multiple levels, sometimes referred to as a parking deck. The benefit to surface lots is that they are significantly less expensive to develop, construct, and maintain per car than a parking deck. The negative to surface lots is that they require many more acres of land than a parking structure to meet the needs of PAF.

With so much land, many entrepreneurial PAF managers with large surface lots, such as stadiums, arenas, and amphitheaters, look for ways to create revenue when they are not used for PAF events. Some of the more creative uses have been spawned by the New Jersey Sports and Expositions Authority's management of their vast parking spaces. These parking-lot-only revenue-producing events included the Meadowlands Grand Prix, carnivals, flea markets and automobile manufacturer test drives. The complex is also developing a destination theme park to use its lots during non-stadium events called Xanadu. The concept of expanding the use of surface lots is also being pursued by the Kraft Family, owners of the New England Patriots and Gillette Stadium. The Kraft's are currently developing Patriot Place using many of their surface lots that will eventually include major retail shops such as Bass Pro, a hotel, and numerous conference and convention spaces.

SUMMARY

Event and ancillary revenue sources and services contribute to the achievement of promoter/producer and guest expectations and satisfaction. The revenues they generate are essential to the financial success of the PAF.

As explained in this chapter, there are several types of revenue that a PAF can derive from events. Primary revenue is generally defined as facility rent and was discussed at the beginning of this chapter. Secondary revenue, or what the industry defines as ancillary revenue, has many different forms and can be collected using many different methods.

Prior to contracting with an event promoter/producer or team, the PAF manager will normally develop a pre-event estimate that includes the event rent and all of the expenses that will be charged to the event. These charges are usually based on size of event (capacity or square footage); duration (number of hours or days); and number of staff needed to safely, securely, efficiently, and effectively operate the event.

In addition to the rent and expenses, the PAF will endeavor to capitalize on the captured audience attending the event to collect secondary ancillary revenue. As stated previously, this can take on many forms, all of which are important.

The food and beverage operation, which can include concession stands, premium seating service, restaurants as well as hawking in the seating areas, is extremely important to all PAFs.

Additional ancillary revenue services may include ticketing services; event merchandising services; parking services and parking lot events; marketing, advertising, promotion, and publicity services; television, radio, and closed circuit services; utility fees and services; labor fees; space rental; and equipment fees.

A major decision faced by all public assembly facility managers is who should manage the food and beverage operation and the sale of novelty items. Should it be managed in-house or contracted out to a service provider? And, if contracted out, what type of contract (management fee-based, percentage of gross sales, or percentage of net sales) would be most beneficial to the facility? Regardless of how these services (and all other ancillary services) are provided, the facility manager must maintain control over product/service quality, menu selections, and product/service pricing.

The quality of the food and beverage operation can affect the reputation of the PAF both positively and negatively. It is the responsibility of the facility manager to monitor the quality level of both product and service rendered to the facility's guests. Efficient operation of the food and beverage service is directly related to the kitchen and food preparation facilities available. Also important are the location and quality of the point-of-sale facilities. Appropriate display of signage listing menu items and their prices is most important. And, operating in a highly competitive marketplace, the facility manager must keep informed of industry trends related to products/services offered and the mode of delivery. Armed with this information, the manager needs to make those adjustments, if any, deemed appropriate.

The merchandising of event-related products can also be a revenue generator. PAF managers must make appropriate contractual agreements with the suppliers and/or vendors of these products. Event parking is another major revenue source. The parking location must be in close proximity to the facility, it must be clean and safe, and its employees must be user friendly. Due to the amount of money generated by parking, usually cash, appropriate measures must be employed to ensure payment from each entering vehicle is received and that all collected fees are accounted for and deposited with the business office.

The opportunities to generate ancillary revenue are restricted only by the vision and creativity of the facility management team. The wise and successful PAF manager will solicit and investigate all suggestions for additional ancillary services and will make every effort to implement all that are appropriate. The PAF manager today must become and think as an entrepreneur. This in and of itself will help the PAF manager seek and achieve job security in a profession that has numerous aspects that are beyond their control.

REFERENCES AND ADDITIONAL READINGS

Bigelow, Chris. 2008. *Foodservice Management*, unpublished manuscript. Coppell, TX: International Association of Assembly Managers, Inc.

Bigelow, Chris. 2008. *Novelties and Merchandise*, unpublished manuscript. Coppell, TX: International Association of Assembly Managers, Inc.

Cotino, Richard M. 1996. *Handbook of Equipment Leasing*, 2nd ed. New York, NY: AMACOM.

Durham, Amy. 2006. "Tomorrow's Food and Beverages." *Facility Manager* (August/September: 24-28). Coppell, TX: International Association of Assembly Managers, Inc.

Esckilsen, Lee. 2008. Public Assembly Facility Management Lectures. Johnson & Wales University, Providence, RI.

Russo, Frank. 2008 . "Event Management" in *Successful Sport Management*. Ed. Guy Lewis and Herb Appenzeller. Durham, NC: Carolina Academic Press.

Shock, Patti J. And John M. Stefanelli. 2000. *On Premise Catering: Hotels, Convention Centers, and Clubs*. Hoboken, NJ: John Wiley & Sons, Inc

CHAPTER 8

EVENT MANAGEMENT

CHAPTER OUTLINE

INTRODUCTION
THE EVENT PLANNING PROCESS
- ELIMINATING THE DISTRACTIONS
- EVENT PLANNING AND PRODUCTION PLANNING
- EVENT PLANNING NEEDS OF LOCAL PRODUCTIONS
- THE PRODUCTION RIDER
- EQUIPMENT AND STAFFING NEEDS
- THE DESIGN PHASE: DIAGRAM LAYOUTS AND FLOOR PLANS
- ESTABLISHING EVENT TIMELINES

MANAGING THE EVENT FROM THE FRONT-OF-HOUSE
- EVENT MANAGEMENT EMPLOYEE DESCRIPTIONS
- FRONT-OF-HOUSE STAFFING
- PATRON AND GUEST COMMUNICATION
- USING VISUAL AND AUDIBLE MESSAGES
- CROWD PROBLEMS AND PATRON ISSUES
- EVENT SPACE AND STAFF CAN SHAPE CROWD BEHAVIOR
- CROWD MANAGEMENT
- INCIDENT REPORTS
- SETTING AND ADJUSTING EVENT STAFFING LEVELS
- PUBLIC IMAGE

MANAGING THE EVENT FROM THE BACK-OF-HOUSE
- EVENT PRODUCTION
- THE EVENT FILE (PRODUCTION MINUTES)
- BACK-OF-HOUSE SECURITY
- MANAGING RISKS IN THE EVENT ENVIRONMENT

EVENT SAFETY AND SECURITY
- SECURITY PLANNING
- ACADEMY FOR VENUE SAFETY & SECURITY
- ADMISSION CONTROL AND OCCUPANT INGRESS/EGRESS
- EMERGENCY PLANNING AND CRISIS COMMUNICATIONS
- TRAINING

SUMMARY
REFERENCES AND ADDITIONAL READINGS

INTRODUCTION

Before the entrance doors open, the lights dim, the puck is dropped, or the curtain rises, the *event management* process has been well under way. Event management is one of many important functions for which a public assembly facility manager must assume responsibility. This chapter focuses upon the public assembly facility management's relationship to each and every event or activity that takes place in the facility and details the preparation and planning required.

Although public assembly facilities may vary in terms of mission, function and configuration, they are each designed to produce events such as trade shows, conventions, meetings, conferences, concerts, athletic events, or performing arts productions. Producing events serves many purposes including the generation of revenue, fulfilling the community's programming needs, and enhancing the quality of life for those residing within the community and surrounding areas. To successfully produce these events requires extensive planning and attention to detail on the part of the public assembly facility's event management staff.

The commitment of the public assembly facility's time and space for a specific purpose through contracts, agreements, or leases is ultimately the beginning of the event management process in a public assembly facility. The most critical aspects of the event management process are (1) the communication of pertinent details (dissemination of information) and (2) the resulting coordination of those activities. The role and responsibility of event management is that of integrating the necessary resources at the right time and location to effectively deliver the experience. In short, the event manager, regardless of venue type, is responsible for bringing about the tangible deliverables that are promised or committed. To accomplish this outcome, this chapter will focus on a number of specific steps and the associated tools needed for event management. Among the more salient points to be covered are the production rider and production requirements, event documentation, guest services staffing, safety, security, *crowd management, emergency preparedness*, and *crisis management*.

In the production of every event, public assembly facility managers and their staffs interact with all of the involved parties such as the performer, the talent agent, the promoter/presenter/producer/planner (hereinafter called *promoter*), as well as the event attendee. Ultimately, the public assembly facility manager is the central figure charged with balancing the relationships among these parties as they work collectively toward producing the event. In some instances, one or more of these parties may work independently with the facility manager and only when the event occurs do all of the stakeholders come together at one place and time.

THE EVENT PLANNING PROCESS

Regardless of the type of public assembly facility or the nature of the event, there are similarities in the way facility managers initially approach the event. Once an event is booked, staffing assignments are determined based on factors such as the type and size of the public assembly facility, the number of staff available, and the nature of the event. In a university setting, for example, events scheduled for the sports arena may be assigned to one staff member while events to be held in the institution's performing arts center may be assigned to someone else. Some public assembly facilities may have staff dedicated to event coordination while others may require certain managerial employees to function in various roles, one being that of event coordinator or manager on duty.

Event-day surprises can be frustrating and perplexing. For example, imagine discovering the day of a concert or play that the show has a new set which is much larger than the production rider indicated, thereby forcing the removal of seats that were already sold or planning for 1,000 people to attend a women's basketball game only to have 6,000 people seeking admission. A concerted effort to minimize problems is the clear theme and objective of effective event management. A sound planning process will eliminate chances of details falling through the cracks. Event management staff, particularly seasoned personnel, can often anticipate event problems and forewarn the public assembly facility manager. Facility management is able to more easily communicate and discuss these concerns with the event promoter if they share a positive rather than a neutral or negative relationship. Structuring a forum for these kinds of discussions is a serious and sometimes difficult management task because it is time-consuming and takes the department managers away from their primary responsibilities. Some managers, even the talented and more experienced ones, struggle with being able to view event presentation from an overall, global perspective. It is the public assembly facility manager's responsibility to create a management team rather than just a group of independent department managers. Left to operate in relative vacuums, individual management departments, such as security, facility operations, box office, marketing, and so forth, may adopt objectives that are beneficial to their particular unit but detrimental to the overall success of a particular event, or they may fail to disseminate event information critical to the successful operation of the other units. Effective event management requires a cooperative, positive effort and communication among all units of the organization.

ELIMINATING THE DISTRACTIONS

While the planning process may vary from facility to facility, the objective for every event should be to plan and prepare in a way that both the performer and the audience are focused upon each other and are not subjected to distractions when they come together. (See figure 8-1 for an example of a hidden distraction). If this objective is achieved, the performance will be successful, thereby enhancing

EVENT DAY DISTRACTIONS

A well-known comedian talked about playing to two identical audiences in Las Vegas. He had contracted to present a Friday and Saturday evening performance in order to accommodate the delegates attending a very large convention. The first night was magic-every joke worked, his timing felt perfect, he had the audience in the palm of his hand. The next night-nothing! The audience was distant, uninvolved, lifeless, and miserable. The second show did not go as well. As he was leaving the backstage area, he noticed the stage manager's event document which indicated the temperature at show time on Friday was 78 degrees but on Saturday it was 67 degrees Fahrenheit. In visualizing the Saturday evening audience he recalled that at least half were women wearing sleeveless dresses. He concluded that women don't laugh when they are cold and neither do the men who brought them. From that point on, one of this entertainer's performance requirements was that the room temperature be at least 72 degrees.

FIGURE 8-1

the public assembly facility manager's potential to gain future business from both the guests and the promoter. However, if planning is overlooked or goes awry and distractions occur, the manager's relationship with guests and promoter is diminished along with the potential for future business. Guest distractions contribute to a negative experience and may include poorly lit parking lots, rude event personnel, unclean restrooms, long concession lines, poor acoustics, and uncomfortable temperatures. Likewise, distractions for promoters and artists may include not having the right equipment available when needed, unclean dressing rooms, poorly catered meals, and failure on the part of the facility's staff to accommodate special requests. Imagine a load-in for a large convention without the exhibit booths being properly located, piped, and draped. What type of message does that convey to the client's convention coordinator? In an increasingly competitive marketplace, facility managers and their staffs must consider every detail carefully. In other words, setting the stage for an event to be successful must not be left to chance but rather demands careful attention from conception to the event's completion. A sellout for one event may lead to future sellouts if the guests, promoters, and artists have had a good experience.

EVENT PLANNING AND PRODUCTION PLANNING

Event planning and production planning begin once an event has been booked and contracted. Following booking, there are critical points where department managers, involved staff members, and promoters need to discuss every aspect of the event in detail. In the course of these discussions, important issues and challenges specific to the event will be identified and addressed. Most problems are easier to deal with if identified early. As a rule, the later a problem is discovered, the harder it may become to resolve.

The public assembly facility management team has a number of event planning responsibilities that include

- providing both market and venue information/regulations/restrictions to the promoter in the event planning stage
- providing a qualified and motivated workforce as required — a "crew" for setting up, taking down, and operating equipment necessary for the presentation and a front-of-house staff to deal with the attending public
- providing, either partially or solely, safety and security for the event, the working staffs and crews, and the event attendees
- providing the promoter with a properly prepared facility and assisting him/her in developing an advertising and promotion campaign if necessary
- coordinating ancillary services for guests (food and beverage, parking, etc.)
- planning and preparing for all emergency situations.

Before booking an event, the promoter should be provided with what many public assembly facility managers refer to as a *promoter packet*. This packet is designed for the promoter new to the facility and contains basic information such as

- line drawings of spaces available for rent
- seating diagrams
- layout of meeting rooms and breakout spaces
- list of house-owned equipment and corresponding rental rates
- list of available labor and corresponding rates
- list of hotel locations
- maps of the area
- names and addresses of service vendors
- house/facility rules and regulations
- rigging plot diagrams

An important part of the packet is a description of the facility's operating philosophy along with specific information about available catering, parking arrangements, merchandise and retail sales, tax collection, business license requirements, fire and safety codes, and any other restrictions or requirements particular to the facility and the community's jurisdictional codes. A well thought-out and designed information packet should answer many of the general questions promoters have when deciding whether or not to book the public assembly facility for their event.

In the past, some promoter packets were produced as fairly expensive brochures and pamphlets. Today, the marketing method of choice for many public assembly facilities in this phase of the information dissemination process is to include the necessary information on their Internet website. For the most part, web pages are less expensive to produce and update than printed pieces, generally easy to navigate, and are universally accessible. The Internet has transformed the way public assembly facilities do business. In this instance, for those promoters unfamiliar with a specific public assembly facility, viewing a facility's Internet website quite often takes the place of an onsite visit. The level of information provided through the website is only limited by the creativity of the facility's marketing department. Numerous websites not only provide the promoter with facility information, they also present links to other websites such as the convention and visitors bureau, local hotels, and event calendars. An important element of facility web sites is the ability for promoters and meeting planners to actually download venue floor plans in a variety of formats, including .pdf — adobe acrobat (probably the most common format); .dwg — autocad (used by many entertainment show designers and professional decorating companies for exhibits, etc.); and .flp — optimum settings (a software program used by many meeting planners for room setups).

Event management and its planning is the act of organizing and coordinating multiple details, some concurrently and others in sequence, to produce a tangible experience for an audience. The more organized and detailed the planning process, the more likely the event's success will be with minimal problems for the event manager the day of the event. Generally, the events that require the greatest coordination are touring shows, theatrical performances, conventions, and commercial music concerts. On the other hand, banquets, assemblies, and small group meetings may require less staffing, but may also require extensive coordination due to the client's expectations.

From several perspectives, touring theater and concert productions are similar. Both tend to travel between performances, from site to site, using buses for the talent and supporting cast and trucks to haul their equipment and props. They will perform in a number of different public assembly facilities during the course of their tour, some for one-night stands, some others for multiple performances on consecutive days. Because of performance frequency while "on the road" and the expense of transportation, standard criteria for essential support services and products that are more common and generic are specified and requested at each public assembly in which they will appear. Establishing these specifications helps the act maintain consistency in the quality of their performance. These standards also provide for efficiency in the load-in and load-out process even though the process takes place in different locales, on different stages, and in different public assembly facilities. Some of the tasks included in the process are transporting show equipment; off-loading and assembling props and/or sets; preparing costumes; accommodating requests from performers, promoters, and crew members; and installing sound and lighting units and sound reinforcement equipment. At the end of the performance, the process is reversed as the show's equipment, props, staging, and costumes are broken down, moved to the loading docks, and stowed on the trucks.

Staging a convention, exhibition, or large meeting demands much the same effort and coordination as that required for touring theater and concert productions. Convention centers must have established policies and procedures relating to convention, exhibition, and meeting setups, advance delivery of equipment and materials from the organizers and exhibitors, provision of electrical service and audiovisual equipment, exhibit booth sizes, pipe and draping and furnishings, food and beverage service, meeting room capacities and configurations, exhibit breakdowns, and the movement of materials and equipment for shipping or pick up at the loading dock.

EVENT PLANNING NEEDS OF LOCAL PRODUCTIONS

Smaller events, meetings, and theatre concerts, particularly those produced by local amateurs/non-professionals, often require special attention during the event planning stage. Providing the local promoter with an opportunity to meet with the public assembly facility's staff is the best way to avoid surprises on the day of the event. Simply providing the local promoter with the promoter packet may not be sufficient if the local promoter is not a professional and lacks the background and experience necessary to understand all the aspects related to producing an event. It's not unusual for an amateur promoter to have contracted with an act and signed off on the production rider before signing a lease agreement with the public assembly facility.

Producing a concert, exhibition, trade show, athletic competition, and so on can be complicated and risky to the public assembly facility's image and financial standing. Most public assembly facility managers will concur that the more difficult events to manage are those produced by local good-hearted, non-professionals who simply do not understand the risks involved or the details, intricacies, and necessary planning associated with a well-orchestrated event. Therefore, the public assembly facility manager must create policies, procedures, and processes that guide and encourage promoters, whether professional or non-professional, to collaborate with the public assembly facility's department managers in achieving positive event outcomes.

THE PRODUCTION RIDER

To make this detailed process work, a document is developed by the act/event explaining in detail each of the elements required by the production in order to produce a quality performance. This document is called the production rider (also referred to as the performance rider or contract rider) and is part of the performance contract signed between the promoter and the show producer, performer, or talent agency. Once signed, the promoter is agreeing to provide everything stipulated within the production rider. While all events have production riders, in fact, theatrical, touring show, concert production, and convention/exhibit riders are typically more complex. Riders may include the following:

- Labor requirements
- Administration/production office requirements
- Dressing room requirements

- Staging requirements (stage, sound, lights, rigging, and special effects)
- Staff call times for both load in and load out
- Parking access for equipment and trucks, artists, and other show personnel
- Hotel accommodations, if required
- Catering for crews and entertainers
- Backstage security requirements

Once the act/performer is contracted, the promoter becomes responsible for making sure the production rider requirements are met. If the promoter fails to provide what the production rider stipulates, the act/performer has the prerogative to cancel the performance and expect compensation from the promoter for breach of contract. Consequently, the promoter should always have knowledge of the production rider requirements prior to booking an event. By providing the public assembly facility with a copy of the rider and its requirements, the promoter further assures his/her ability to comply with the contract production rider expectations.

The promoter relies on the public assembly facility manager to fulfill many of the conditions of the production rider. Therefore, it is critical that the promoter meets with facility management to ensure that the facility can actually fulfill each of the facility-related requirements stipulated in the production rider either independently or with assistance from external entities. Typically, this initial meeting could include the promoter, the facility manager, event manager, facility's operations manager, and departmental representatives from security, marketing/promotions, and the business office. A careful review of the production rider by the working staff should uncover any problems that must be solved or negotiated before the promoter signs the contract. It must be clearly understood that unless the contract between the promoter and the facility includes agreements as to what requirements of the artist's rider the facility agrees to fulfill, there is no legal obligation to do so. Anything in the artist's rider that the public assembly facility does not agree to fulfill still remains the responsibility of the promoter and the artist. Many, if not all, of the rider's requirements will have associated costs. The public assembly facility manager should be certain these costs are identified and agreed upon as to who should pay for each item. A key issue is who can agree to expenses. An attachment to contract is used to designate who is authorized by the promoter to make financial commitments on his/her behalf, including charges by the facility. Having this attachment in place as a part of the contract/lease allows for a clearer and more efficient operational relationship during the entire course of the event.

Occasionally, the promoter may want to complete the facility lease agreement and establish an on-sale date before the public assembly facility manager and/or operations manager has reviewed the production rider. To avoid such requests, the facility's operating policies, which should have been brought to the attention of the promoter in the event booking stage, should clearly state that tickets will not go on sale before a lease agreement is signed and the production rider reviewed and its conditions accepted. The promoter may challenge this posture since she/he ultimately shoulders the responsibility for ensuring that the production rider requirements are met. The fallacy of this argument is that there can be instances in which a rider requirement cannot be accomplished. For example, an agreement between the artist and promoter to use pyrotechnics during an indoor performance is explicitly prohibited and illegal in some jurisdictions. Nonetheless, any request to prematurely complete the lease agreement should be denied or at least tentatively agreed to "subject to…," because, whenever the requirements of the production rider are not fulfilled, it is the facility and its employees who are subjected to the reaction of the upset performers and production crews.

As stated earlier, while the production rider is generally specific to touring shows, theater, and concert productions, all events have some form of production criteria that the event depends upon, formal or informal, which serves the same or similar purpose. Convention centers generally use a *banquet event order* (BEO) to confirm catering reservations and room setup diagrams to stipulate necessary seating arrangement, audiovisual equipment, floor plans, show booth locations and so forth. Every event should have a similar type of document stating exactly what the public assembly facility management and those producing the event have agreed upon with respect to room arrangements and necessary production equipment and who is responsible for providing each production element. Particular attention must be paid to timing requirements for live televised events. Whether a convention, trade show, athletic contest, a banquet, political speech, theatrical performance, Fourth of July celebration or an awards program, live televised events have their own particular timing demands. These events must start on time and often must be programmed to conclude at a specified time. If television commercial breaks are involved, they must be accommodated and accounted for within the event production timeline. Special effects must be ready for implementation upon demand signal. All associated with the event production must be organized in a manner that will ensure that the timing requirements are met in order to facilitate a smooth televised presentation.

EQUIPMENT AND STAFFING NEEDS

While the following discussion focuses more on issues included in riders for touring shows, many of the requirements are applicable to all events, although they may be implemented differently. In effect, the rider spells out what is needed to produce the event such as labor, equipment, special effects, the artists' needs, and other unique requests. For example a BEO might include table decorations, servers' dress, service times, sound/lights for a program, plus other items. Just as it is not feasible for a traveling attraction to carry all the necessary production labor personnel with it (such as stagehands, riggers, loaders, drivers, runners, followspot operators, and so forth), it is also not feasible for it to carry all the equipment needed to produce the event. The production rider should outline in detail the specific type/kind of equipment and personnel that will have to be provided from local sources to operate such equipment. Usually it becomes the responsibility of the facility's staff to procure that equipment and the necessary operators available as needed.

Many full service public assembly facilities have their own fork lifts, spotlights, tables and chairs, crowd control barriers and/or bike rack barricades, performance stages, electrical hook-ups, water/gas/compressed air lines, telephone lines, Internet connections, dressing room furniture, and a-frame ladders. Typically, equipment owned by the public assembly facility is available to the promoter on a separate rental basis, but may be included in the contract agreement. Rental and services expenses are documented on a separate equipment rental invoice and the total included on the event settlement sheet for reimbursement by the lessee. Event promoters are provided with a rental rate card depicting cost of equipment and services as a part of the contract agreement process. Special equipment can usually be rented if the request is made within appropriate timelines. Unusual equipment requests will generally surface early in the discussions between the public assembly facility's operations manager and the event promoter.

While the production rider clearly determines the number of stagehands, riggers, loaders, equipment operators, etc., required by the event, there is no such document that definitively outlines the staffing needs for the front-of-house staff. The front-of-house staff is primarily composed of part-time employees who are recruited, trained, employed, and supervised by the public assembly facility's management. It is not unusual for some facilities including performing arts, small auditoriums/civic centers, university facilities, etc., to use volunteers. The actual number of front-of-house staff required for a particular event is determined by the public assembly facility management based on judgment as to the staffing level necessary to ensure the comfort and safety of the guests attending the event. Staffing levels are influenced by the type and size of the event and its past history, the facility's physical configuration, and also by the staffing history of the public assembly facility. The front-of-house staff includes ushers, ticket takers, medical or first aid staff, security personnel, ticket sellers, and custodians. In short, front-of-house staff personnel (event staff) are present only when there is an event.

THE DESIGN PHASE: DIAGRAM LAYOUTS AND FLOOR PLANS

Once the promoter, event manager, and the operations manager have made their initial decisions concerning space accommodations for the various aspects of the event, such as room sets, equipment needs, and parking, it becomes the responsibility of the facility to create a detailed diagram of the spaces committed, a listing of the equipment provided, and the projected labor necessary to produce the event. (Figures 8-2 and 8-3 are sample diagrams.) Computer software is available that enables the operations manager to produce scaled drawings of the space(s) the client has requested. When designing the floor plan, some additional factors that must be addressed include room capacity (official capacity versus the number of people that can fit in a theater style configuration versus a classroom configuration or the number of tables that can be set for a buffet style banquet versus a banquet with wait service), fire code restrictions, and functionality (positioning the stage or head table at the opposite side of the entrance doors so latecomers will not interrupt the program).

BANQUET SET-UP DIAGRAM

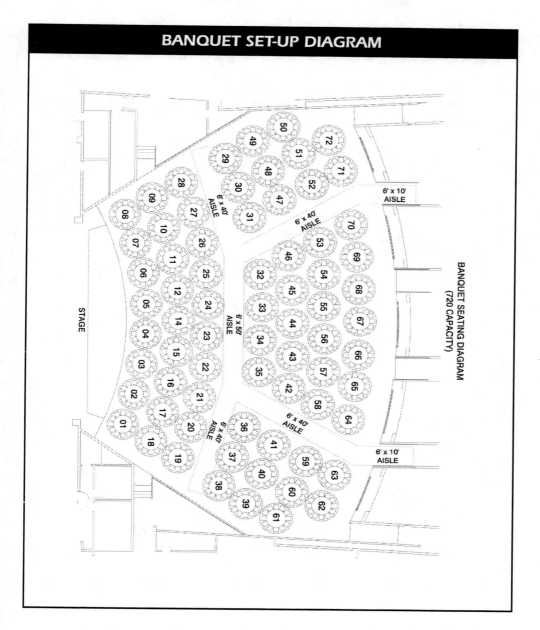

FIGURE 8-2

Providing the operations staff with detailed space drawings and a list of required equipment and services provides a very useful tool when setting up for the event. The more scheduled event activity there is within the public assembly facility, the greater the need for detailed space drawings and lists. For example, if a public assembly facility has multiple events scheduled for the same time or day,

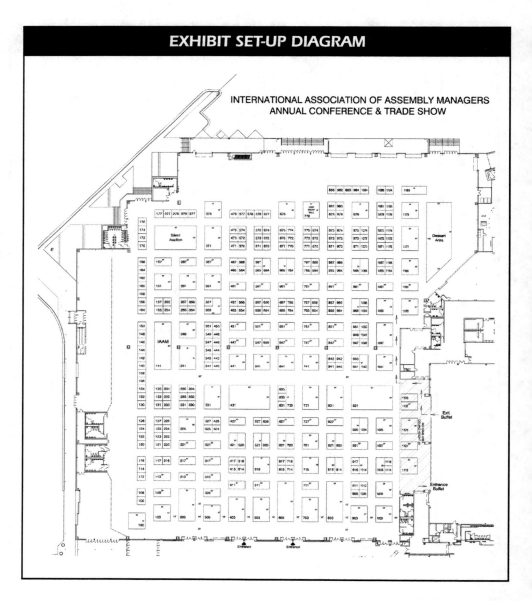

FIGURE 8-3

particular care must be taken to verify that room times committed to each event do not overlap, that sufficient time is provided in order to changeover the room, and that there is sufficient equipment available to cover everyone's requests (such as not mistakenly committing four lapel microphones when the facility only has three).

Potential problems may be discovered in the event planning process during the design phase conducted by the operations department. Before proceeding with further planning, the client should be required to approve and sign off on the diagrams and accompanying details prescribed. Although this will not ensure against last-minute changes by the promoter, it will give the operations department a level of protection and the right to charge the client for any additional services requested and provided. If additional equipment/services are requested/added to the event, the client should be required to authorize a written *change order* and a revised *cost estimate* should be issued to eliminate any financial surprises.

ESTABLISHING EVENT TIMELINES

Another tool for event planning is the *event timeline*. (See figure 8-4 for an example of an event timeline.) A meeting to develop the event timeline will assist the event manager with scheduling issues and identifying potential problems. During this meeting, the *running schedule* will be outlined with an in-depth discussion of "what happens when." Depending on the specific issues and the size of the event, individuals representing the following areas could be involved:

- Facility management
- Event promoter/producer
- Event managers/coordinators
- Representative from local agencies such as police, fire, public transportation, etc
- Box office manager
- Operations manager/IATSE steward
- Parking and traffic manager
- Food and beverage/merchandise manager
- Engineers
- Housekeeping supervisor

Quite often for small and routine events, only the promoter and a liaison from the public assembly facility meet. The liaison then disseminates the information to others as needed.

As the public assembly facility staff reviews the event's schedule on an hour-by-hour basis, issues and concerns may arise that will require clarification and discussion. Issues such as event staff parking, load-in and load-out schedules, meal and rest breaks, dress and decorum, and the event's start, intermission, and ending times all have different implications for the various groups that make up the work staff. Bringing the staff together and creating a timeline that accommodates the needs of each area will enable the staff to assess the event comprehensively and efficiently. In essence, the front-of-house must relate to the needs of the back-of-house and vice versa. Although simple in concept, the feedback gained from a meeting of this nature generally proves very useful in reducing distractions or surprises on the day of the event.

EVENT TIMELINE

EVENT TIMELINE

May 28, 2009
Doors @ **5:30**pm
Show @ **6:30**pm
End @ **10:30**

Single Scale Seating

Sections: **Floor &
Bowl Seating**
$25.00

Who	What	When	How
F	**Conversion IN**	5/23/09 completed	Event floor, All dashers set and removed, plugs in place
F	**Locker, Catering, & Production rooms**	5/23/09 completed	Remove materials, clean, vacuum, sanitize, set open,
SH	**Stage set**	5/27/09 3:00am	Sand Hollow will set a 40x60 stage. Positioning will be determined by BM.
P	**Production Set**	5/28/09 8:00AM – 12:00PM	Trim all from previous show - Dasher & coverage drape, prep lighting set, FOH prep, spots, headsets, com link, power, patches, Greenroom, Please cover all cables after placement. Prep 2 30' trusses for wings.
P	**Dressing Room Set**	5/28/09 8am-11am	Refresh all drapery, furniture, tables, chairs, analyze for secure and tight set
F	**Load in prep**	5/28/09 8:30am	Set out all forks, open roll up door, clear tunnel of refuse, set ramp for dasher dam lip, prep flagger & sign 7 cone set
F	**Cones set**	5/28/09 8:45am	Place cones on lane, set all signage, Flagger reports at this time for load in.
P, SH, E	**Load In**	5/28/09 9-11am	Sand Hollow will load in show, Electrician arrives @ 9:00, flagger on street and down below in garage.
F	**Facility restore**	5/28/09 11-2pm	Replace plug, set stairs, tighten all rails, set ready for show
P, SH, E	**Lunch advantage**	5/28/09 12pm-2pm	Try to grab a bite and take advantage of show production slow
P, F	**Pre show checks**	5/28/09 3pm-4pm	Check all technical aspects, trim drapery, stairwell check, bathrooms ready, stanchions set, door check, merch set. Set Floor entry signage outside
ALL F, P, ES, BO, M, EM GM	**Arena Check**	5/28/09 4pm-4:30pm	Check arena for show readiness, adjustments if necessary, setup front street entrance signs and prepare entry. All fluorescents in e-level tunnels out, breezeway & backstage tunnels lights out, all drapery adjusted and ready, all doors & seats secure & safe, concourse clear, backstage lights out up to red door.
ES, EM, GM	**Event Briefing**	5/28/09 4:45pm	Cover security requirements, last call, obstructed view seats, relocation areas & procedure, CMS, ES coord, GM, & EM (staff posted on grove to usher people in line with floor tickets to go to front street entrance.)
ALL	**Doors**	5/28/09 5:30pm	All staff in positions, doors to be called by MOD, house lights ready & on headset, custodial ready, Front street ready, merch ready.
ALL	**Show**	5/28/09 6:30-10:30	Show Duration
F	**Cones set**	5/28/09 10:00pm	Place cones on lane, set all signage, Flagger reports at this time for load out. if necessary assist truckers into position. A few cleanup crew members report at this time, along with a few conversion crew
ALL	**Crowd Load out**	5/28/09 10:30 - 10:45	Begin ushering crowd off of the floor area
ALL	**Load out**	5/28/09 10:45 – 1:00	Load out begins, remove load in plug & dashers, remove entire house setup with the exception of needed setup for MMA
F	**Post Event Cleanup**	5/28/09 11:00pm	Remainder post event cleanup & conversion crew reports to restore facility
SH, F	**Stage Out**	5/29/09 2:00am – 3:30am	Stage to be removed

Notes:

_____

_____

_____

_____

FIGURE 8-

MANAGING THE EVENT FROM THE FRONT OF THE HOUSE

Well trained event managers understand the importance of attending to the event management details associated with the areas within the public assembly facility which are typically occupied by the general public or event attendees referred to as front-of-house. These areas typically include lobbies and concourses, concession stands, public restrooms, the box office, parking lots, seating, and exhibit areas. Great emphasis is placed on the training required for the part-time employees who deliver services to the facility's guests while they occupy the front-of-house spaces in the public assembly facility. It goes beyond the delivery of those services in the most efficient and effective manner to ensuring the safety and security of every guest regardless of the circumstances that can and do disrupt the guests' event experience. Effectively managing the variables associated with front-of-house operations will help ensure that event attendees have a safe and enjoyable event experience, but will also contribute to the overall image the facility enjoys within the community. This section will discuss the importance of the communication tools that event managers employ in their duties to deliver excellent customer service to the facility's guests as well as the event management techniques employed in dealing with patron issues, in particular, crowd management.

EVENT MANAGEMENT EMPLOYEE DESCRIPTIONS

Typical titles for employees who are the promoter's contact point and deal with event-related issues include event services manager, event supervisor, and event coordinator. Although not always, these positions are typically a part of the facility services and operations department, and the role of those holding these positions is to facilitate the event planning and implementation processes. Again, each of these positions may be filled by a single individual or through a collaborative effort depending on the public assembly facility, the specific event, and the volume of events booked.

Regardless of how the positions are filled, promoters expect the role of the event manager to be assumed by a knowledgeable person or persons employed by the public assembly facility. If the facility's size or event volume does not justify assigning a dedicated employee to coordinate the event-related information and to make appropriate decisions, then others must accomplish these tasks such as the booking manager, the operations manager, or, at times, the facility manager. In every instance, someone must assume the responsibilities for coordinating activities and disseminating information to the promoter from the facility as well as coordinating and relaying information from the promoter back to the appropriate facility personnel.

SELECTED EVENT MANAGEMENT POSITIONS

EVENT SERVICES MANAGER
The event services manager reports to and works under the direction of the operations manager. This person controls and monitors the customer contacts aspect of the public assembly facility operations by planning, monitoring, directing, delegating, controlling, and managing the event's coordination, wardrobing, security, crowd management, telephone, and outside contractor service function; performs related responsibilities as required.

SENIOR EVENT COORDINATOR
The senior event coordinator is responsible for planning, organizing, and controlling events within the facility as assigned and assists the event services manager in supervising the day-to-day activities of event services, to include but not limited to supervising event coordinators, preparing event outlines and scaled drawings of event areas, coordinating equipment distribution, event billing, monitoring event assigned, and such other functions and duties as required by the event services manager.

EVENT SUPERVISOR
Performs professional and supervisory work assisting in the utilization of entertainment, recreational, and convention facilities. Duties are varied and require some independent action as well as a thorough knowledge of facility's rules in assisting with the supervision of the day-to-day activities. Employee has regular contact with inside and outside sources related to the planning for and providing of services needed by facility's users.

EVENT COORDINATOR
The event coordinator is responsible for organizing and controlling events within the facility as assigned and monitors the logistical interfacing of these events, to include but not limited to the preparing of event outlines and scaled drawings of event areas and coordinating equipment distribution and event billing. The duties will include all event coordination tasks after events are booked through their conclusion. Ensures tenant requirements are met and facility rules, regulations and policies are adhered to by serving as a liaison between the facility and the tenants; assists tenants in the planning of their own events; and performs related responsibilities as required. Position reports directly to the senior event coordinator.

FIGURE 8-5

Job descriptions for the management positions noted in Figure 8-5 are presented in the *IAAM's Position Description Handbook* (IAAM, 1994) that address these event management positions. The positions are not necessarily presented in hierarchical order. Any particular facility may have all or none of these positions.

Front-of-House Staffing

As stated, the front-of-house staff is a mixture of staffing positions ranging from ushers to armed, uniformed security/police when appropriate. The public assembly facility's event manager usually determines the components of the event staffing mix based on variables such as projected attendance, type of event,

PATRON SERVICES STAFFING

Event Personnel	Quantity	Hours	Rate	Payroll Tax		Total
Ushers and Ticket Takers	17	5.75	$6.50	$	209.67	$ 845.05
Early Arrival Usher for walk up	2	9.00	$6.50	$	38.61	$ 155.61
Usher Captains	3	5.75	$8.00	$	45.54	$ 183.54
Event Staff Supervisor	2	12.00	$11.00	$	87.12	$ 351.12
T-Shirt Security All Day	2	17.50	$11.50	-		$ 402.50
T-Shirt Security	23	7.00	$11.50	-		$ 1,851.50
T-Shirt Security Coordinator Fee	1	FLAT	$25.00	-		$ 25.00
CMS - Security	3	5.75	$17.00	$	96.77	$ 390.02
CMS - Coordinator Fee	1	FLAT	$25.00	-		$ 25.00
CMS - Supervisor	1	7.00	$20.00	$	46.20	$ 186.20
Uniformed officers	2	6.00	$37.50	-		$ 450.00
Box Office On Sale Labor	1	2.00	$8.00	$	5.28	$ 21.28
Box Office Lead	1	3.75	$8.00	$	9.90	$ 39.90
Box Office Labor	1	2.75	$6.75	$	6.13	$ 24.69
Box Office Labor	1	4.75	$6.75	$	10.58	$ 42.64
Merchandise Labor	1	4.75	-	-		$ 403.08
Custodial	1	5.00	$8.93	$	14.73	$ 59.38
Custodial	1	5.00	$8.50	$	14.03	$ 56.53
				TOTAL:	$	5,513.04

Setup and Post Event Personnel	Total
Conversion	$ 1,000.00
Post Event Cleanup	$ 760.10
TOTAL:	$ 1,760.10

Misc Expenses	Total
Credit Card fee (2.60%)	Please Insert
Floor Tape	$ 25.00
Furniture Rental Insurance	$ 12.50
Catering	$ 4,967.85
TOTAL:	$ 5,005.35

Production Personnel and Equip.	Total
Stage Rental	$ 1,500.00
Run of Show	$ 95.76
Load In	$ 233.08
Load Out	$ 35.91
Sand Hollow - Production In	$ 3,076.00
Sand Hollow - Show Call	$ 700.00
Sand Hollow Production Out	$ 1,780.00
Sand Hollow - 15% Admin Fee	$ 833.40
ICM Fork Rental	$ 55.73
TOTAL:	$ 6,809.88

Payouts	Total
Bravo Entertainment (cash)	$ -
TOTAL:	$ -

Show Revenue	Total
SAS Gross ticket Sales	$ 69,625.00
Suite Sales	$ -
TW Gross ticket sales	$ 19,800.00
Concessions	$ 4,349.14
Merchandise	$ 3,721.11
TOTAL:	$ 97,495.25

TOTAL SHOW EXPENSES:	$ 19,088.38		TOTAL SHOW REVENUE:	$ 97,495.25

FIGURE 8-6

time of year, time of day, weather, community expectations, the event's history, community influences, facility restrictions, legal regulations, etc. Because the public assembly facility management has the responsibility for decisions that directly affect the promoter, such as front-of-house staffing decisions, it is wise to provide the promoter with an estimate of these associated costs, as well as other costs, prior to the start of the event. (Figure 8-6 is an example of the staffing schedule for an event.)

Prior to event day(s), if promoters believe the event to be "overstaffed," there are ample opportunities for them and the event coordinator to look at an alternative staffing scheme. Staffing and cost estimates not only give the promoter an early awareness of one of the larger event expenses, they also provide the event coordinator some insight into the security manager's approach to ensuring the safety of the event. This process provides vital information to the decision makers at a time and manner that allows them to review, react, and adjust the staffing plan, if deemed necessary. Again, the reason for engaging in this process is to prevent event day surprises from occurring.

PATRON AND GUEST COMMUNICATION

Policies adopted by the public assembly facility that have a direct effect on guests should be prominently displayed and advertised. Some policies remain constant whereas the implementation of others may depend on the event. For example, constant policies would include prohibiting smoking or carrying weapons within the confines of the facility while policies related to the use of cameras and recording devices or the age limit for children being required to have (or not have) their own ticket may change depending on the event. In all instances, every effort should be made to inform guests of these policies in a timely manner.

USING VISUAL AND AUDIBLE MESSAGES

Graphics and/or signage are an important part of the crowd management program. Properly conceived and professionally produced, graphics often can better and more rapidly inform guests than can facility employees. Graphics may be permanently installed or posted only when needed. For example, signage posted in a very visible manner at the entrances to a facility displaying the facility's policy regarding prohibited items may save the guest from the embarrassment of having such an item confiscated during an event or from the inconvenience of finding a safe storage place for the item or having to discard it prior to gaining admission. Public address systems and message boards provide two excellent means for immediately delivering communications to large numbers of guests. It is extremely important for the public assembly facility manager to provide the public address/ message board operator with pre-recorded messages/instructions that are to be used in the event of emergencies. This same information should be provided to the event receptionist. This is especially true if a situation occurs that necessitates evacuating guests from the public assembly facility.

CROWD PROBLEMS AND PATRON ISSUES

While it is virtually impossible to develop detailed procedures covering every potential problem event staff may encounter, the event manager will have preplanned responses to predictable and repetitive problems. Dedicated event staff will tend to "do something" whenever a problem does occur. Unfortunately, without clearly written and understood procedures, these well meaning staff members may initiate an action that does not meet with management approval or solve the problem.

A manual containing approved procedures for dealing with general activities such as traffic control, parking, opening the house for an event, resolving seating and ticketing problems, dealing with unruly guests, ejections from the premise, medical emergencies, demonstrations, and so forth should be provided to each employee and then reviewed and discussed on a routine basis. The manual should also address procedures and responsibilities for potential major incidents such as bomb threats, fires, riots, shootings, terrorist activities, etc. Special attention should be given to procedures related to the evacuation of guests from the facility and its grounds in emergency situations. In addition, the facility should provide all appropriate personnel specific policies and procedures applicable to each event; this can be accomplished verbally or in writing.

Event Space and Staff Can Shape Crowd Behavior

Design and use of space can exert subtle influences on a public assembly facility's guests. In fact, some of these influences are so subtle guests remain totally unaware of their behavior being modified by the facility's design. On the other hand, guests are very much aware of the feelings they experience as they interact with the facility's event staff. Much of the public assembly facility's public image, as previously stated, results from the guest's interactions with the front-of-house staff, including ushers, ticket takers, greeters, security guards, ticket sellers, and parking attendants. Guests also interact with food/beverage and merchandise workers. Therefore, each of these individuals becomes, by default, the caretaker of a facility's valuable asset, its public image. With this dynamic understood, the public assembly facility manager must recruit, hire, train, and monitor personnel accordingly.

In a sense, the question becomes what is customer service and where does crowd management begin? The two are inseparable. When staff controls ingress by taking tickets, monitoring turnstiles and doors, checking for prohibited items, enforcing building/event policies, and implementing the evacuation plan, if necessary, it is managing the crowd by providing customer services: guests are admitted efficiently and effectively, provided with directions to their seat or other locations and are able to enjoy their time at the facility in a safe environment.

Crowd Management

Each audience has its own personality: country and western concert audiences are considerably different from those attending alternative rock performances. Fans attending a sporting event at a stadium one weekend may be very different from those in attendance the following weekend. Security personnel should not allow themselves to be lulled into believing "an audience is an audience" and dealing with each in the same manner. Every audience is different. A thorough understanding of crowd management, as opposed to crowd control, can assist the security management team in understanding the differences in crowds and in making appropriate crowd management or crowd control decisions. (See Appendix A, Figure 8-7 for crowd management definitions and duties.)

The exact number of security personnel placements, especially for the front-of-house, is determined by the event's potential for crowd management challenges. For example, a symphony orchestra performance will require less "visual uniform presence" than a hard rock show where alcoholic beverages are served. A trade show centered on home improvement products and projected to attract 20,000 attendees over the course of a weekend might require a security director, door guards at each entrance/exit area, and a first aid team. On the other hand, an alternative rock show projected to attract an audience of 8,000 may require the presence of uniformed security/police, door guards at each entrance/exit area, a first aid team, and a host of T-shirt security personnel.

Sometimes, crowd management problems that occur at events have virtually no connection with the event or the public assembly facility. The facility and the event simply become involved because the feuding elements, either by accident or design, decide to confront each other at that site and during that event. For example, there have been numerous incidents in which inner city youth gangs have caused violent disruptions at high school football and basketball games. In these instances, neither the competing teams nor the high school arena or stadium in which the contests were being held had anything to do with the conflicts.

After watching 10,000 college football fans rush onto the field and tear down the goal posts following a dramatic ending to a hotly contested game, it becomes crystal clear that once a large crowd decides to do something, there is very little the public assembly facility's security management team can do to stop them. As frightening as this may appear, it is equally unsettling to realize that if a fan were to sustain an injury in an incident of this nature, the public assembly facility's management team and/or its owners may potentially be held liable.

The public assembly facility's security manager is charged with the responsibility to assess each event and recommend the appropriate staffing requirements. The security manager assumes the role of liaison between outside law enforcement agencies and the facility's security personnel, including contract security if used. Creating and maintaining relationships with local law enforcement agencies is critical. Depending on the event, these agencies should be involved at the event planning stage so they will be knowledgeable of the event thereby enabling them to respond faster and more effectively if a crisis were to occur. Security managers should be collecting as much intelligence about upcoming events as possible.

Information may be obtained from networking with other public assembly facility security managers, following the reports of touring attractions through the trade publications, observing crowd behavior of those in the ticket line when the event goes on sale, and visiting or talking with other public assembly facility's staff where the event is performing in order to understand the behavior to be expected of the act's fans. Each of these information sources is beneficial in keeping the security manager sharp and informed.

INCIDENT REPORTS

Whenever an incident occurs, facility personnel should be instructed to record all pertinent information relative to the incident on an *Incident Report Form*. (See Appendix A, Figure 8-8 for a sample form.) These report forms should be kept on file for no less than the time period allowed by state law (or other legal jurisdictions) for filing a lawsuit by the party(ies) involved in the incident. Only authorized individuals should have access to these reports. Medical information related to those involved must be kept confidential and only shared with individuals or agencies authorized by law and/or those authorized by the specific individual's consent. Accountable staff members should be required to complete these reports following the event before their departure from the facility.

SETTING AND ADJUSTING EVENT STAFFING LEVELS

Often when a public assembly facility prepares for doors opening, the casual observer will note a huge ratio of event staff personnel per patron, frequently anywhere from one to 100-250. Depending on the event, the maximum number of employees on duty is at the time the doors open. Due to the sporadic "on-again/ off-again" nature of the public event business, the majority of patron service and event staffing roles are filled by casual and part-time labor. Because these service providers are usually in front line roles, in direct contact with the public, extensive efforts need to be made by the public assembly facility's management to develop customer friendly attitudes and programs.

PUBLIC IMAGE

One of the most valuable assets of any public assembly facility is its public image: how the public feels about the facility. The facility's public image is also formed in part by its success in accommodating community needs through its programming and the level of maintenance and housekeeping afforded the facility and its adjacent grounds. Another very important aspect in determining the facility's public image is the quality of the interactions between the guest and the front-of-house event staff, a workforce primarily composed of part-time employees. Consequently training is absolutely critical. Every day, managers entrust the image of their public assembly facility to those employees who might be the least trained, marginally supervised, poorest paid, and least committed to the overall enterprise.

For many guests attending an event at a public assembly facility, the annoying parking guard, the stressed ticket seller, the surly ticket taker, the inattentive usher, or the employee unable to provide initial first aid or cardiopulmonary resuscitation (CPR) due to lack of training becomes "the facility." Negative encounters with these individuals may dramatically alter the guest's perception of that facility. The only way to reduce the potential for employees acting in a negative fashion (or not acting at all) is to have a training program that truly emphasizes the need for positive guest relations and that imparts in the employee a sense of ownership in the success of the event production.

MANAGING THE EVENT FROM THE BACK OF THE HOUSE

Responsibility for managing the event from the back-of-house perspective usually resides within the facilities services/operations department often under the supervision of the operations manager or technical director. Areas of the public assembly facility usually associated with the back-of-house operations include the stage, dressing rooms, mechanical rooms, loading docks, kitchen, commissary, equipment storage rooms, and operations staff support areas. While the operations managers work with a variety of staff, including touring show production personnel, to present each event which ensures that the magic of live events is present, they also are most often involved and responsible for, in part, the facility-wide risk management and emergency preparedness plans, which is the result of their oversight responsibilities for the physical plant.

EVENT PRODUCTION

One of the fundamental functions of a public assembly facility is to provide a space in which events are produced. Event production is the art and science of bringing two distinctly different groups of people together at the same time and space to share the experience of a live event. Artists perform for an audience, athletes compete for their fans, and vendors display their products for their clients at a specified time in public assembly facilities during an event. When the performance, competition, or display occurs, it is referred to as the event. The process of bringing all of the various elements that comprise an event is referred to as event production.

THE EVENT FILE (PRODUCTION MINUTES)

The event file is a valuable tool created by the event manager to document planning activity and track progress. The event manager might maintain a written diary or a running commentary to document events. This diary chronologically documents the event, starting with the booking memo and concluding with event debriefing meeting notes. The diary is a log of the interactions among the event manager, promoter, and the attraction. Upon conclusion of the event, the diary, along with the contract, production rider, settlement sheet (which includes labor, equipment, and other charges), box office statement, certificates of insurance, event drop counts, ticket stubs, deadwood, etc., becomes a part of the event file. These documents provide management with an understanding of the entire event process and factual information needed to respond to any questions. Having access to a detailed description of the last time the event played at the public assembly facility can provide valuable information to the facility's current staff as well as to the act or attraction itself.

Another valuable management technique is for facility managers to have on their desks when arriving the following day at least these four reports: first aid log, general incidents (public contact) report, box office statement and settlement, and an event summary that includes traffic and parking.

BACK-OF-HOUSE SECURITY

Everything behind the stage such as dressing rooms, buses, trailer trucks, common catering areas, meet and greet areas, etc., are referred to as back-of-house. Security personnel, either in-house or subcontracted, normally provide protection for these areas. Decisions related to their number, positioning, and hours on location are usually outlined in the production rider. Even though the production rider spells out back-of-house requirements, public assembly facility managers must remember that ultimately they are responsible for the safety and security of the act, the audience, and the working staffs, and therefore it must be made clear to all parties that the final decision-making authority resides with the facility's management.

MANAGING RISKS IN THE EVENT ENVIRONMENT

Protecting the assets of the facility and reducing its liability are key roles of facility management and are often considered back-of-house functions; responsibilities are, more often than not, delegated to the facility services/operations department. Although risk management is a facility-wide discipline and may be implemented by management, many of the functions may be performed by operations due in part to oversight of the physical plant. In case of fire or other reasons for evacuation, procedures, processes, and communications are preplanned, established through training and implemented, both internally and externally, with the appropriate local agencies.

In cooperation with the facility manager and facility services and operations department, the event manager plays a key role ensuring that the event is operated in a safe and secure manner. Responsibilities in risk management areas include:

- Event certificate of insurance
- Proper contract administration
- Risk assessment
- Security and crowd management planning, including planning to "harden" the facility against threats and provide effective screening and admission protocols
- Emergency and crisis management planning
- Alcohol management

- Fire code and life safety planning
- Staff training for risk management responsibilities

While events designed to attract large numbers of guests to the facility are desirable from a business perspective, they also bring with them an increased degree of responsibility. During all such events, event managers literally hold the safety and well-being of the guests in their hands. Whether the audience is a small meeting group or 100,000 sport fans, the responsibilities and need for preparation remain the same. The satisfaction, well-being, and safety of guests, employees, performers, contractors, and all others depend upon the care taken by the public assembly facility manager and the event management staff. The facility manager must convey this sense of responsibility to each and every employee. From the parking lot to the performance itself, the well being of everyone must be safeguarded.

Readiness for dealing with disastrous circumstances during a public event is critical to effective event management. The list of possible problem areas includes:

- Medical emergencies
- Fire/fire alarm
- Bomb threat/explosion
- Mechanical/equipment/structure failure
- Power failure
- Natural disasters/severe weather
- Civil disturbance/riots/other criminal acts
- Hazardous material release
- Terrorism
- Building evacuation
- Air conditioning contamination
- Food poisoning
- Suspicious mail/packages

EVENT SAFETY AND SECURITY

Public assembly facilities exist to hold and produce events, of many different types. Each event creates a unique set of situations and environments. It is, therefore, important that facility management adopt and practice an event planning process that logically and methodically prepares for each event. This event planning process must address the operating requirements of the event as well as consider and address the risks and threats that may be associated with all events, or by the nature of a specific event.

A facility manager's goal is to keep guests, employees, licensees, athletes, and performers safe. In order to achieve this goal, facility managers must incorporate complete safety and security planning and programming at all times to guard all assets as well as personnel and to evaluate the risks and threats associated with facility operations during event production. This is an ongoing process within which there is always potential for threats, which may present themselves in many different forms and dimensions.

SECURITY PLANNING

Through the 1990s, facility and event "security staff" were focused on routine crowd management and policy enforcement roles; increasingly, security staff also was trained to provide quality customer service.

In the aftermath of the September 11, 2001, terrorist attacks, security planning has taken on new emphasis. For high profile events, large budgets are devoted to upgrading the facility's capabilities to deter and defend against terrorist attacks. Safety and security measures, though present in most venues, are now more overt in nature and extensive in options, but must repeatedly be reviewed and evaluated for circumstantial/situational conditions. Typical enhancements to security include perimeter protection measures such as installation of bollards and closing of streets; heightened admissions control procedures, including the use of metal detectors; more rigorous employee screening and background checks; improved credentialing of employees, contractors and facility visitors; more extensive use of closed circuit television (CCTV) monitoring; and modification of HVAC air intakes to eliminate the possibility of introduction of biological or chemical agents by terrorists.

Most facilities and major events also use sophisticated programs to assess security risks and threats. A typical assessment model includes these elements:

Asset assessment – An asset assessment involves the identification of those things within an organization that might be the target of a threat. Assets include facility equipment, personnel, information, activities or events, and the facility itself. Key questions that should be asked during the process of conducting an asset assessment might include the following:

- What are the core functions and processes of the facility?
- What are the critical building elements, including structural and informational?
- For each asset, what is its value, i.e., to what extent would its loss cause a debilitating impact on the facility?

By identifying the important assets and answering these key questions, an organization takes the first step towards focusing its resources on that which is most important. Asset identification also is important because all of the additional assessments will flow from it.

Threat assessment – Webster's Dictionary defines threat as an expression of intention to inflict evil, injury, or damage, or an indication of something impending. To a facility manager, a threat is the bad thing that could happen to the assets the manager is responsible for. Threats exist in many different forms. They can be from an external force such as an act of terrorism; they can be unsafe conditions or situations that are highly likely to cause an accident; they can be acts of God such as severe weather, or any other thing that can go wrong. When a threat becomes an actual action or situation, it becomes an emergency. At this point, the facility's emergency response plan must be implemented. This will be discussed further in Chapter 9.

Vulnerability assessment – Vulnerability assessments identify weaknesses within an organization that could be exploited by a threat. This is also the time to identify the vulnerability of specific assets related to undesired events, and evaluate existing countermeasures (protections) and their effectiveness in reducing or eliminating those vulnerabilities. The vulnerability assessment begins by examining the critical infrastructure of the facility. This includes the building itself, personnel, and operational policies and procedures, and it requires venue managers to evaluate the effectiveness of the current level of protection. Given various threats and threat scenarios, facility vulnerability assessment might consider factors such as the facility's level of visibility in the community, the facility's value to the community, the facility's target value to an adversary, potential for collateral damage, and the facility's "hardness" or "softness" in providing access to aggressors.

Risk analysis – The purpose of this analysis is to establish a level of risk for each asset. During the risk analysis phase, a venue manager begins to prioritize the assets of the venue based upon the potential consequences of their being lost or damaged. This is also when one begins to establish the degree of impact of such loss relative to each of the identified assets; the likelihood of an attack by a threat; the likelihood a vulnerability will be exploited; the relative degree of the risk based upon the countermeasures required. When considering the cost of a risk, the facility manager must consider not only the direct costs (replacement value, loss of use, etc.) but also the indirect costs (reduction in employee morale, patron psychological feelings, etc.) when doing a cost/benefit analysis. A final consideration must be that whatever countermeasure is considered, it must not introduce another hazard to the situation. It just doesn't make sense to reduce or eliminate one risk by replacing it with another.

Using some type of quantitative rating system is helpful in establishing priorities. For instance, a staff brainstorming session on threats at a facility could yield hundreds of possibilities. By rating the likelihood of a particular threat, facility management can establish priorities and attempt to develop complete plans for only those threats of highest risk. (Figure 8-9 is an excerpt from one of the IAAM planning guides that show use of a decision tree.)

IAAM's "Best Practices Planning Guides for Safety, Security and Emergency Preparedness" assist the event manager in assessing risk factors and determining threat levels. Utilizing the decision tree checklist, event organizers are encouraged

DECISION TREE

Sample Decision Tree Questions:

■ Has the Office of Homeland Security issued a "Severe Condition" (Red) Warning?
   No   Yes ── **Management should consider canceling the event.**
   |

■ Has the event been classified as a Secret Service "Special Event" under the
   Office of Homeland Security?
   No   Yes ── **Management should implement Level #4 measures.**
   |

■ Is the event being broadcast nationally or internationally?
   No   Yes ── **Have specific and credible threats been received by the event organizers or police?**
   | Yes ── **Management should implement Level #3 measures.**

FIGURE 8-9

and directed to evaluate various environments that may exist and provides the accompanying response recommendations. (Figure 8-10 provides a list of resources available for safety and security planning.)

RESOURCE CENTER

IAAM has developed extensive planning guides and training materials for facility managers to use in designing and training for security, emergency planning, life safety and crowd management. Most of the informational material, including reference links and downloadable material can be found at IAAM's Center for Venue Management Studies at IAAM's web site at:
http://www.iaam.org/CVMS/CVMSsafety.htm

Below are some resources that are available:
■ Safety and Security Best Practices Planning Guide for Theatres and Performing Arts Centers (member only download).
■ Safety and Security Best Practices Planning Guide for Arenas, Stadiums and Amphitheatres (member only download)
■ Safety and Security Best Practices Planning Guide for Convention Centers/Exhibit Halls (member only download)
■ Safety and Security Best Practices Planning Guide for Emergency Preparedness (member only download)

Emergency Planning Resources and Links
■ Homeland Security Advisory Vehicle Borne Improvised Explosive Devices
■ SSTF State Handgun Laws
■ SSTF Weapon Position Statement
■ Facility Pre-Employment Information and Verification: The First Level Of Security Defense
■ FBI Alert to Stadiums
■ Safeguarding Building Ventilation Systems

Also, see safety and security publications available for sale at:
http://www.iaam.org/Products/catalogue.htm

FIGURE 8-10

Academy for Venue Safety & Security

The Academy for Venue Safety & Security was created in 2004 by the International Association of Assembly Managers (IAAM) as an intense training academy in security planning and life safety management for the public assembly facility industry. The Academy for Venue Safety & Security (AVSS) is an IAAM school designed to teach and promote the best practices of safety and security protocols, methods, and procedures. Venue management professionals are provided information, tools, and methodologies to protect guests, customers, employees, vendors, athletes, and performers, as well as property and assets through risk identification, implementation of risk management practices and procedures, emergency planning, preservation of economic viability, and facilitation of recovery.

Beginning in 2007, the IAAM Academy for Venue Safety & Security adopted a track system for curriculum organization and course scheduling. Each track focuses on a broad-based topic critical to safety and security. All tracks consist of a series of courses designed to educate AVSS students by providing instruction, applicable tools, and experience, and will typically conclude with a practicum on the topic. The core curriculum AVSS tracks are 1. Risk Management; 2. Emergency Planning; 3. Security Operations; and 4. Training. More information about the IAAM Academy for Venue Safety & Security can be found on the IAAM website (www.iaam.org).

Admission Control and Occupant Ingress/Egress

Traditionally, event managers have been concerned with guest entry (*ingress*). They work diligently to provide the most efficient way of allowing ticketed guests to enter the facility. In the same vein, they must be just as diligent in providing guests with the most efficient routes for exiting (*egress*) the facility. Public assembly facility entrance and exit points, as well as the concourse flow pattern, require special attention.

Access control takes place at all physical entrances to the various areas of the facility complex, including parking lots, loading docks, patron entrances, backstage, and employee entrances, etc. During events when heightened security is required, a security perimeter may be established: an outside line perhaps coinciding with outside fencing of the facility and its parking areas. Examples of access control techniques from IAAM's "Safety and Security Planning Guide for Arenas, Stadiums and Amphitheaters" (IAAM, 2002) include:

- Inspect all bags, including equipment bags and other containers of persons entering the venue.
- Require each licensee, organizer, team, etc. to provide a pass list, certified by management, of all representatives who will enter the venue.
- Venue management and lessees will not issue credentials to non-essential personnel or other persons.

- All event employees, media, contractors, exhibitors, and vendors must wear IDs issued by management. All temporary employees, contractors, vendors, media, and visitors should be issued daily passes that correspond to the "color of the day." Passes should not be issued until verification from their point of contact within the venue has been established. All temporary passes should be returned to security upon exiting.
- Photo IDs must be worn at this level of heightened security.
- No persons other than authorized user personnel and guests should be permitted in the dressing rooms, i.e., players, performers, spouses, coaches, media, staff, cleaning, maintenance, catering, etc.
- Artists and team members should not bring guests, other than immediate family, a significant other, or friend into the back-of-the-house areas.

During periods of heightened security, access controls and search techniques combine to sanitize the event areas of the facility. Similar to what happens at airports when access controls are breached and airport terminals are evacuated, public assembly facilities also must have procedures for when facility security sanitation is not maintained. Entrance control requires that all exit/entry doors be checked to ensure that the panic hardware is functioning properly.

In the desire to control ingress, facility tenants will sometimes ask that panic hardware be disabled or take it upon themselves to disable these devices. Since the public assembly facility management is ultimately responsible for the safety of the attending public, it is clearly the event manager's responsibility to make sure the panic hardware installed on every marked exit door remains operable at all times. In most jurisdictions, disabling panic devices constitutes a serious criminal offense.

Historically, management personnel have been concerned with guest entry issues and, for the most part, have developed excellent resolutions. However, since the advent of worldwide terrorist activity, public assembly facility managers have to be concerned with controlling key locations against unlawful entry either onto the property or into the facility itself. This vigilance must be maintained on a twenty-four hour basis, every day of the year.

Regardless of when the facility was constructed, facility managers must determine whether sufficient barriers exist to prevent unauthorized entry onto the property and whether there are sufficient buffer areas or clear zones between those barriers and the facility. If deficiencies are detected, it becomes the manager's responsibility to initiate corrective measures to ensure as much as possible the safety of the public assembly facility and its guests.

EMERGENCY PLANNING AND CRISIS COMMUNICATIONS

Emergency planning is an ongoing activity that should involve every department within a facility. From the event manager's point of view, *emergency preparedness* takes on heightened importance during events because of the high stakes in a facility occupied by many people. The event manager must have the knowledge and competence to carry out emergency responses if necessary. Emergency response will include appropriate actions from a broad range of facility occupants, including event staff such as ushers and security personnel, medical staff, facility management, police, and fire officials. The emergency plan will include a chain of command protocol that includes an incident command system specifying who is in charge, during what times, and under what circumstances specific to the various types of potential emergencies. For instance, in many locales and emergency plans, the facility's general manager or his/her designee may have responsibility for ordering a building evacuation in circumstances where police or fire officials do not have obvious jurisdiction, such as in the case of a bomb threat. (Figure 8-11 is a sample bomb threat checklist.) This is an extremely important aspect of public assembly facility management.

Emergency plans should be specific to the facility and its locale. For instance, some facilities, based on their geographic location may have need for hurricane preparedness, tornado preparedness, blizzard preparedness, earthquake

---

ATF BOMB THREAT CHECKLIST

Exact time of call:
Exact words of caller:

QUESTIONS TO ASK
1. When is bomb going to explode?   2. Where is the bomb?

3. What does it look like?   4. What kind of bomb is it?

5. What will cause it to explode?   6. Did you place the bomb?

7. Why?   8. Where are you calling from?

9. What is your address?   10. What is your name?

CALLER'S VOICE (circle)

Calm	Slow	Crying	Slurred	Stutter	Deep	Loud	Broken	Giggling	Accent
Angry	Rapid	Stressed	Nasal	Lisp	Excited	Disguised	Sincere	Squeaky	Normal

If voice is familiar, whom did it sound like?
Were there any background noises?
Remarks:

Person receiving call: Telephone number call received at:
Date: Report call immediately to:
                                           (Refer to bomb incident plan)

Bureau of Alcohol, Tobacco and Firearms (ATF), 2003   **FIGURE 8-11**

preparedness, etc. Such plans need to be coordinated with state and local offices of emergency management and/or local police and fire departments.

In addition, it is important to know the location of fire and safety items and electrical controls in each area of a facility. When an emergency situation arises, having this information immediately available is critical. All appropriate personnel should be familiar with this information. Further, diagrams such as these should be posted in multiple locations in the areas involved and at a central location.

Another important element of emergency planning is crisis communications. In the event of an emergency, the event manager may have a role in managing not only internal communications, but also communications with other stakeholders such as families of facility occupants, public officials and facility owners, the press and media, vendors and suppliers. Each facility should have a crisis communications plan to manage these various activities.

TRAINING

Public assembly facilities deal with a variety of audiences, each with its own characteristics. With this in mind, the security, emergency, and crowd management plans must be developed in a way that allows management to account for the different needs and characteristics of each audience. In developing a crowd management training program for the front-of-house employee, most public assembly facility managers come to realize that often the best approach is to expose all staff to a broad-based facility orientation followed by training specifically related to the individual's area of assignment or possible assignment.

In all aspects of the training program, customer service and guest safety must be emphasized as the primary goals. For example, newly hired ushers should be required to attend an orientation session that acquaints them with the facility's physical layout and the location of areas such as concessions stands, restrooms, first aid stations, telephones, and seating sections. It is vitally important for these personnel to understand where these places are located because the majority of questions asked by guests relate to these locations.

They should also be required to attend a session that focuses on the specific role they play in the overall event presentation. For instance, ushers should be taught how to assist in solving seating, ticketing, and public safety issues. They also need to understand their role in the event of a necessary facility evacuation, and they must be provided guidelines to assist them in determining when to request assistance from a supervisor. All public assembly facility crowd management training should include components related to facility hardware, design, and use. Other components should include personnel training, a procedures manual, and graphics and audiovisual materials. Finally, all new employees should attend a session devoted to the concept of guest service.

A significant amount of information is provided and reviewed during employee training and orientation sessions. It is unrealistic to assume employees, particularly part-time employees, will make the effort necessary to comprehend and retain all of this information. Consequently, all employees should be provided with a copy of the employee manual that contains detailed information about which each employee should be knowledgeable. Both event-specific and general information should be contained in the manual. Some public assembly facilities use an "Event Handbook" that all employees must carry with them while working.

The IAAM has developed and/or endorsed several event staff training programs that are available to public assembly managers. For training event staff, IAAM publishes video training programs, most with instructors' guides and resource manuals, on the following topics:

- Guest relations skills
- Dealing with the problem patron
- Providing services to guests with disabilities
- Safety awareness
- Basics of crowd management
- Basics of emergency planning
- Preparation for terrorism attacks

Other training and informational programs and materials are available from the IAAM and from the various other organizations and associations noted in Appendix D.

SUMMARY

Event production starts with the selling of facility time and space. Event management requires the interaction of a variety of people generally associated with the facility operations department.

Management of the client/tenant relationship is crucial to event management. All public assembly facility managers must assume the responsibility of fostering and maintaining these relationships. Public assembly facilities generate income through the leasing or rental of their facility for events as well as through the ancillary revenue streams, including catering, food and beverage, novelties, and parking.

Every effort must be taken to prevent the occurrence of event day surprises. All anticipated problems and issues should be addressed and resolved prior to event day. To avoid these distractions requires cooperation from and effective communication among all units of the public assembly facility's organization.

Once an event has been booked and contracted, the planning and production of the event commences. It is important to have a promoters' packet available, especially for those promoters new to the facility. These packets need not be expensive, but must be informative, and may be available on the facility's web site.

Entertainment events should have a production rider, signed by the promoter and the performer/agency, detailing all elements required by the performer in order to provide a quality performance. Once the production rider is developed, it becomes the responsibility of the promoter to ensure the requirements are met. In most instances, the promoter relies upon the public assembly facility manager to fulfill these conditions. However, the facility manager should deny all requests of the promoter until the lease or rental agreement is completed.

Events undertaken by local groups, especially those produced by non-professionals, require special attention during the planning stage. All events should have detailed diagrams specifying room arrangements for meetings, dining functions, and other uses.

A schedule of event timelines should be created and adhered to. An event document similar to a diary should be maintained for each event. Everything about the event, including any incidents, should be recorded in a clear and detailed manner. This document is very valuable in evaluating the event and in future planning for the event.

In many instances, the public assembly facility manager is expected to assist in providing equipment and staff required by the event such as front- and back-of-house personnel, part time labor, and house or rental equipment. The cost of providing for these needs is billed to the event and its promoter.

Crowd management and crowd control issues must be discussed and planned for each event. Decisions must be made regarding the type and level of security necessary to ensure the safety of the guests, the performers, and the facility's personnel based on the event's history, the anticipated audience's demographic profile, the current political climate, and the facility's design and hardware. Security personnel, as well as all employees, should be trained in crowd management techniques. Each employee should know how to respond to crowd control issues, especially in the event an order is issued to evacuate the facility.

Each employee must be an ambassador for the public assembly facility. Interactions between guests and employees must be positive at all times. In making policy and procedure decisions, the effect upon guests must be seriously taken into consideration. It is especially important that policies and procedures directly affecting guests be communicated to them in order to avoid potential problems resulting from enforcement.

Successful events require much coordination from back-of-house operations staff. Event managers often use an event file to document planning activities and to track progress. The final event file or diary might include planning documents and reports such as the lease contract, the production rider, the settlement sheet (which includes labor, equipment, and other charges), the box office statement, certificates of insurance, event drop counts, ticket stubs, and deadwood.

The facility's overall risk management plan includes many duties carried out during events by the event management and operations staffs. Security staff carry out important roles in controlling access to facility entrances and back-of-house areas such as dressing rooms, loading docks, locker rooms, and stage entrances. All event and operations staff must be trained to carry out duties in the case of some type of an emergency during an event, such as medical emergencies, fires or fire alarms, bomb threats, mechanical failures, natural disasters, or terrorism attacks. IAAM provides many resources useful for training staff in the areas of safety and security.

REFERENCES AND ADDITIONAL READINGS

Berlonghi, Alexander. 1990. *The Special Event Risk Management Manual.* Dana Point, CA: Event Risk Management.

Berlonghi, Alexander. 1996. *Special Event Security Management, Loss Prevention, And Emergency Services: The Guide for Planning and Documentation.* Dana Point, CA: Event Risk Management.

Cote', Ron, P.E. (Editor). 2009. *The Life Safety Code Handbook.* Quincy, MA: National Fire Protection Association.

Goldblatt, Joe. 2001. *Special Events: Twenty-First Century Global Event Management*, 3rd ed. Hoboken, NJ: John Wiley & Sons, Inc.

Goldblatt, Joe and Kathleen Nelson. 2001.*The International Dictionary of Event Management* Hoboken, NJ: John Wiley & Sons, Inc.

IAAM (International Association of Assembly Managers, Inc.). 1994. IAAM Position Description Handbook. Coppell, TX: IAAM.

_____. 2008. *IAAM Academy for Venue Safety & Security* Training Manual. Coppell, TX: IAAM.

_____. 2002. *Venue Security After September 11* Audioconference Package. Coppell, TX: IAAM.

_____. 2002. *Venue Emergency Planning After September 11* Audioconference Package. Coppell, TX: IAAM.

_____. 2003. *Convention Center Security Planning and Risk Management Update* Audioconference Package. Coppell, TX: IAAM.

_____. 2003. *Performing Arts Venue Safety & Security Update*. Coppell, TX: IAAM.

_____. 2003. *Emergency Planning at Public Assembly Facilities*. Coppell, TX: IAAM.

_____. 1999. *Managing the Crowd*. Coppell, TX: IAAM.

_____. 1997. *Customer Service Begins With Me: Superior Guest Relations at Public Assembly Facilities*. Coppell, TX: IAAM.

_____. 1995. *Safety Awareness at Public Assembly Facilities*. Coppell, TX: IAAM.

_____. 1993. *Service Excellence: Patrons With Disabilities*. Coppell, TX: IAAM.
_____. 1994. *Service Excellence: Dealing with Guests' Problems and the Problem Guest*. Coppell, TX: IAAM.

Maloy, Bernard P. and Charles R. Higgins. 2000. *No Excuses Risk Management*. Carmel, IN: Cooper Publishing.

Kent, Penny (Editor). 2006. *The Art of the Show*, 3rd ed. Dallas, TX: IAEM Foundation.

Silvers, Julia Rutherford. 2003. *Professional Event Coordination*. Hoboken, NJ: John Wiley & Sons, Inc.

Tarlow, Peter E. 2002. *Event Risk Management and Safety*. Hoboken, NJ: John Wiley & Sons, Inc.

CHAPTER 9

FACILITY OPERATIONS AND EVENT SERVICES
"The Back of the House"

CHAPTER OUTLINE

INTRODUCTION
FACILITIES OPERATIONS MANAGEMENT
- RISK MANAGEMENT
- REGULATORY COMPLIANCE
- SHIPPING AND RECEIVING
- INVENTORY MANAGEMENT
- CAPITAL REPLACEMENT
- GREEN MANAGEMENT

ENGINEERING
- MECHANICAL AND ENGINEERING
- MECHANICAL SYSTEMS
- PREVENTIVE MAINTENANCE

TRADES AND CRAFTSMEN
HOUSEKEEPING AND CUSTODIAL SERVICES
EVENT SERVICES
- TRANSPARENT EVENT MANAGEMENT
- RECONFIGURATIONS/CONVERSIONS/CHANGEOVERS
- PERFORMANCE/PRODUCTION RIDER
- STAGEHANDS AND SHOW LABOR
- RIGGING
- TEMPORARY EVENT EMPLOYEES
- WORKING WITH UNIONS
- CUSTOMER/CLIENT SERVICES
- EVENT EQUIPMENT
- MARSHALLING AND STAGING YARDS

SUMMARY
REFERENCES AND ADDITIONAL READINGS

INTRODUCTION

Evenings, weekends, and holidays, day after day, the Operations and Event Services (OES) department is responsible for making the public assembly facility (PAF) functionally ready, safe, and secure for every customer, promoter, performer, and employee involved in an event.

Depending on the type of PAF and its event year or season, these facilities are constantly being transformed from one event to the next. This transformation is sometimes called *conversion* or *changeover*. In addition, the PAF constantly repairs and maintains the facility to keep it operating safely, securely, efficiently, and effectively during times when the facility is not booked for an event.

To successfully meet these challenges requires a significant organization, communication, and management structure that enables the PAF to adapt to each and every event that is scheduled. The functional areas that typically define an OES department vary depending on the type of facility and geographical location of the building, but typically include

- Reconfigurations/conversions/changeovers
- Coordination and management of event contract riders
- Event equipment operation (scoreboards, LEDs, electronic signs)
- Engineering (HVAC/refrigeration/life safety systems/utilities)
- Technical services (IT/AV/phone/Internet)
- Housekeeping and custodial
- Maintenance and repair
- Trades (electricians, plumbers, mechanics, carpenters)
- In-house security
- Parking
- Exterior landscaping and snow removal
- Pest control
- Sanitation, recycling, and trash removal

The typical back-of-the-house organizational chart may include some of the following positions, depending on the type of PAF, size and geographical location:

- Director or VP of operations
- Operations manager
- Assistant operations manager
- Engineers
- Electrical-mechanical technicians
- Technical director
- Stage manager
- Trades stewards
- General trades (union) employees
- Maintenance staff
- Custodial supervisors

(See Figure 9-1, Operations Organizational Chart)

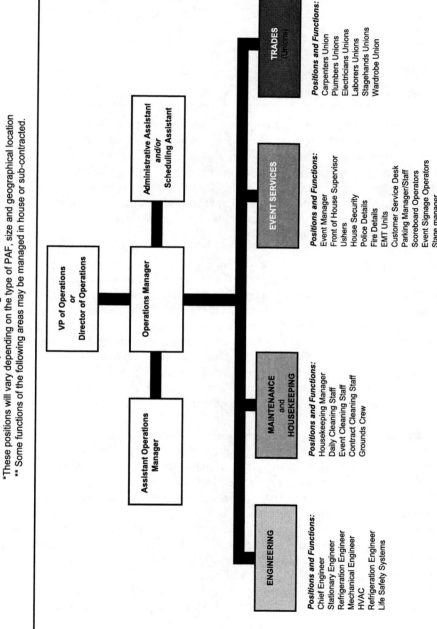

Figure 9-1

Operations Organization Chart

*These positions will vary depending on the type of PAF, size and geographical location
** Some functions of the following areas may be managed in house or sub-contracted.

This chapter is intended to describe the internal workings of an OES department and the high levels of cooperation and communication that are essential between the front-of-the-house functions and back-of-the-house functions to successfully and safely manage and operate a PAF before, during, and after an event as well on dark days.

FACILITY OPERATIONS MANAGEMENT

At its fundamental core, delivery and achievement of the PAF's objectives depend on a solid facility OES department. Regardless of type, size, ownership, or number of events, common operational services and activities must occur in order for the facility to function in a safe, efficient, and effective manner. Facility OES departments are generally responsible for the facility's physical environment that includes its state of maintenance, repair, air quality, life safety, the logistical delivery of event production requirements, and the overlapping life safety/security and control of the building.

This chapter focuses largely on the *back-of-house* operations or functions that facilitate the delivery of services to the client and customer. Ultimately, facility OES departments must have a concentrated focus on providing a clean, safe, and comfortable event environment where each customer can "see and enjoy" the event. Understanding the dynamic impact that facility operations has on the overall success at meeting its mission should encourage and require that the PAF manager devote significant attention, support, and resources to the OES department and its staff. For the purposes of this chapter, the term *client* will also refer to the promoter, producer and/or tenant. Also in this chapter the term *customer* will also refer to guest and patron.

Generally, facility OES departments have two distinctively different components, and both are critical to the success of the PAF and its mission. One is devoted to the operational aspects of the physical plant, mechanical and facility maintenance, and the other is focused on event services. On one hand, the facility's operational services must continually keep the facility safe, clean and in good repair while also facilitating building conversion to fulfill all event-related requirements. To achieve the PAF's objectives, the facility OES department must be flexible and responsive to the varying event-related needs of customers and clients. It must accomplish this while constantly performing year-round tasks such as maintaining and repairing the physical plant; attending to the cleanliness and aesthetics of the facility, its landscaping and parking lots; and inspecting, maintaining, and repairing the equipment necessary to produce the facility's events.

When facility OES functions are managed in-house, the organization of the department is generally based on the tasks to be performed. The facility OES manager is responsible for the supervision of the department's various unit managers. The number of unit managers varies depending on factors such as size and type of facility and type and volume of events.

As shown in Figure 9-1, it is common for a PAF OES department to be divided into four basic sub-departments: engineering, maintenance/trades/craftsmen, housekeeping and custodial, and event services. PAFs employ individuals with a myriad of skills. Tasks may be unique to the facility type. For instance, a stadium may have a groundskeeping crew; a theatre may have a technical director; and arena may have a Zamboni driver; and a convention center many have a banquet manager. Each department supervisor is charged with the responsibility for directing and supervising their staff that may be part- or full-time employees (or a combination of both) depending on the PAF event schedule. Although engineering, maintenance and trades, housekeeping and custodial, and event services generally reside in the facility OES department, the tasks assigned these sub-departments can be significantly different. Consequently, each sub-department requires workers with skills and abilities specific to that unit. Each area of a facility OES department should be supervised by a manager who is knowledgeable and experienced concerning the specifics of the work to be performed, the employees who will perform the tasks, and the PAF's objectives.

Allowing individual OES sub-departments to lose sight of the PAF's overall mission tends to encourage the emergence of unfortunate, but inevitable, conflicts. Understanding this particular dynamic should encourage the management to adopt techniques that assist both full-time and part-time employees to focus on the facility's mission and to understand and appreciate their contribution to the overall success of the PAF. The PAF and OES managers may accomplish this objective by insisting that all full-time OES managers and supervisors implement the facility's recruiting, hiring, training, and rewards systems for all of their full-time and part-time employees. Other management tools include having up-to-date job descriptions, providing manuals and handbooks that clearly explain the facility services and operations department's policies and procedures, scheduling required employee training sessions, requiring documentation of employee skill levels, and using effective employee evaluation and reward techniques.

RISK MANAGEMENT

The PAF sports, entertainment and event environment is very exciting but can potentially produce very dangerous situations. The primary responsibility of the PAF manager is the safety and security of the customers, clients, and employees. For that reason, the managers need to adopt a proactive approach to the well being of everyone in their facility. This type of proactive thinking can also be referred to as "optimistic pessimism," that is, planning for all the myriad of potential negative situations that can occur and finding ways to prevent them from happening, if possible, and, if they are not preventable, having a plan to manage the consequences.

There are typically two elements of risk management that need constant attention, and they are non-event and event risk management.

Non Event Risk Management – These are the risks associated in operating the PAF during the non-event days or dark days and the time before and after an event when the customers are not in the building and the OES department is going through a series of activities to set-up, load in, load out, tear down, clean up, and convert/changeover/reconfigure the facility for the next event. The back-of-the-house can become a very hectic and potentially dangerous environment depending on activity levels in the facility.

Event Risk Management – This type of risk management is concentrated on managing the facility during the event, i.e., periods of time just before (walk-up), during (event) and after (the blowout) the event. The event risk management plan should consider many factors, such as make-up of the crowd, history of the event, alcohol usage, amount of noise during the event, event surprises (pyrotechnics), and whether the lights are on or off during the event.

As a requirement of the PAF director's fiscal accountability, the facility OES department is responsible for many safety and risk management tasks, and must be continuously alert to remove hazards that may cause accidents. Such tasks might include installing and maintaining florescent tape or paint on steps, de-icing of exterior pedestrian stairs and walkways, storage of hazardous materials (HAZMAT), maintaining lens screens over light bulbs, etc.

The OES department may also be responsible for emergency preparedness and crisis communications plans. Designing evacuation routes, emergency communications, and response systems is operational in nature. Implementation of plans occurs whether the building is occupied or dark. Additional care must be taken to ensure that, in the event of a disaster, programs and records (electronic and hard copy) and/or their duplicates are secured. Business recovery may depend on backup information being stored separately off-site.

REGULATORY COMPLIANCE

Maintaining the facility's compliance with a broad range of regulatory codes is often another responsibility of a facility OES department. Local regulatory jurisdictions usually will oversee compliance of PAF in a number of ways, but invariably will refer to various national codes. In the United States, some of the more common are the Occupational Safety & Health Administration (OSHA) regulations, which seeks to protect the safety and health of workers; the Americans with Disabilities Act (ADA), which protects both employees and patrons from discrimination due to both mental and physical disability; and fire, life safety, and building codes such as those developed and recommended by the National Fire Protection Association (NFPA). Other countries have similar code requirements. The management of the OES department is usually the entity assigned this responsibility.

Additionally, the facility OES department is responsible for numerous periodic inspections ranging from elevator maintenance certification to fire extinguisher validations. Failure to comply with some of these responsibilities not only places the client and customer in danger, but also can put the PAF in a liability position or financial jeopardy.

The OES department must pay careful attention, depending on its geographical location, to the removal of ice and snow in order to provide for the safety of customers, clients, and employees. Many PAFs do not have adequate equipment to deal with this removal task and consequently enter into a subcontract for the service.

The facility OES department should require periodic inspection by the engineering sub-department in the areas of fire suppression, fire sprinklers, and smoke detection systems. Auxiliary generators used to produce electric power for emergency lighting and public address systems during periods of electrical outages should also be routinely tested and maintained. It is imperative that, during periods of electrical outages, emergency power be available to provide for the safety of the facility's customers, clients, and employees. Emergency power systems are a legal requirement for PAFs in most jurisdictions.

SHIPPING AND RECEIVING

Public assembly facilities that host trade shows, exhibitions, or similar activities require vendors to ship large amounts of materials to the facility in advance of the event and, upon its conclusion, to ship their materials back to their place of business or to another site. PAFs therefore might have a shipping and receiving unit and assign staff specifically to oversee the shipping and receiving functions.

The shipping and receiving unit should be adequately staffed and equipped to receive shipments of materials and equipment from delivery services in both a timely and organized manner; to manage an identification system that enables the clerk to associate the equipment with the correct exhibition activity; to stage the materials properly in order to maximize their efficient movement to the exhibition space; to organize the process of removing the materials from the exhibition space at the end of the event and prepare them for shipping; and to manage the required documentation associated with the receiving and shipping processes. It is not unusual for trade and/or exhibit events to use a private contractor, referred to as the Official Services Contractor, to perform these functions.

INVENTORY MANAGEMENT

The OES department in many PAFs is responsible for managing an inventory control system that might include recordkeeping, periodic scheduled and unannounced inspections, lock maintenance and key controls, and surveillance and security systems. Due to the nature of a PAF with its revolving doors, constant events, and thousands of customers and clients, keeping track of the millions of dollars of fixtures, furniture, and equipment (FF&E) is a daunting and endless task. Inventory management is a responsibility in which all PAF administrators must be accountable. Some PAFs hire personnel or contract with an inventory control specialist to manage their system.

The creation and maintenance of operations and event FF&E inventory records documenting the existence, location, and condition of every piece and type of equipment owned or leased by the PAF is a demanding task. Items contained in inventory may include turf equipment, forklifts, floor cleaning machines, pressure washers, tools, cleaning materials and equipment, carpeting, office furniture, computers, kitchen equipment, telephones, storage racks, lockers, etc. Items contained in the event FF&E inventory might include catering equipment and table cloths, tables and chairs, sound and lighting equipment, audiovisual equipment, and other such items.

In some PAFs, the inventory control system includes a labeling and numbering system whereby each item is etched, labeled, and/or numbered with a tag. These labels, in addition to identifying the item, may also display a barcode that when scanned provides additional information about the item such as its manufacturer, model number, date of purchase, date of service entry, etc. Knowing the date that crucial items such as light bulbs and fixtures are put into service enables the inventory staff to track the amount of hours that a light bulb or fixture has been on compared to the amount of hours that the bulb or fixture has been rated to last by the manufacturer so the OES staff can change the bulbs as they near the end of the manufacturer's projected life and avoid having them go out during an event and possibly harming the event or creating a danger for the customers.

In addition to a system to track FF&E, it is also the responsibility of the OES department to monitor and inventory supplies such as paper products, cleaning supplies and chemicals, light bulbs, and other such products. These supplies are difficult to monitor and inventory but must be tied directly to anticipated use based on expected attendance for previous and upcoming events.

Similar to an external auditor, the inventory control staff may randomly spotcheck selected items from the facility's inventory list. In case a discrepancy is discovered or something is unaccounted for, a thorough and complete accounting of the OES s entire inventory may be required. Larger PAFs with extensive equipment inventories frequently employ their own full-time inventory control specialist. When this occurs, the inventory control specialist is able to immediately label, number, and barcode each new inventory item and add it to the control list thereby facilitating the ability to conduct periodic checks more frequently in order to verify the presence, location, and condition of all inventory items. Establishing procedures that address the process for deleting (taking out of service) outdated, non-functional, sold, or traded items from the inventory control list is also critical. Creating an inventory of all keys to locked areas and to whom each key is issued is also very important to maintaining the facility's security and access control. A part of the key inventory may also include conducting periodic inspections of all locks and any required maintenance.

As previously discussed, it is also essential that controls be in place for accounting for the receipt and use of materials and supplies, such as paper goods for restrooms, cleaning supplies, grounds herbicides and fertilizers, office supplies, and other facility supplies depending on the building. An inventory system for these areas provides many benefits:

- Recording materials and supplies when they arrive informs administration a transaction is complete and payments may be made.

- Recording the use of materials and supplies and therefore the need to reorder.

In the case of event-related usage, such as restroom paper goods, the information can identify usage that can be calculated on a per capita (PC) basis. This information is an important management tool in determining the amount of product necessary for an event or series of events. It is also an excellent tool when creating an annual budget. The budget planner uses the per cap for supplies usage and multiplies it by the projected annual event attendance to determine the annual budget amount.

On an individual event basis, if the product used is to be charged back to the client, the formula provides the usage amount. The client might be charged on a PC basis, or if an event of several days, such as a religious convocation/ convention or consumer show, on a re-stocking basis. The re-stocking approach is simply to be fully stocked at the beginning and end of an event, with the amount of product used to re-stock being the amount on which a charge is calculated.

The knowledge an inventory system exists also acts as a deterrent to theft or misappropriation and holds management and supervisors responsible for creating and exercising controls.

CAPITAL REPLACEMENT

PAFs are built to be used by the customers and promoters they serve. The more events that are booked and the more customers who attend those events, the earlier the facility and its equipment will wear out. Regardless of how good the facility OES efforts may be, equipment, like light bulbs in the previous example, has a limited lifespan and eventually wears out. Whether it is door hinges and closures or mechanical bearings and motor windings, new equipment must be purchased and installed on a regularly scheduled basis.

Planning ahead for such inevitable replacement is an important role of the OES department. Knowledge of anticipated equipment and facilities usable life span is an important step towards planning for replacement. If a carpeted area receives a lot of traffic, it will show the wear sooner. A plan to schedule such maintenance is called capital replacement and, viewed over a three- to five-year period, enables management to anticipate line-item expenses for each year's budget. Management may establish a Reserve for Replacement fund with a three to five percent budget allocation annually.

GREEN MANAGEMENT

One of the newest concerns that PAF Managers have become increasingly aware of is the need to operate their facility with an emphasis on the environmental impact that the building and its events create. Everyone in our society is being asked to be a better steward of our environment. PAFs can "go green" through activities such as recycling event waste, using nontoxic green cleaning chemicals, using energy efficient lights and lamps, and closely monitoring the consumption of utilities by using automated systems. Using green techniques will continue to be required standard operating procedure for all PAF directors and their staffs and will permeate all aspects of facility operation. Those involved in new PAF design, construction, and renovation, especially for convention centers, are implementing LEED (Leadership in Energy and Environmental Design) certification standards to create buildings that are more environmentally friendly.

LEED began in 1994 as a broad-based coalition of non-profit organizations, government agencies, architects, engineers, developers, builders, product manufacturers and other industry leaders. Through a consensus process, LEED has developed a comprehensive system of six interrelated standards for new construction covering all aspects of the development and construction process. LEED was created to accomplish the following:

- Define "green building" by establishing a common standard of measurement
- Promote integrated, whole-building design practices
- Recognize environmental leadership in the building industry
- Stimulate green competition
- Raise consumer awareness of green building benefits
- Transform the building market

Green Building Council members, representing every sector of the building industry, developed and continue to refine LEED. The rating system addresses six major areas:

- Sustainable sites
- Water efficiency
- Energy and atmosphere
- Materials and resources
- Indoor environmental quality
- Innovation and design process

Individuals recognized for their knowledge of the LEED rating system are permitted to use the LEED Accredited Professional (AP) acronym after their name, indicating they have passed the accreditation exam given by the USGBC.

IAAM conducted a Green Survey in 2008 to determine how many IAAM members were using LEED standards and green techniques in their facilities. A sampling of the results included:

- 63 % of the respondents felt that it was important for their facility to be environmentally friendly or "green"
- 5.1 % of IAAM facilities were LEED certified but 48.6 % were considering compliance
- 25.1 % of respondents indicated that they had conducted a "Green Audit" but 47.4 % were considering one
- 53.8 % of the respondents had conducted an energy audit
- 67.6 % of the respondents use a CMMS (Computerized Management Maintenance Software)
- 95.8 % of respondents recycle paper and cardboard and 65.5 % recycle wood, metal, and plastic
- 84.2 % of respondents use "green" cleaning products
- 12.7 % of respondents indicated that their facility used solar or other sustainable energy sources

ENGINEERING

The engineering sub-department (and in some types and sizes of PAFs can be a stand alone department) of the OES department is one of the most critical areas of a PAF for many reasons. Engineering can be referred to as the "heart" of the PAF. It is responsible for the flow of life-sustaining air and water throughout the PAF. If this department and its systems do not function efficiently and effectively, there could be dire life safety and financial consequences. The vital areas that require servicing and monitoring on a frequent basis include:

- Circulating fresh air and air quality in the PAF (for indoor facilities)
- Air conditioning and inside environmental temperature (for indoor facilities)
- Potable water flowing throughout the PAF (for all PAFs)
- Refrigeration circulating systems (for PAFs with ice making requirements)
- Facility electrical consumption (for all PAFs)
- Life safety systems such as fire suppression and sprinkler systems (for all PAFs)

MECHANICAL AND ENGINEERING SERVICES

The terms mechanical and engineering services refer to those activities associated with the management of the facility's mechanical systems. Engineering services is also responsible for supplying utilities and other resources essential for both the facility and the event being staged. In exhibition and convention centers, the engineering services department may also have responsibilities that include maintaining electrical power distribution equipment, determining the most efficient and effective ways to provide electricity to the facility's clients, and the installation and removal of temporary electrical outlets.

Exactly where the line is drawn between OES and engineering services depends on several variables: size of the facility, the facility's mission, the number and types of activities hosted, and whether the facility has access to other external departments for required areas of support. In many facilities, the functions are combined in one department.

Most PAFs have some level of in-house maintenance, staging, and housekeeping services support. That support might be actual in-house support, meaning the employees are directly employed and managed by the PAF, or it might be provided by other departments (e.g., municipalities, universities, etc.) or through a contractual arrangement between the facility and a private contractor. A municipally owned PAF might have an on-site OES department to deal with general maintenance and housekeeping services but rely completely upon the municipality's public works department for major repairs and HVAC environmental support. It is not unusual for a university-managed performing arts center, particularly one with a modest event schedule, to draw all of its maintenance and housekeeping support from the university's maintenance, grounds, and housekeeping departments. In all probability, the performing arts facility would receive its water, electrical power, and HVAC support from the respective university departments as well. In situations of this nature, the PAF could employ a superintendent to oversee the facility's operation and to serve as a liaison between the facility and the parent organization.

In public PAFs with an ice surface for hockey, traveling shows and/or public skating, it is not unusual for a refrigeration engineer to be in charge of the ice and the ice making equipment. The refrigeration or ice engineer is responsible for installing, maintaining, and removing the ice; painting and logo placement; maintaining the ice surfacing equipment (such as a Zamboni); and managing the maintenance program for the ice making equipment. Depending on union contracts, the ice engineer or the union laborers and possibly the stagehands might install and remove the dasher boards and glass that surround the hockey rink playing surface. In some cases, the ice engineer works under the supervision of the facility OES manager. The sheet of ice that the players skate on is, in effect, the stage for the event.

MECHANICAL SYSTEMS

Central control of the PAF's facilities is often referred to as the *physical plant*. This environment is one of the key responsibilities of the engineering staff. In today's PAF management, mechanical systems have become very sophisticated through technological advancements.

To provide for constant and vigilant oversight of these systems, many PAFs have what is sometimes called the *motor control center* or Mechanical Services Office (MSO). This area of the facility is where manual and automated control circuitry may be centralized for master control of the facility's mechanical, life safety, security, and comfort environments. For instance, engineers may be able to minimize utility consumption by automatically adjusting demand through load shed or by systematically sequencing motor startups. Typically located in the back-of-house near the loading dock or shipping/receiving zones, the MSO may have many surveillance security and alarming systems, fire detection and enunciator panels, and switch gear for HVAC, refrigeration and their monitoring.

Newer, more energy efficient lighting systems can also be installed that will only come on when someone enters the room. From automatic timed shut off of water faucets to metered toilet flushing, today's PAFs can have built-in systems that make it economically viable, efficient, and green to operate while minimizing utility use and labor. During inclement weather conditions when freezing temperatures or snow loads become a concern, engineers are able to monitor systems and make appropriate adjustments or changes from remote locations. Some of these systems are referred to as:

- BAS – Building Automated Systems
- EMS – Energy Management Systems
- CAFM – Computer Aided Facility Management
- FMIS – Facility Management Information Systems

Because of the sophisticated technology involved in these newer systems, in-service training and licensing is required for many of these specialized mechanical areas. It is often more cost efficient and effective to employ the services of outside companies to perform periodic scheduled and preventive maintenance tasks. Maintenance and repair of equipment requiring specialized service such as elevators, escalators, fire suppression equipment, security alarm and surveillance systems, air handlers, cooling towers, etc., are generally outsourced to the original component manufacturer or private companies through service and maintenance contracts.

PREVENTIVE MAINTENANCE

Extending the life of the facility and its operating equipment and systems can be a daunting task, particularly if the facility has been run-down and/or management has chosen to defer maintenance. Unfortunately, when PAF owners are confronted with the need to reduce expenses, one of the first cuts tends to be the facility's maintenance and repair budget. Deferred maintenance may be encouraged for one reason or another (usually financial) but will eventually take its toll on the PAF. Clearly, deferring maintenance will reduce short-term operating costs. However, owners must understand that the cost of repairing or replacing neglected equipment becomes far more expensive than the cost of providing routine maintenance and that deferred maintenance decisions predictably result in very expensive long-term costs. Inevitably, it will affect what the clients and customers experience.

It is the facility OES manager's responsibility to produce adequate preventive maintenance schedules based on the number and attendance of events and to ensure and document the completion of all assigned maintenance tasks. A complicating factor in keeping to a maintenance schedule is the facility's schedule of event activities which must take precedence. However, a PAF manager needs to intentionally schedule time on the event calendar for major maintenance projects such as rigging inspections and floor maintenance.

A well designed preventive maintenance program takes into consideration the life cycle of the facility and its equipment as well as optimum maintenance activities necessary to maximize use with minimum cost. To initiate such a program, the facility OES department may categorize the various properties of the physical plant, e.g., equipment, hardware, painted surfaces, flooring, exterior, grounds, etc. A maintenance schedule for each category's elements can be assigned a timeline for attention and formalized in a departmental action plan. Graffiti, especially in restrooms can be reduced if a systematic cleaning and/or removal process is diligently followed. The key is to have a system in place for upkeep to reduce the aging process as much as possible.

Adequate funding for PAF scheduled and preventive maintenance is also critical to the facility's life span. Many PAF managers believe the facility OES department's annual budget should be, depending on the age of the facility, at least one percent of the facility's current value.

Responsibility for the maintenance of a PAF can be delegated to the facility's engineers and trades, the maintenance staff of a larger umbrella public works type of department, or a private contractor. Exactly which approach best benefits the facility depends upon a number of variables such as the availability of services from an umbrella group, availability of skilled labor, costs of service, and type of maintenance and repairs anticipated. The best approach is simply the one that, after careful examination and consideration of all options, produces desired results at an acceptable cost and on time.

TRADES AND CRAFTSMAN

A *trade* is usually defined as an occupation requiring manual or mechanical skill and often requiring licensing. In an OES department, there are several types of positions that fall under this description. The trades that are used in most PAFs include electricians, carpenters, plumbers, painters, and mechanics. Depending on the jurisdiction, trades in a PAF may be covered by an international brotherhood or, more commonly, a local union of the international union. Trade or labor unions are important to a PAF in that they supply a trained workforce that is usually controlled by the terms of a labor agreement.

The trades and craftsmen provide the skilled labor to perform the maintenance duties and responsibilities of a PAF. These employees spend a substantial portion of their time maintaining and repairing the facility and its equipment with the exception of the mechanical areas that are maintained by the engineers. Job descriptions for maintenance personnel vary depending on the job level. Depending on the jurisdiction and the availability of licensed tradesmen, maintenance workers may only be required to have a general knowledge of, rather than certified training in, areas such as carpentry, plumbing, painting, electrical, and mechanical work.

Most maintenance employees have a minimum of a high school diploma and may have also sought additional training in their chosen trade through a two year technical college to develop their skill. The majority of maintenance workers are hourly employees who are paid based on their skill level and seniority and are usually eligible for overtime compensation and shift differentials (unusual shifts beginning after midnight), depending on the laws and regulations of the particular jurisdiction and union contract.

Depending upon the needs of the PAF, some maintenance positions may be filled by a union through a collective bargaining agreement that covers skilled labor with licenses or certificates in one or more specific fields. In many instances, the most senior member of a union in a PAF, determined by number of years employed and/ or skill level, are designated as the shop leaders, or stewards, who supervise both the certified and non-certified workers often referred to as assistants.

At one time, entry to the maintenance department of the facility OES profession was primarily through the apprentice position process. After serving a period of time or a number of events as an apprentice and passing licensing examinations in one or more of the traditional maintenance skills areas, the employee became eligible for promotion to a tradesman/craftsman position. The vocational/ technical school training in many of the maintenance areas currently available in many countries has significantly altered the need for, and nature of, the apprenticeship system.

Today's tradesman and craftsman often hold a license in one or more of the common maintenance areas such as plumbing, electrical, mechanical, or carpentry and they are expected to have a general working knowledge of them all. These employees may also possess skills in general shop work, general mechanics, electrical and gas, milled steel welding, metal fabrication, heating/ventilation/air conditioning (HVAC), painting, and computer applications in the facility services and operations areas. Tradesmen and craftsmen assignments could include tasks such as inspecting and changing light bulbs, changing air filters in the facility's air handlers, checking and repairing seats, checking and maintaining safety hardware, and providing equipment maintenance and repair.

HOUSEKEEPING AND CUSTODIAL SERVICES

Of all the work that occurs in a facility, keeping the facility clean, sanitary and presentable is undoubtedly the least glamorous activity of the OES department. However, housekeeping and custodial services are critical components to the successful management and operation of a PAF. Although housekeeping services may be underappreciated and undervalued, a clean and comfortable facility environment is one of the most essential elements to repeating and increasing attendance. Generally, housekeeping services relate to those tasks directed toward keeping the facility safe, clean, and appealing to clients, customers, employees and owners.

The housekeeping services unit faces many challenges. One is to establish a standard for cleanliness for those areas not regulated by statute. Another is to successfully identify, recruit, train, and supervise competent and dependable employees and to motivate them to work difficult shifts such as overnight, weekends, and holidays. The many tasks that fall under the housekeeping services domain, if not properly performed, may result in the facility being sanctioned or closed by public health or safety agencies.

Within every PAF, housekeeping services are required, and each area may have its own standard by which acceptable cleanliness is measured. The cleanliness standard for the office area, for example, may be quite different from that for a private dining room. Housekeeping attention provided to open-air seating in a sports stadium is different from that afforded to premium seating areas in many types of facilities. The key dynamic affecting the level of housekeeping service provided beyond statutory requirements and industry standards is based upon customer's and client's expectations. Consequently, it becomes the responsibility of the housekeeping services supervisor to recognize the different levels of expectations and to develop operating procedures for the housekeeping services staff that specify what must be done in order to meet these expectations.

The housekeeping services supervisor's job includes maintaining lines of communication to custodial and housekeeping staff. The housekeeping services supervisor outlines the activities of the day and informs the service crews of particular challenges related to the day's or evening's events or activities. These meetings also represent an opportunity for supervisors to remind their crew of the facility's housekeeping services objectives and to reinforce the relationships that exist between housekeeping services and the facility's other units.

It is not uncommon for a PAF to have full-time housekeepers and/or custodians in order to maintain the facility's offices and those areas generally open to the public during non-event periods. Keeping the general meeting rooms, the lobby, the main office space, and other public areas within the facility clean and presentable is normally a responsibility assigned to the full-time housekeeping services staff for both consistency and security.

Cleaning the arena, stadium, auditorium, convention, or exhibit center following an event usually requires more personnel than just the facility's full-time housekeeping services staff. Tasks of this magnitude are often assigned to cleaning crews employed on a part-time, as-needed basis. Some facilities use full-time staff to serve as crew leaders. To clean a PAF after a concert in a larger facility may easily require a crew of 100 or more workers in order to perform the labor necessary to transform the facility back into one that is clean, sanitary and presentable. Often such work begins after midnight and must be completed in sufficient time to allow the facility to host another event in the morning.

A common method used by PAFs to secure the services of part-time, as-needed cleaning crews is to go through the RFP process and subcontract with a private company that provides such labor. The contract between the PAF and the contractor usually stipulates that the facility's housekeeping services supervisor must advise the contractor of the facility's labor needs within a specified advance-notice timeframe. The contractor then provides the labor, and supervision if necessary, and subsequently bills the PAF for the services rendered based upon the rates specified in the contract. It is important that the facility reserves management rights and quality control in monitoring the work performed and the overall contract requirements.

OES EVENT SERVICES

The role of the OES department is crucial to the delivery of event services that both the customers and clients demand in this emerging era of high ticket prices and technologically advanced expectations. It can be said again, customers don't buy tickets to a PAF, they purchase tickets to an event with the expectation to be entertained in a clean, safe, secure, and well maintained environment. Clients arrive at a PAF with the anticipation that the PAF will be comfortable, setup, and staffed according to their production rider.

Transparent Event Management

Most importantly, customers can expect that the event will take place in an atmosphere that will enable them to "see and enjoy" the event to the extent that the PAF and its services are "transparent." This means that when the customers leave the PAF the only memory was how educational the conference was or what the final score of the game was. If the customers remember that the facility air temperature was too hot, the concession stands sold out of bottled water, or the bathrooms ran out of paper supplies and were not kept clean during the event, then the PAF is at fault for the customer's diminished experience. The hands of the clock can never be turned back on that negative.

It's equally important that the facility and its OES staff do nothing that negatively impacts the event performance. Some examples are the rink ice temperature being too warm and slow; the basketball floor too slippery; or the sound system repeatedly having feedback or inadequate volume. The OES department needs to make sure that everything is ready and has been tested, not once, but many times to ensure optimum performance during the event.

The OES manager should adopt an "optimistic/pessimistic" approach in an effort to be proactive. The OES staff needs to always remember that the PAF entertainment and sports business is a time sensitive environment. Once the event has taken place, you can't go back and change the outcome for the client or the experience for the customer. A PAF is in the business of "selling experiences" and must strive and constantly endeavor to provide the highest quality customer service in a way that enhances the event experience, not detracts from it; The OES manager wants to create "transparent customer service."

If customers or clients have a negative experience, they may not come back. Clients do not and will not book facilities that carry a negative reputation. Even though customers do not buy tickets to a PAF (they purchase them to experience an event), the PAF and its poor condition and customer service may be the reason they don't buy tickets in the future.

Reconfigurations/Conversions/Changeovers

The role of the OES staff members selected to produce an event is considered to be the more glamorous or exciting side of the OES department. This is the functional component of the facility's OES that is directly involved with the client performance activity, without which the logistical deliverables that produce event outcomes could not exist. Fundamentally, the OES production staff is responsible for assisting the client with producing the physical and technical environment required to achieve the successful and desired event objectives.

There are a number of similarities between an OES production services staff, sometimes referred to as the stage crew, and those of maintenance and housekeeping services, the primary example being the need for part-time labor. The stage crew supervisors are responsible for identifying, recruiting, training, and employing part-time labor, which in many cases is done in cooperation with the stagehands union.

At the outset of the client taking temporary residence in the facility, or any part thereof, OES management is obligated to make the appropriate changes from the occupancy of the previous event to the new event. Typically, this activity is known as a *conversion* or *changeover*. This is the act of transformation that occurs between events that provides the necessary environment for next use.

In some cases, this may simply be the elimination of all obstacles by providing a clean and open space. Other situations, as in the conversion from a basketball game to an ice hockey configuration, may require significant conversion activities requiring significant physical changes to the venue.

Performance/Production Rider

As described in Chapter 8, the event client or promoter often provides a production rider that includes a detailed description of the production support and assistance required from the PAF to conduct their event. Many of the specific requirements may be carried out by the OES department. The typical production rider may ask the PAF to provide workers in one or all of the following categories:

- Riggers to hang and detach equipment above the stage
- Stagehands to operate event-related equipment
- Runners to perform pick-up and delivery tasks
- Equipment operators to operate forklifts and other mechanical and hoisting equipment
- Electricians to handle power/energy connection and distribution for the event
- Carpenters to build sets/props
- Wardrobe staff to help arrange, clean, organize, and sometimes repair costumes
- First aid/emergency medical technicians (EMTs) to deal with medical emergencies that may occur while the event is being set up, during the event itself, or while the event is being broken down

(See Appendix A, Figure 9-2 for a sample production rider.)

Touring attractions, concerts, circuses, exhibitions, etc., usually provide their own production crew, termed the *road crew*, which includes workers such as the production manager and the sound and lighting director. Generally, touring shows do not provide their own laborers such as loaders, forklift drivers, riggers, wardrobe assistants, and general labor. It is usually the PAF's responsibility to provide such personnel. Labor requirements such as starting time, number of people, skill sets, and estimated time to complete tasks are normally specified in the production rider. Unloading trucks, operating forklifts and hoists, assembling stage equipment, hanging and removing rigging, setting tables and chairs, and loading equipment are typical tasks required by traveling attractions and accomplished by the local stagehands and/or part-time labor force. The expense of providing these workers is usually borne by the event's promoter, is referred to as a "pass through expense," and typically appears on the settlement as "reimbursed labor."

The production rider may also request the presence of additional security guards in order to protect the attraction's equipment, buses, and vans along with the dressing rooms, back-of-house, and other areas. Additional housekeeping services employees may be requested as well to keep dressing rooms, catering areas, and "green rooms" (room in a facility set aside as a hospitality area for artists to meet the media and VIP guests) cleaned to an extremely high standard. Supervision of housekeepers and security guards may be the responsibility of either the OES manager or a designated event supervisor depending on how the department is organized.

Typically, the PAF provides this extra labor with the expense being charged back to the promoter as a reimbursable expense. Other labor requests that may be included in the production rider include stagehands who actually work on stage during a performance; spotlight operators; house light operators trained to operate the facility's emergency lighting and general illumination; house electricians familiar with the facility's electrical equipment; and sound and lighting technicians operating the facility's sound and lighting equipment. Depending on the size, type, and technical requirements of a traveling event, the show may bring its own sound and lights and personnel to operate them.

STAGEHANDS AND SHOW LABOR

Virtually all PAFs utilize a large number of part-time employees to produce the events for which the facilities were designed. A performing arts theatre may have a professional manager and a small, full-time, non-event day staff. However, on event day, the number of event staff may swell considerably when the additional part-time stagehands, front-of-house staff, security and parking guards, catering employees, and others are on hand to successfully stage the event. Event-related labor, particularly for arenas and theatres, may be divided into five categories: set up and tear down; move-in/move-out labor; production labor; clean up labor; and conversion or changeover labor.

- Set up and tear down labor is the staff needed to prepare the facility and its equipment prior to move in and to return the facility to the same condition after the event has loaded out of the facility.
- Move-in and move-out labor is the people required to unload and load an event, organize and assemble equipment, pack equipment prior to the event, and dismantle, and pack equipment at the end of the performance as well as remove equipment from the facility.

- Production labor is staff required during the course of the actual event and in many facilities is referred to as the *show call*. This type of labor may require the services of employees possessing higher skill levels than that normally available from in-house and subcontracted labor. In such instances, these workers generally belong to an organized labor union and command a higher rate of pay.
- Clean-up labor is the in-house or sub-contracted staff that is necessary to clean the facility to a standard that is both sanitary as well as clean. This needs to be completed to the extent that when guests enter the facility for the next event, it is difficult to tell that another event preceded it.
- Conversion or changeover staff is the labor needed to change the configuration of the PAF from one event to the next, such as hockey to basketball or concert to circus.

Decorators also are an event labor category common to certain types of PAF such as convention and conference centers. In small to medium size PAFs, decorators are typically sub-contractors that are responsible for laying carpet, dressing and setting tables and chairs, piping and draping exhibit booths, etc. Larger, busy convention centers normally have a decorating unit within their organizational structure with its manager reporting to the facility OES manager. In the same way that arenas, auditoriums, and theatres often rely on part-time stagehands, many convention centers rely upon part-time employees for food preparation, beverage service, and dining/banquet room wait service. Just as a union or private contractor may supply stagehands for the arena, specialty contractors may be used to provide part-time decorators, wait staff, or kitchen employees. Again, the best arrangement for each public assembly facility depends upon its activities, size, local politics, regulatory laws, and mission statement.

RIGGING

Rigging for events involves the use of cables and motorized hoists to lift and position lighting, audio, video, scenery, special effects, and related items. This practice poses special and serious risks for PAF management because, most of the time, these objects are suspended over the heads of performers, guests, and facility employees. Each type of PAF has specific types of rigging. In a performing arts venue, stage rigging is an integral element of the stage design. At arenas, stadiums and convention centers, temporary (arena-style rigging) is often used. In addition, nearly all facilities have some type of permanent rigging that suspends components such as scoreboards, speakers, chandeliers, etc. PAF management has liability responsibilities for all rigging that takes place in the facility, even if it is installed by clients and their contractors. A rigging safety plan usually includes the following:

- Building load capacities marked on a rigging plot plan by a structural engineer
- Fall protection plan and equipment, such as safety harnesses and life lines

- Training programs and certificates of ability for rigging staff
- Constant monitoring and evaluation of safety procedures and rigging equipment conditions
- Policies and procedures that require supervision and inspection of rigging by competent and certified personnel on a regularly scheduled basis

The facility's OES manager, the PAF structural engineer, and stagehands should always be involved when questions arise concerning facility structural issues. When a PAF is being designed, the architect and structural engineer calculate the effects of additional weight and stress being placed on the facility's roofs, walls, floors, and structural beams. These stresses include snow load in northern climates and wind shear in windy climates.

Appropriate safety margins are incorporated into the structural design for more recently constructed or renovated PAFs to accommodate anticipated production and tension loads that may add stress to the structure. Once the construction phase is completed and the PAF is about to receive its certificate of occupancy, weight limits for the various aspects of the facility must be confirmed and documented by the contractor and submitted to the appropriate structural engineer for certification. It is the responsibility of the engineers to monitor activities held in the facility in order to ensure these weight limits are not exceeded. The weight limits for all of the load points and structural steel should be sent in writing to the prospective client and promoters during the booking process.

It is wise and prudent to periodically engage the services of an architectural and/ or structural engineering firm to confirm the facility's ability to accommodate the load requirements of touring shows that hang equipment and to perform an overall structural audit of the facility. Usually the structural engineer will review the event's load requirements and develop a plot plan based on the ceiling's steel structure to help the riggers place loads on beams using dead hangs (one point of connection) based on weight or bridled hangs (two or more points of connection) to distribute the weight of heavy objects such as speaker clusters.

Temporary Event Employees

One of the OES manager's many responsibilities is to develop a pool of trained, reliable, and accessible personnel. The size and source of the pool that the PAF draws from depends on a number of variables including the number and types of events the facility stages, the particular work skills required by the booked attractions, local labor union policies and regulations, regulatory laws, and the availability of qualified workers. The pool may come from the students from a local college or university, civic off-duty fire and police personnel, labor contractors, or the local theatrical and stage employees union.

A number of issues affect the decision as to how best to organize and manage the PAF's event labor pool. In some instances, development of this pool may be the direct responsibility of OES management. When this occurs, laborers might become part-time employees of the facility and work on an as-needed basis, be supervised by the facility's stage manager, be paid directly by the facility, and may be eligible for some elements of the facility's employee benefits package. In this scenario, clients requiring the use of laborers submit their request to the OES manager who then fills the *labor call* from the facility's pool. Rates of pay are established by the facility along with other personnel costs charged to the event. The personnel reimbursement rates are typically calculated and are carried forward onto a general rate card provided to all potential clients of the PAF. Other standard charges for equipment and other facility services might also be included on the same rate card.

The client is billed for the labor provided, and the PAF's management receives its payment (referred to as reimbursable labor) at the settlement meeting. In this arrangement, workers are paid in accordance with the facility's regular payroll and/or union labor rate schedule. Labor management costs incurred by the facility, such as insurance, payroll preparation and distribution, training, records management, and overhead, are typically calculated and charged to the parties requesting the labor.

Commercial labor contractors are also a source for part-time event staff. The PAF may enter into a contractual agreement with a labor contractor to provide the staff requested by clients. The contractor develops and maintains the labor pool, establishes the rate of pay as allowed or required under the contract, and provides the event with the requested labor workers. The PAF usually provides supervision for the workers through its facility OES departments and also guarantees the contractor payment for services rendered.

After the labor requirements have been finalized, the event manager informs the contractor of the event's labor needs and schedule. In this scenario, PAF management makes the labor call and the provider fulfills the request. For each event, the PAF manager submits a bill to the client for the labor provided and then collects the amount due on behalf of the contractor as part of the event settlement.

Working with Labor Unions

It is common practice in most PAFs to have a working relationship in the form of a bargaining agreement with labor unions to supply various types of skilled and unskilled event staff. Prior to entering into a relationship and agreement with a union, representatives of the PAF's management and the union's management must negotiate a labor contract. This contract, which is generally subject to periodic renegotiation, establishes pay rate schedules and employee benefits, minimum crew compositions, employee training, work rules and guidelines, and employee supervision.

Some facilities may elect (others are legally obliged) to use the local stage employee worker's union for stagehand work. In the United States, the International Alliance of Theatrical and Stage Employes (IATSE) union is capable of meeting most production-related labor requests for *production calls,* while the International Brotherhood of Teamsters (IBT) may coordinate truck loaders for unloading vehicles carrying event equipment including vans and trucks of all sizes. The union's local business agent (BA) identifies, recruits, and trains potential employees; certifies skills and abilities; negotiates wages and rates of pay; and establishes working rules with the PAF management on an annual or bi-annual basis.

It is extremely important for the facility to retain management rights in the sense that the PAF can object to hiring individuals who have a history of being unproductive or disruptive. It is also essential that the cost of using union employees is competitive with the cost of using non-union employees in order to keep costs in line with competing PAFs.

Some of the effective labor relations or union labor motivation practices that can be implemented and used while maintaining management rights of a PAF include

- Communication of work schedules as far in advance as possible
- Tickets for union employees to events that are not sold out such as family shows (e.g., circuses and ice shows)
- Holiday receptions
- Employee of the month programs
- Preferential and secured parking close to the PAF

The union will also provide employee oversight in the form of a supervisor or steward. Sometimes labor requests and requirements for an event scheduled in a union contracted PAF can be submitted directly to the facility's union steward or the local union secretary. The union fills the labor call and the union bills the event's promoter directly or through the facility. In many instances, all financial activities between the client or promoter and the union might be separate and distinct from those between the PAF and the promoter.

Some shows, before they go on tour, contract with the international union administration to negotiate stagehand services in every community throughout the tour. Known as *yellow card* shows, these shows are typically theatrical events like Broadway shows or family entertainment such as ice shows.

Again, the number and type of activities presented, local politics, and the facility's ownership and governance type are usually the prime variables that determine which employee source or combination of sources are used. In some jurisdictions the law will affect the labor supplier decision. In those jurisdictions with right to work statutes, it is illegal to require an employee or potential employee to hold union membership. In such jurisdictions, union members can be employed, but non-union workers cannot be systematically excluded.

CUSTOMER/CLIENT SERVICES

Facility OES departments are critical to providing customers and clients with superior service and creating positive experiences that are clean, safe, and comfortable. The OES department can also be an important source of ancillary revenue for the facility. Today, with the customer experience expectations so extraordinarily high and the client's trucking and shipping of equipment so expensive to put on the road, clients are increasingly dependent upon local suppliers and purveyors to provide necessary products and support services. Many of these support services are generic, off-the-shelf items that either can be obtained locally or provided in-house by the facility OES department.

Some of the more common services provided to clients are business- or production- related equipment such as audiovisual services, decorating supplies, and office equipment such as fax machines, telephones, etc. For the PAF, these extra services to the client can become business opportunities to generate additional ancillary revenue.

It is also important for the OES manager to work with the marketing and sales department as well as the premium seating coordinators. The OES manager and marketing manager can develop a list of companies that the PAF is purchasing utilities, supplies, and equipment from and solicit their interest in purchasing tickets, event sponsorships, signage, and premium seating leases.

EVENT EQUIPMENT

A PAF manager has the responsibility of having up-to-date equipment and supplies which meet industry standards to support each and every customer, client, and event that is booked into the facility. Depending on the type of facility and the events booked, the list of typical event supplies can be divided into two categories: facility event equipment and supplies and client event equipment and supplies. Some of the facility's event equipment and supplies and hopefully all of the client equipment rental and supplies will be charged back to the client's event. These lists vary by facility type, but might include

Facility event equipment and supplies
- Portable and adjustable stage with wings, handrails, and stairs
- Portable basketball floor and goals
- Refrigerated floor for ice skating/hockey
- Indoor synthetic turf for soccer/football
- Scoreboard
- Durable, comfortable front-lift portable chairs
- Rectangular and circular tables in varying widths
- Paper supplies
- Utility connections

Client event equipment and supplies
- House sound system
- Spotlights
- Forklifts
- High lifts
- Dollies and handcarts
- Catering equipment
- Crowd control barriers
- Turnstiles
- Bar code reading units

MARSHALING AND STAGING YARDS

Large special events often require extensive "staging" areas to manage incoming traffic. At a convention center, staging areas may allow parking for and security searches of the large number of trucks arriving with trade show and convention materials. At stadiums and arenas, incoming special events such as rodeos, circuses, and large concerts may require significant space dedicated to staging the event or performance. Such areas may be reserved for queuing purpose of contestants, herding or sorting of animal acts or rodeo performers, or simply for overnight parking of trucks, buses, and other vehicles and equipment.

The OES shipping and receiving unit may be responsible for managing the staging areas, including developing the policies and procedures communicated to incoming events and supervision of the staging areas during load-in and load-out. Providing a centralized process for receiving shipped materials is essential. In some cases, particularly with hazardous materials or under extreme security alerts, separate, even off-site, facilities will be dedicated to screening materials destined for the venue.

Implementation of written policies and procedures for receiving, documenting, securing, and distributing delivered shipments offers all parties an important level of protection. Appropriate shipping and receiving policies and procedures also facilitate the transfer of item ownership and provide an additional monitoring opportunity for the shipping and receiving staff, as well as the facility OES manager.

Summary

The facility OES department manages the back of the house, which is the heart and nerve center of the PAF. The OES department is organized in many ways in different types of facilities, but the basic components typically include a management function referred to as Facility Operations Management and four basic sub-departments:

- Engineering, which has oversight of the physical plant and its mechanical systems
- Trades and Craftsmen, which are assigned with the tasks of keeping the building repaired and maintained, including staff such as plumbers, carpenters, electricians, painters and mechanics
- Housekeeping and Custodial Services, which is responsible for the cleanliness and sanitation of the facility
- Event Services, which is tasked with providing the highest standards of safety, security, and customer service for both the customers and clients while performing their duties and responsibilities so that no one is distracted. Avoiding distractions is referred to as transparency, and it is not an easy task!

PAF management must create, implement, and monitor programs designed to train all full-time and part-time OES staff on how to meet and exceed customer and client expectations. OES, as one of the core components of a venue, is the department of the PAF responsible for delivering services anticipated by the customers and clients. Charged with the care and stewardship of the physical plant, this department must maintain and plan for replacement of the physical assets of the facility. Risk management and emergency preparedness are core components of this department's mission.

It is the responsibility of the OES managers and staff to keep the PAF safe, secure, clean, and comfortable. A well maintained environment is critical to providing a satisfactory atmosphere for guests and clients. Safety must be the first consideration in every facility OES decision, as well as providing event-related services with a high quality of guest relations skills.

References and Additional Readings

Convention Industry Council. 2007. *The Convention Industry Council* (CIC) Manual, 8th ed. McLean, VA: Convention Industry Council.

Donovan, Harry. 2002. *Arena Rigging: A Practical Guide for Riggers, Designers & Managers.* Seattle, WA: Rigging Seminars.

Feldman, Edwin B. 2000. *Managing Housekeeping and Custodial Operations* Handbook. Latham, NY: National Trade Publications.

Glerum, Jay O. 2007. *Stage Rigging Handbook*, 3rd ed. Carbondale, IL: Southern Illinois University Press.

Lewis, Bernard T. 1999. *Facility Manager's Operation and Maintenance* Handbook. New York, NY: McGraw-Hill.

Robbe, Deborah. 1999. *Expositions and Trade Shows*. New York, NY: John Wiley & Sons, Inc.

U.S. Green Building, 2009. Leadership in Energy and Environmental Design (LEED). http://usgbc.org.

Rondeau, Edmond P., Robert Kevin Brown, and Paul D. Lapides. 2005. *Facility Management*. New York, NY: John Wiley & Sons.

Wireman, Terry. 2005. *Developing Performance Indicators for Managing Maintenance*, 2nd ed. New York, NY: Industrial Press.

APPENDIX A

ILLUSTRATIONS

LICENSE APPLICATION

The following information is requested by the St. Charles Convention Center management to assist in the review and consideration of your request for lease of the Convention Center facilities. The accuracy and completeness of the information provided below are very important insofar as this information will be a critical factor in considering your request. Be as detailed and specific as possible. Until Convention Center management officially approves this application and a formal License Agreement is fully executed, there is no legal or binding commitment between the Convention Center and the rental applicant.

EVENT NAME: _____

TYPE OF EVENT: Consumer Show ☐   Trade Show ☐   Convention ☐   Other ☐ (describe below)
EVENT DESCRIPTION: _____

ESTIMATED DAILY ATTENDANCE: _____
SPACE REQUESTED: _____

DATES REQUESTED (specify ingress/egress and event): _____

REQUESTED EVENT AND INGRESS/EGRESS TIMES: _____

PAID ADMISSION EVENT: Yes ☐   No ☐   If yes, state ticket prices: $_____
NAME OF LICENSING ORGANIZATION: _____
Address: _____
City: _____   State: _____   Zip: _____
Tax I.D. Number: _____   Or SSN: _____
NAME & TITLE OF PERSON WHO WILL SIGN THE LICENSE AGREEMENT: _____

HOW DID YOU LEARN OF THE CONVENTION CENTER? _____

FIGURE 3

LICENSE APPLICATION - PAGE 2

BANK & CREDIT REFERENCES:

1. _____

       Name   Telephone Number   Account Number

2. _____

       Name   Telephone Number   Account Number

3. _____

       Name   Telephone Number   Account Number

REFERENCES WITHIN INDUSTRY:

1. _____

       Name   Company   Telephone Number

2. _____

       Name   Company   Telephone Number

3.

       Name   Company   Telephone Number

PREVIOUS EVENTS:
(List name and type of show, when it was held, facility contact name and phone number)

1. _____

_____

2. _____

_____

3. _____

_____

OTHER COMMENTS: _____

_____

_____

SIGNATURE: _____

                   Name   Title   Date

Reprinted with permission of Saint Charles Convention Center and Global Spectrum.

FIGURE 3-5

RUN OF SCHEDULE

MEDIA	THU 1	FRI 2	SAT 3	SUN 4	MON 5	TUE 6	WED 7	THU 8	FRI 9	SAT 10	SUN 11	MON 12	TUE 13	WED 14	THU 15	FRI 16	SAT 17	SUN 18	MON 19	TUE 20	WED 21	THU 22	FRI 23	SAT 24	SUN 25	MON 26	TUE 27	WED 28	THU 29	FRI 30	Daypart	Total # Spots	Rate / Unit	Total Gross
KBUL 98.1 FM					5	5	5					5	5	5					5	5	5										ROS	45X	$43.00	$1,935
KOH 780 AM					5	5	5					5	5	5					5	5	5										ROS	45X	$40.00	$1,800
KRNO 106.9 FM												5	5	5					5	5	5										ROS	30X	$42.00	$1,260
KTHX 100.1 FM					5	5	5					5	5	5					5	5	5										ROS	45X	$35.00	$1,575
KJZS 92.1 FM					7	7	7					7	7	7					7	7	7										ROS	63X	$10.00	$630
KOZZ 105.7 FM					5	5	5					5	5																		ROS	26X	$40.00	$1,000
TOTAL																																253X		$8,200

ACPS=$32.41

FIGURE 4

Civic Center
Box Office Statement

gagement_____   Play Dates_____November 14, 200X
ow_____Saturday, November 15, 200X

e ʊac	Manifest Cap	Free Passes	Passes and Special Rates		TOT Not Sold at Full Price	TOT Sold	Tick Price	House Receipts
			G-Type	T-Type				
	2226	32			55	2139	22.75	48662.25
	5468	209			1130	4129	18.75	77418.75
								00.00
								00.00
								00.00
								00.00
								00.00
								00.00
								00.00
al	7694	241	0	0	0 1185	6268		

				Total House Receipts	126081.00
	State Tax	TOT State Tax	City Tax	TOT City Tax	
ket Price					Less State Amusement Tax 6989.30
06	1.26	2695.14	0.42	898.38	Less City Amusement Tax 2343.53
36	1.04	4294.16	0.35	1445.15	
0	0.00	0.00	0.00	0.00	Total Net 116748.17
0	0.00	0.00	0.00	0.00	
0	0.00	0.00	0.00	0.00	Less City B & O Tax 583.74
0	0.00	0.00	0.00	0.00	
0	0.00	0.00	0.00	0.00	Total Final Net 116164.43
0	0.00	0.00	0.00	0.00	
0	0.00	0.00	0.00	0.00	
0	0.00	0.00	0.00	0.00	

		Total	Total To Date
Gross Receipts		126081.00	126081.00
St. Amuse. Tax		6989.30	6989.30
Ct. Amuse. Tax		2343.53	2343.53
Total Net		116748.17	116748.17
City B&O Tax		583.74	583.74
Final Net		116164.43	116164.43

ather: Cold/Cloudy   Temp: 28 degrees

	Number	Dollars
ʊance	6268	126081.00
sh	0	0.00
al	6268	126081.00

endance

	Today	To Date
l	6268	6268
np	241	241
al	6509	6509

We certify that we have personally checked
the above statement and it is in every way correct.

_____

FIGURE 5-7

IAAM ARENA
INCOME STATEMENT
APRIL 30, 200X

	MONTH ENDING	YEAR TO DATE
OPERATNG REVENUES		
RENT	60,000	400,000
REIMBURSED EXPENSES	26,000	310,000
CONCESSIONS	80,000	520,000
CATERING	24,000	280,000
ADVERTISING	10,000	100,000
COMMISSIONS	6,000	40,000
MISCELLANEOUS	0	5,000
TOTAL OPERATING REVENUES	206,000	1,655,000
OPERATING EXPENSES		
EXPENSES	185,000	1,485,000
INCOME FROM OPERATIONS	21,000	170,000
NON-OPERATING INCOME / DEDUCTIONS		
INTEREST INCOME	3,000	29,000
HOTEL / MOTEL TAX	16,000	141,000
CC RENEWAL / REPLACEMENT FUND	(3,000)	(30,000)
TOTAL NON-OPERATING INCOME / DEDUCTIONS	16,000	140,000
NET INCOME (LOSS)	37,000	310,000
PRIOR SURPLUS	2,248,000	2,100,000
HOTEL / MOTEL TAX	(16,000)	(141,000)
SURPLUS	2,269,000	2,269,000

FIGURE 6

IAAM ARENA
BALANCE SHEET
MONTH ENDING APRIL 30, 200X

ASSETS			LIABILITIES AND EQUITY		
CURRENT ASSETS			**CURRENT LIABILITIES**		
CASH	36,000		ACCOUNTS PAYABLE	164,000	
PETTY CASH	1,000		NOTES PAYABLE	100,000	
PAYROLL FUND	0		LOAN PAYABLE	60,000	
TEMPORARY INVESTMENT	8,000		CONSUMER SALES TAX	4,000	
ACCOUNTS RECEIVABLE	334,000		F.I.C.A.	2,000	
INVENTORY	128,000		WORKERS COMPENSATION	1,000	
	33,000		ADVANCE DEPOSITS	0	
TOTAL CURRENT ASSETS	540,000		**TOTAL CURRENT LIABILITIES**	331,000	
SUNDRY ASSETS			**EQUITY**		
PREPAYMENTS	20,000		HOTEL / MOTEL TAX	2,000,000	
DEPOSITS	8,000		CONTRIBUTIONS	1,500,000	
TOTAL SUNDRY ASSETS	28,000		SURPLUS	2,269,000	
FIXED ASSETS			**TOTAL EQUITY**	5,769,000	
BUILDING EQUIPMENT	190,000		**TOTAL CURRENT LIBABILITIES**		
KITCHEN EQUIPMENT	218,000		**AND EQUITY**	6,100,000	
CONCESSION EQUIPMENT	132,000				
TOOLS	24,000				
BOX OFFICE EQUIPMENT	16,000				
OFFICE EQUIPMENT	36,000				
COMMUNICATIONS EQUIPMENT	51,000				
TRANSPORTATION EQUIPMENT	64,000				
BUILDING IMPROVEMENTS	4,801,000				
TOTAL FIXED ASSETS	5,532,000				
TOTAL ASSETS	6,100,000				

FIGURE 6-2

IAAM Arena
Detail Revenue/Expense Statement

ACC#	Account Title	This month	Year to Date
	Operating Revenues		
500	Rent	60,000	400,000
510	Concessions	80,000	520,000
515	Catering	24,000	280,000
520	Reimbursed Expenses	26,000	310,000
530	Advertising	10,000	100,000
540	Miscellaneous	0	5,000
550	Commissions	6,000	
40,000			
	TOTAL OPERATIONS REVENUE	206,000	1,655,000
	Operating Expenses		
	Building Maintenance		
601	Supervision	4,000	48,000
602	Labor	10,000	120,000
603	Building Maintenance	100	8,000
604	Equipment Maintenance	1,000	8,000
605	Operations	1,700	35,000
606	Office Expenses	100	300
607-A	Electric	7,000	88,000
607-B	Water/Sewer/Etc.	1,100	12,700
607-C	Gas	13,600	50,000
	TOTAL BUILDING MAINTENANCE	38,600	370,000
	Concessions		
611	Supervisions	2,000	20,000
612	Labor	5,000	28,500
614	Equipment Maintenance	500	
800			
615	Operations	300	300
616	Office Expenses	200	400
617	Food Supplies	22,000	160,000
	TOTAL CONCESSIONS	30,000	210,000
	Catering		
621	Supervision	2,000	20,000
622	Labor	5,000	68,800
624	Equipment Maintenance	400	1,000
625	Operations	300	16,000
626	Office Expenses	100	200
627	Food Supplies	8,200	94,000
628	Contracted Services	0	0
	TOTAL CATERING	16,000	200,000
	Event Operations		
631	Supervision	1,500	15.000
632	Ushers	4,000	34,000
633	Ticket Takers	5,000	36,000
634	Equipment Rentals	1,000	4,000
635	Operations	6,000	60,000
636	Security	3,500	21,000

Continued on next page

FIGURE 6-3

REVENUE/EXPENSE STATEMENT - CONTINUED

637	Materials & Supplies	2,000	42,000
638	Spots & Stagehands	16,400	81,000
	TOTAL EVENT OPERATIONS	39,400	293,000
	Box Office		
641	Supervision	2,500	20,000
642	Labor	5,000	28,000
643	Outlet Expenses	300	600
644	Equipment Maintenance	200	500
646	Office Expenses	300	
900			
647	Advertising/Promotion Expenses	17,700	50,000
648	Contract Fees	0	0
649	Equipment Rental	0	0
	TOTAL BOX OFFICE	26,000	100,000
	Administrative		
661	Supervision	6,000	45,000
662	Labor	4,000	28,000
663	Insurance	5,400	58,000
664	Equipment Maintenance	200	400
665	Telephone	1,000	12,000
666	Office Expenses	600	8,000
667	Travel	750	6,000
668	Legal Services	0	2,200
669	Misc. Administrative Expenses	50	400
	TOTAL ADMINISTRATIVE	18,000	160,000
	Accounting		
671	Supervision	500	10,000
672	Labor	1,800	7,000
673	Payroll Services	300	7,000
674	Equipment Maintenance	100	1,000
676	Office Expenses	200	1,000
677	Audit Expenses	100	6,000
679	Federal / State Tax Expense	0	0
	TOTAL ACCOUNTING	3,000	32,000
	Employee Welfare Expenses		
681	Vacation / Holiday	0	0
682	Sick Leave	400	1,200
683	Unemployment Insurance	700	3,000
684	Group Insurance	4,000	34,000
685	FICA	4,800	37,400
686	Workers Compensation	2,800	21,000
687	Education / Seminars	300	7,400
688	Pension	1,000	6,000
689	Miscellaneous	0	10,000
	TOTAL EMPLOYEE WELFARE EXP.	14,000	120,000
	TOTAL OPERATING EXPENSES	**185,000**	**1,485,000**

FIGURE 6-3

EVENT FINANCIAL SETTLEMENT STATEMENT

MID-SIZE ARENA
EVENT SETTLEMENT STATEMENT

EVENT: HEAVY METAL ROCK 'N ROLL CONCERT
DATE:
PROMOTER:

DESCRIPTION OF ACTIVITY	AMOUNT	TOTALS
INCOME		
Gross Ticket Sales	322,204.50	
TOTAL INCOME		$ 322,204.50
EXPENSES		
Facility Rental Fee (12% capped @ $18,000)	18,000.00	
Box Office Commission (4% capped @ $2,000)	2,000.00	
Stage Labor-Hands, Riggers, Electrician, Runners	7,511.89	
Custodial-Set-Up, Show, Clean-Up	2,880.15	
Guest Services-Ushers, Ticket Takers, T-Shirt Security	4,980.20	
Uniformed Police	3,030.00	
Parking Services-Attendants	1,014.25	
Emergency Medical Services	450.00	
City Fire Expenses	551.20	
Show Expenses:	-	
Forklift Rental	298.25	
CO-2 Refills	155.06	
Telephone Line Installation	600.00	
Pyro Technicial	300.00	
Vehicle Rental #1	150.00	
Vehicle Rental #2	30.00	
Vehicle Rental #3	190.00	
Dressing Room Furniture Rental	282.00	
City Business License	65.00	
City Floor Plan Approval	120.00	
City Pyro Permit	150.00	
TOTAL EXPENSES	$ 42,758.00	
NET INCOME		$ 279,446.50
TOTAL AMOUNT DUE AT FINAL SETTLEMENT		$ 279,446.50

AGREED

Promoter	Facility Management

Date	Date

FIGURE

EVENT EVALUATION FORMS TO DETERMINE ALCOHOL SALES

Toby Keith Concert

Event Date(s):   **Doors Open at:** ___7:00 p.m.___   **Event Starts at:** ___8:00 p.m.___
                       Event Ends at: ___10:00 p.m.___

	Sport	Flat Show	O Ent.	Concert*
Type				x
Comment				

	Rock	Pop	C&W	Other
Concert Type*			x	

	Low Key	Variable	Exciting
Intensity			x
Comment			

	Light	Competitive	Aggressive
Energy	x		
Comment			

	Lax	Informal	Formal
Decorum		x	
Comment			

	Under 25	25-35	Over 35
Age		x	
Comment			

	Male	Female	Non-Specific
Gender		x	
Comment			

	No Alcohol	Neutral	Alcohol
Expectation			x
Comment			

	Under 2,000	2-3,000	3-4,000	4-5,000	Over 5,000
Attendance Projected					x
Comment					

	Family	Couple	Friend Group
Attendance Pattern		x	
Comment			

Seating Configuration	Flat	Floor Only	Balcony Only
	Festival Floor	Seated Floor	Tables Floor
		x	

Reported Incidents
History: No reported incidents, high energy show, sell-out crowds.
Other Comments/Factors: Beer Garden area is too small to control and accommodate a sell-out crowd.

FIGURE 7-6

Toby Keith Concert
Security Needs and Alcohol Sales

EVENT PROFILE

Type	C&W Con.	History:
Intensity	Exciting	No reported incidents, high energy show, sell-out crowds.
Energy	Light	
Decorum	Informal	
Age	25-35	
Gender	Female	Other Comments:
Expectation	Alcohol	Beer Garden area is too small to control and accommodate crowd.
Attendance Projected	Over 5,000	Recommendation: Allow patrons to carry beverages to balcony
Attendance Pattern	Couple	seats but not to floor.
Seating Configuration	S - Floor	
Will Alcohol Be Sold?	Y N	

If yes:

Alcohol Sales

# of POS	POS Locations/	ID Checking	Products Sold	Start Sales	End Sales
1	Sky Club	at bar	all	w/ doors	10:00 PM
1	B Concourse	assisted	b&w only		9:30 PM
1	C Concourse	assisted	b&w only		9:30 PM
Total 3					

Security

	Uniformed Officers	T-Shirt Security	Professional Event Staff
Number:	6	2 0	0
Stations:	Roaming	Floor - 6	
		Vomitories -10	
		Lobby - 4	

FIGURE 7

DEFINING CROWD MANAGERS

IAAM conducted a study on staffing responsibilities for crowd management and identified the following roles:

Four levels of crowd management responsibility were identified:

1. *Crowd Assembly Facilitator (CAF)*–front-line event staff providing direct services to patrons. Example job titles are usher, ticket taker, parking attendant, peer security.

2. *Crowd Assembly Supervisor*–During an event, CAFs report to the Crowd Assembly Supervisor, who oversees activities of CAFs during an event.

3. *Crowd Management Administrator*–Professional staff person with necessary experience and expertise to design and implement all facility security, crowd management, and emergency preparation activities.

4. *Crowd Management Instructor*–A crowd management professional, trained under an IAAM-endorsed curriculum, who has the knowledge and skills to develop and conduct in-facility training programs for Crowd Assembly Facilitators and Crowd Assembly Supervisors. Instructors may be regular staff or consultants.

Staffing Definition
Crowd Assembly Facilitator
Crowd assembly facilitators assist facility or event administrators in providing a safe and enjoyable environment for their guests by implementing the facility/event policies and procedures. Crowd assembly facilitator duties include contributing to the safety of facility and event, managing the movement and activities of crowd/guests, assisting in emergencies, assisting guests with specific concerns related to their enjoyment and/or involvement with the event by communicating with the guests in a polite and professional manner.

Duties of a Crowd Assembly Facilitator
<u>Training</u>
Knowledge of event and facilities.
Perform communications function.
Risk management.
Crowd dynamics management.
Assist guests..
Implement facility/event policies and procedures.
Conflict identification and mitigation.
Major emergency response.

<u>Assisting Guests</u>
Maximize accessibility to guests.
Anticipate guests' needs.
Use good guest service techniques.
Answer questions or assist to find answers.
Provide direction to appropriate locations.
Respond to guest concerns.

Continued on next page

FIGURE 8-7

Implement Facility/Guest Policies and Procedures
Learn and apply appropriate policies and procedures.
Observe violations of policies and procedures and report to supervisor.
Inform guests of violations of policies and procedures and ensuing consequences.
Review policies and procedures as appropriate.
Proactively monitor changes to policies and procedures.
Report problems not addressed in policies and procedures to supervisor.

Risk Management
Participate in pre-event orientations.
Conduct pre-event review of assigned work area.
Review check-list of safety hazards.
Identify and mitigate safety hazards and report to supervisor.
Confirm assigned work area and equipment readiness to supervisor.
Operate and maneuver equipment in safe manner.
Report incidents and property damage to supervisor.
Identify, mitigate and report medical emergencies to supervisor.
Return assigned equipment in good working order.

Crowd Dynamics Management
Adjust to crowd demographics.
Anticipate crowd activities and behavior.
Maintain the usability of means of egress.
Make guests aware of their responsibilities.
Observe crowd for potential problems and report to supervisor.
Monitor flow of crowd during duration of event.
Identify changing crowd behavior and demeanor and report to supervisor.

Knowledge of Event and Facilities
Review schedule of event activities.
Review venue/event diagram.
Review event specific policies and procedures.
Review event specific alcohol policies and procedures.
Review specific event ticketing and credentialing policies.
Familiarize oneself with event seating requirements.
Familiarize oneself with type and activities of the event.
Identify key event/facility personnel.
Maintain control of limited access areas.

Conflict Identification and Mitigation
Identify credential/ticketing/seating problems.
React according to policies and procedures regarding problem guests.
Mitigate credential/ticketing/seating problems.
Resolve guest complaints/problems.
Avoid arguments with guests.
Avoid physical contact with guests.

Continued on next pa

FIGURE 8

Training

Attend employment orientation.
Fulfill certification as legally required.
Attend facility/event orientation.
Fulfill specific facility training requirements.
Read assigned and posted material.
Attend pre and post event briefing sessions.
Participate in job assignment training from supervisor at events.
Maintain focus on role during event.
Share competence with other employees.
Interact positively with guests and employees.
Follow chain of command.
Attend continuing education as appropriate.
Participate in on-going training.
Participate in performance evaluation.

Perform Communications Function

Employ good listening skills.
Adapt communication to crowd diversity.
Adhere to proper written and verbal communication channels.
Follow supervisor instruction.
Utilize proper written, verbal, and non-verbal communication techniques.
Report communication breakdowns to supervisor.
Be competent with communication equipment.
Keep communication relevant.
Utilize event/facility terminology.
Communicate with all personnel associated with the event.
Maintain the integrity of confidential information.
Recognize non-verbal crowd communication.
Utilize signage in communication process.
Respond appropriately to all public address announcements.
Complete required written documentation.

Major Emergency Response

Maintain guest safety as a priority.
Assist guests with special needs.
Follow appropriate instructions applicable to fire, weather, earthquake,
crowd incidents, terrorism, hazardous materials, transportation mishaps, and power loss.
Participate in drills.
Report all fires immediately regardless of size.
Permit individual guests to leave if they wish during an emergency.
Execute assigned tasks or responsibilities as provided in event of emergency.
Provide appropriate information.

Definitions for other staff roles can be found at: http://www.iaam.org/CVMS/CVMSsafety.htm

FIGURE 8-7

INCIDENT REPORT

DATE __April 4, 2009__

TIME OF INCIDENT __8:00 p.m.__
TIME OF REPORT __8:05 p.m.__

LOCATION: ⟨Lower Level⟩   Sect. ___12___
            Mezzanine Level   Row _____
            Upper Level   Seat(s) _____
            Bleachers   Concourse ____
            Parking Lot _____
            Concession Stand _____
            Other _____

TYPE: Altercation   T.E.A.M. Player
            Foul Ball   Abusive Language
            Alcohol Possession   Other _____
            ⟨Fall⟩

EMPLOYEE   __Bob Smith__   BADGE # _234_

DESCRIPTION OF SUBJECT

RACE _____   SEX _____   HEIGHT _____   WEIGHT _____
HAIR COLOR _____   EYE COLOR _____

SUBJECT AND WITNESS INFORMATION

SUBJECT'S NAME __Jan Mason_____
ADDRESS __1234 Bay Street, Apt. 4_____
CITY __San Francisco__   STATE _CA_   ZIP CODE _94904_
PHONE NUMBER _____
STATEMENT __"I slipped on some kind of liquid. I hurt my back."__
_____
_____

WITNESS' NAME __John Mason__   RELATION TO SUBJECT __Husband__
ADDRESS __Same as above_____
CITY _____   STATE _____   ZIP CODE _____
PHONE NUMBER __( ) same_____
STATEMENT __"I heard a noise and looked back and she was on the__
__ground."__

FIGURE 8

PRODUCTION RIDER

SHOW ADVANCE

SHOW DATE(S): _____   VENUE: _____   CITY: _____

LABOR CALLS

LOAD IN: __9:00 AM__   SECOND CALL: _____   SHOW CALL: __6:00 PM__   LOAD OUT: __10:00 PM__

STEWARD:	_____	HANDS:	_____	STEWARD:	_____	STEWARD:	_____
HEADS:	_____	RUNNERS:	_____	DECK HANDS:	6	HEADS:	_____
LOADERS:	4	PROD. ASST.	_____	HOUSE SPOTS:	4	LOADERS:	4
HANDS	18			ELEC/HSE LTS:	1	HANDS	22
UP RIGGERS:	4					UP RIGGERS:	4
DN RIGGERS:	1					DN RIGGERS:	1
ELECTRICIAN:	1			LOAD OUT:	9:00 PM	ELECTRICIAN:	1
FORK OPS:	1					FORK OPS:	_____
RUNNERS:	3			FORK OPS:	1		
				LOADERS:	4		

RUNNING TIMES

SOUND CHECK NFG:	3:00 PM	Band 1	6:30 PM - 6:50 PM
SOUND CHECK GC:	4:00 PM	Band 2	7:10 PM - 7:40 PM
SOUND CHECK OP:	5:00 PM	Band 3	8:10 PM - 9 PM
DOORS:	5:30 PM	Headliner	9:30 PM - 10:20 PM
SECURITY MEETING:	4:00 PM	CURFEW:	10:30 PM

STAGE AND FOH RISERS / POWER / SPOTS / BARRICADE

STAGE SIZE:	60'w x 40'd x 5'h	FOH SOUND POSITION:	16'w x 16'd x 0'h
SL WING:	16'w x 24'd x 4'h		on floor at 75' from DS
SR WING:	16'w x 24'd x 5'h		
	wings recessed 4'	FOH LIGHT RISER:	12'w x 8'd x 2'h
			directly behind sound
UPSTAGE WING:	_____		
		RIGGING POINTS:	14 Lights, 6 Sound
AUDIO POWER:	200 Amp & 50 Amp	BARRICADE:	tour carrying 120'
LIGHTING POWER:	400 Amp & 200 Amp		we will need bike rack for FOH
	120/208 Volt 3Phz, 5 Wire		
		SPOTS:	Require 4 FOH spots

VEHICLE INFO / PARKING

# PRODUCTION TRUCKS:	3	# BAND BUSES:	2
# MERCH TRUCKS:	2	# CREW BUSES:	2
# SPONS FOH TRUCKS:	2	# SPONSOR BUSES:	1
TRAILER ON BUS:	1	# SUPPORT BUSES:	1
AND:	Van & Trailer	RUNNER VEHICLES:	3

Page 1

FIGURE 9-2

PRODUCTION RIDER - CONTINUED

CATERING

	TIMES	NUMBERS*	NOTES
BREAKFAST:	8:30 AM - 10:30 AM	35	
LUNCH:	12:00 PM - 3:00 PM	45	9 vegetarian, 3 veg
DINNER:	5:00 PM - 8:00 PM	60	12 vegetarian, 4 veg

*note -- these are tour numbers only

HEADLINER 1			
DR SET-UP	12 Noon	NOTES:	

HEADLINER 2			
DR SET-UP	11:00 AM	NOTES:	

*Please have 4 Dozen towels & 8 Bars of Soap to production office at load in and additional 6 dozen by 5 pm

SECURITY/FIRST AID

BACKSTAGE	NUMBER	TIMES	FOH	NUMBER	TIMES
BACKSTAGE DOOR:	1	Load In	SOUND CHECK:		
TRUCKS & BUSSES	1	Load In	FOH MIX:	1	Doors
STAGE AREA			WINGS:	2	Doors
BAND DR:	1	Noon	BARRICADE:	8	Doors
BAND DR:			EMTS:		
ROVERS:			SUPERVISOR:		
SUPERVISOR:					

(These are suggested minimums, # to be determined in advance)

DRESSING ROOMS AND OFFICE NEEDS

TOUR PRODUCTION OFFICE
Four tables, Eight chairs
3 Phone lines, 1 Fax line

Headliner BAND ROOM
Real furniture for 8 people
Couches, armchairs, lamps, tables.

ACCOUNTING OFFICE
One table, Four chairs
1 Phone line

Headliner 2 BAND ROOM
Real furniture for 8 people
Couches, armchairs, lamps, tables.

TOUR SPONSOR OFFICE
Two tables, Six chairs
2 Phone lines

Hedliner 1 PRACTICE ROOM
Large enough for 8 people
Needs 110 power and Four chairs.

BAND 2 BAND ROOM
Large enough for 8 people
Love seat, armchairs.

Headliner 2 PRACTICE ROOM
Large enough for 8 people
Needs 110 power and Four chairs.

OPENER BAND ROOM
Large enough for 8 people
Catering table, Ten Chairs

MEET & GREET ROOM
Large enough for 50 people
Two tables, Ten chairs

THANK YOU FOR HELPING US MAKE THIS A SUCCESSFUL TOUR AND A GOOD DAY IN YOUR VENUE!

FIGURE 9

APPENDIX B

CORE COMPETENCIES OF PUBLIC ASSEMBLY FACILITY MANAGERS

BODY OF KNOWLEGE TASK FORCE

CORE COMPETENCIES OF PUBLIC ASSEMBLY FACILITY MANAGERS

Updated 2006

OVERVIEW

The Core Competencies of Public Assembly Facility Managers were developed in 1999-2000 and updated in 2006 by the IAAM Body of Knowledge Task Force. The Core Competencies represent the skills and abilities that managers of public assembly facilities, regardless of facility type, should possess and build upon in order to be judged competent and qualify for the designation of Certified Facilities Executive – CFE.

FUNCTIONS COMMON TO PUBLIC ASSEMBLY FACILITIES
1. Administration (People & Organization)
2. Sales & Marketing (Selling Time & Space, and Event Activity)
3. Fiscal Management (Financial Performance)
4. Facility Services & Operations (Physical Plant & Event Management)
5. Leadership & Management

   I. Administration
      1. Capital Improvement
- Identifying the need
- Forecasting the expense
- Finding the funding
- Budgeting the expense
- Overseeing the project

      2. Construction Management
- Understanding the bidding process
- Understanding technical specifications
- Reading blueprints and architectural drawings
- Supervision of contractors (both on-site and administratively)

      3. Technology
- Basic understanding of computer systems
- Familiarity with basic terminology
- Ability to identify appropriate technologies
- Ability to evaluate emerging technologies

4. Insurance/Risk Management
   - Understanding the terminology
   - Ability to evaluate risk
   - Skilled in risk assessment
   - Ability to conduct cost/benefit analysis

5. Emergency Management
   - Develop communication strategies
   - Develop evacuation plans
   - Coordinate emergency services with responder agencies (police, fire, etc.)
   - Train staff in response preparedness
   - Knowledge of emergency equipment
   - Develop media relations

6. Crisis Management
   - Develop response procedures
     1. Bomb threat
     2. Fire
     3. Weather-related incident (hurricane, flood, etc.)
     4. Chemical/biological threat
     5. Natural disaster (earthquake, tornado, etc.)
     6. Terrorist incident
   - Staff training and preparedness
   - Media relations
   - Insurance issues

7. Human Resources
   - Knowledge of legal and regulatory issues
   - Staff training
   - Staff retention
   - Creating and maintaining workplace morale
   - Employee counseling

8. Contract Management
   - Understanding terminology
   - Negotiation skills
   - Aware of legal issues

9. Governance
   - Understanding the operating policies
   - Knowledge of the operating environment
   - Knowing key persons with authority

10. Tenant Management
   - Understanding landlord responsibilities
   - Understanding tenant's needs
   - Partnering where mutually beneficial
   - Creating a happy marriage

11. Training and Development
   - Needs assessment of staff
   - Knowledge of available resources
   - Develop meaningful training programs
   - Evaluate effectiveness of training programs

12. Legal Issues
   - Knowledge of laws affecting facility
       1. Business regulations
       2. Reporting requirements
       3. Employment laws

13. Disability Services
   - Conduct accessibility assessment
   - Understand legal responsibilities and requirement
   - Staff training

14. Public and Private Management
   - Understanding the difference

II.   Sales & Marketing

1. Sponsorship
   - Ability to develop partnerships

2. Perceived Value of sponsorship to buyer
   - Understanding the difference between advertising and sponsorship
   - Fulfillment of sponsorship contract (promises)
   - Value to sponsors' annual report

3. Community Relations
   - Sensitivity and understanding the community
   - Understanding the direct and indirect impact of the facility on the community
   - Sensitivity of community standards in programming the facility

4. Public Relations
   - Understanding the concept of free advertising
   - Ability to create a press release and public service announcement (PSA)
   - Developing policies for proper use of complimentary tickets
   - Understanding the value of facility's website as a public relations tool

5. Advertising
   - Knowledge of the media (print, radio, television, Internet)
   - Ability to develop an effective advertising campaign
   - Selling the facility to the industry (i.e., event producers and promoters)
   - Selling the facility to the community
   - Selling tickets to a specific event

6. Marketing
   - Creating a demand for the facility
   - Understanding the demographics of the market
   - Conducting market research and analysis
   - Developing a marketing campaign
   - Packaging the product (event, facility, sports team, meeting destination)
   - Understanding and directing the facility's image

7. Booking and Scheduling
   - Developing relationships with event producers, event promoters, talent agents, meeting planners, etc.
   - Knowledge of event production requirements
   - Understanding the facility's capabilities and limitations
   - Knowing the competition
   - Understanding the concept of yield management

8. Event Programming
   - Develop a diverse program of events
   - Be considerate of the primary tenant(s)
   - Develop event acquisition strategies
     1. Standard rental
     2. Co-promotion
     3. In-house promotion/buying and promoting talent
   - Develop events through non-profit/community organizations
   - Foster sponsorship opportunities through event programming

9. Fund-Raising
   - Balance fund-raising with other sources of revenue
   - Understand the "not-for-profit" statues of some facilities
   - Develop grant writing skills
   - Create events and galas as fund-raising tools

10. Premium Seating
    - Golden Circle
    - Club seats
    - Luxury suites
    - Premium seating add-ons (parking, concierge service, catering, dedicated entrance/exit)

11. Convention and Visitors Bureau (CVB) Relations
    - Understanding shared marketing responsibilities
    - Coordinating joint sales efforts
    - Developing booking priorities
    - Understanding economic impact studies
    - Working with sports commissions in U.S. cities
    - Understanding the facility's role in urban/economic development

III. Fiscal Management

1. Budgeting
   - Developing a budget for the facility
   - Ability to monitor and adjust budgets
   - Understanding financial statements (income statement, balance sheet, operating statement, profit/loss statement)
   - Understanding financial operations (accounts payable, accounts receivable)
   - Knowledge of audit controls
     1. Internal audit
     2. External audit
     3. Areas for audit: box office, petty cash, time cards, travel claims, food & beverage commissions, etc.

2. Inventory Control
   - Supplies
   - Equipment

3. Cost Accounting
   - Identify cost systems
   - Allocate expenses
   - Understanding fixed and variable costs

4. Investments
   - Cash flow management
   - Investing box office receipts

5. Capitalization
   - Developing capital improvement budgets
   - Understanding bonding capacities

6. Forecasting
   - Understanding the facility's overall financial performance

IV. Facility Services & Operations

1. Admission
   - Developing admission control systems
     1. Box office operations
     2. Credentials

2. Event Production
   - Developing a thorough understanding of event production elements
     1. Stages
     2. Sound systems
     3. Lighting systems
     4. Portable floors
     5. Seating configurations
     6. Stagehands
     7. Television production
     8. Power requirements
     9. Advancing a show

3. Rigging
   - Load bearing capacities
   - Safety policies
   - Rigging maintenance
   - Risk management
   - Specific trade knowledge

4. Physical Plant
   - Interior maintenance
   - Exterior maintenance
   - Groundskeeping
   - Heat, ventilation, air conditioning (HVAC)
   - Mechanical systems (electrical, plumbing, HVAC)
   - Ice making and ice maintenance
   - Service contracts with third party specialists

5. Housekeeping
   - Custodial labor
   - Custodial supplies
   - Custodial equipment
   - Event custodial duties vs. daily custodial duties
   - Changeovers
   - Inventory control of equipment and supplies
   - Trade specific knowledge (carpet care, window washing, floor refinishing, etc.)

6. Food & Beverage
   - Options – in-house vs. outsource contract
   - Concessions and catering
   - Health department regulations
   - Alcoholic beverage service regulations and licensing
   - Products (basic vs. branded)
   - Sanitation (cleaning & pest control)
   - Service points-of-sale/staffing
   - Accounting & cost controls
   - Auditing (cash & inventory)

7. Merchandise
   - Options – in-house vs. outsource contract
   - Commission rates
   - Locations for sale
   - Staffing
   - Accounting & cash controls
   - Auditing (inventory)
   - Bootleg/counterfeit merchandise

8. Event Management
   - Event Labor (hire, train, and supervise)
   - Ushers, ticket takers, tickets sellers, security, medical, event custodians, parking lot attendants, stagehands
   - Event briefing
   - Event incident reports

V. Leadership & Management

1. Principles of leadership
   - Vision and values
   - Empowerment of subordinates
   - Collaboration with colleagues up and down the organizational structure
   - Risk taking

2. Use of power and authority
    - Balance the power
    - Develop a team

3. Strategic planning
    - Mission statement
    - Goals and objectives

4. Knowing the ground rules
    - History of the organization
    - Guiding principles
    - Policies and procedures

5. Staff development
    - Use job descriptions effectively
    - Use evaluations as a communication tool
    - Provide training and professional development opportunities

6. Mentoring
    - Provide guidance and learning opportunities
    - Impart knowledge and experience
    - Instill confidence

7. Morals and Ethics
    - Maintain highest ethical standards
    - Give respect to others
    - Lead by example

8. Motivation
    - Instill enthusiasm in others
    - Be accessible to subordinates
    - Exercise problem solving skills

9. Decision making
    - Exercise sound judgment
    - Consider more than one option before making a decision
    - Aim for balanced outcomes

10. Sense of humor
    - Maintain a sense of humor
    - Be able to laugh at yourself

11. Communication skills
    - Be clear and concise
    - Never enough communication
    - Use difference communication tools for difference circumstances

12. Time management
    - Learn to use time efficiently
    - Balance work with leisure time

13. Crisis Management
    - Understand the leader's role in time of crisis
    - Step up to the plate

14. IAAM Membership and Participation
    - Professional associations
    - Networking with colleagues
    - Opportunities for service to the industry/profession
    - Educational opportunities
    - Certified Facilities Executive (CFE)

APPENDIX C

CONTRACT COMPONENTS

CONTRACT COMPONENTS TENTATIVE COMMITMENTS/ CONTRACTUAL OBLIGATIONS

A tentatively held date becomes a firm commitment when a formal contractual instrument is issued. It becomes a contract when properly signed by all parties. The scope and importance of the event will usually dictate whether any serious negotiating will be required. Many facilities utilize standard form contracts or license agreements with a "fill in the blank" type format. These types of instruments allow the process to be streamlined and somewhat consistent in format.

Negotiated contracts or license agreements require advance preparation. The assistance of an attorney is certainly a must for the original standard facility document. Whether or not an attorney is needed for individual event contracts is a decision to be made by the manager unless there is a policy requiring a sign-off by the facility's attorney. In addition to the "boiler plate" information that usually appears in most documents, several areas must be addressed prior to negotiation. A comprehensive "laundry list" must be developed with major deal points outlined. Armed with the information, the facility negotiator can focus on items such as special terms, condition, and benefits to be obtained by the parties.

COMPONENTS OF A CONTRACT

A contract is defined as an agreement of two or more parties to do or refrain from doing some lawful thing. The agreement must create obligations on the part of all parties. Every contract must meet four basic requirements:

1. Mutual assent of all contracting parties.
2. The parties must possess the legal rights and capacity to make the contract.
3. Proper and fair consideration of services or provisions must be received by all contracting parties.
4. Offer of terms of the agreement.

The contract must have a lawful objective and a legal method for accomplishing it. In law, a contract is a promissory agreement between two or more parties to establish, change, or rescind a legal relationship. The public assembly facility manager should understand that the prime purpose of a contract is to provide protection to:

1. The owner of the public assembly facility.
2. The organization or individual using the facility.
3. The patron attending the event (whatever that event might be).

There are some very basic components that should be contained in the facility use contract. These items will, in nearly all cases, be seen as a part of the basic contract form:

1. **Form of Legal Document** - i.e., Is it a Contract, License, Lease, Permit, etc.?
2. **Facility Identification** - Include name, address, city, state, zip code, telephone and fax number of the facility. Be sure to include legal nomenclature such as Municipal Corporation, Incorporated, Partnership, Joint Venture, etc.
3. **User Identification** - Include business name, address, city, state, zip code, event contact person, telephone and fax number of the contracting organization. Be sure to include legal nomenclature such as Corporation, Partnership, Sole Owner, D.B.A., Joint Venture, etc.
4. **Event Identification** - What space is being rented for what purpose and the name of the event.
5. **Event Date(s)** - List date(s) of use, including move-in and move-out.
6. **Event Time(s)** - List time(s) of use, including move-in and move-out.
7. **Event Schedule** - State what will be going on during specific date/time frames.
8. **Venue Identification** - List the exact space(s) which will be rented. Thi is particularly important when the facility being rented has many spaces. The User must know that he/she is only renting specific areas and not the whole building, unless that is the case. Be sure to also include language which states that the organization will, or will not, also have use cf the common public areas for ingress and egress to the event(s).
9. **User Fees and Revenue Sources** - State the specific amount of money which will be paid for rental of the space or a percentage of ticket sales, or even a combination of base rent against a percentage of ticket sales. Other User Fees and Revenue Sources include:
    - Equipment use.
    - Labor charges.
    - Merchandise.
    - Parking.
    - Food/beverage.
    - Catering.
    - Flowers, etc.
    - Videotaping, etc.
10. **Payment Schedule** - State a precise schedule of when payments are due for:
    - Advance/Contract Deposit.
    - Minimum Base Rental.
    - Percentage Balance (if appropriate).
    - Commission on Sales (if appropriate).
    - Service/Labor Costs.
    - Equipment Rental Costs.
    - Other.

11. **Insurance Requirements** - Include language to identify the exact type of cover-age, limits of liability and scope, and qualified insurance companies required by the facility. Note a Certificate of Insurance will be required by the facility X days prior to the event. Specific wording of any requirement for making the facility or the governing authority an "additionally named insured" should also be included here. Facility should have right to AUTOMATICALLY provide coverage at User's expense if user fails to provide on time.

12. **Indemnity Clause** - Include specific language holding the facility, its manager, employees, agents and guests harmless from legal action caused by the acts or omissions of the User.

13. **Cancellation Clause** - Definite and specific language must be in place which spells out the allocation of risk between the parties in the event of cancellation by either party.

14. **Attorney Fees** - Most attorneys will insist on a clause which obligates the payment of attorney fees and court costs by the non-prevailing party to the prevailing party in the event of a lawsuit.

15. **Force Majeure** - This is a clause which states that the facility will not be obligated in any way in the event of an act of God, fire, civil riot, strike, lockout, flood, war or other situations over which the facility has no control.

16. **No Partnerships** - Unless there is specific language to the contrary, there should be a section which simply states that there is no partnership relationship between the facility and the User.

17. **Obstruction/Alterations** - Include language with regard to the specifics of not blocking, for example, sidewalks, ramps, entries, doors, corridors, passageways, galleries, vestibules, hallways, lobbies, stairways, elevators, aisles, driveways, fire hose cabinets, heating and air conditioning vents, lighting fixtures and fire prevention water sprinkler systems, to ensure patron safety. No physical alterations to the facility should be allowed without prior written consent of management.

18. **Signature Lines and the Corporate Seal** - There should be sufficient room at the end of the document to allow for all signatures required by the governing authority in addition to that of the User. If the User is a corporation, a corporate seal may need to be affixed to the document over the signature of the corporate secretary.

19. **Personal Requirements** - A mention should be made with regard to any personnel that are necessary to set up, operate, and tear down the event and who will provide those personnel. Note that worker's compensation law varies from state to state. If union personnel are required, this should be stated.

20. **Basic Services Provided by the Facility** - Reference should be made for the provision of heat, light, air conditioning, cleanliness, water, sewer, natural gas, if the facility normally supplies these services as a part of the rental agreement It should be stated if the facility does not provide these services or only provides them at a fee.

21. **Control of Building** - The building should always be under the ultimate control of the facility manager and it should be specifically spelled out in the document.

22. **Changes to Agreement** - Changes to the agreement must be in writing and signed by all parties.

This is not meant to be a complete listing of each clause which should be in a facility use contractual document. In addition to the foregoing, each facility manager should regularly seek the counsel and advise of the facility's attorney to be sure that all requirements of federal, state and local law are properly covered.

In addition, there are many operating aspects and other items involved in the use of a public assembly facility that need to be addressed, although trying to include them in a contract document may be too complex and cumbersome. Many facilities address this issue by developing "policies and procedure" and/or "rules and regulations" documents which are made a part of the contractual agreement by a statement in that latter document so stating. Some areas that might be addressed in the policies and procedures if that approach is used, could include, but not be limited to:

1. *Concessions* - Revenue and expenses connected with food and beverage, merchandise, photography, flowers, etc. would be addressed.
2. *Exhibits* - The terms and conditions for exhibits, including storage, freight, locations, local laws, etc.
3. *Alterations/construction* - Requirements for either approval or prohibitions against nails, balloons, adhesives, etc., if applicable.
4. *Capacity* - State maximum seating, floor loads and rigging requirements, among other items.
5. *Broadcasting/filming* - Specify who has rights to these, under what conditions, and at what formula for determining costs and revenue distribution.
6. *Tickets* - Specify who sells and through what resources, collects money, prints tickets, manifest requirements, box office staffing and statements, seating configurations, complimentary tickets, and trade tickets.
7. *Evacuation of facility in case of Emergency* - Who controls, diagrams, etc.

DEFINITIONS

a. **Contract**: A contract is defined as an agreement upon sufficient consideration to do or refrain from doing some lawful thing. The agreement must create an obligation. Every contract must have at least the following four elements:
   1. Mutual assents.
   2. Parties with the capacity to contract.
   3. Consideration and valid subject matter.
   4. Term.

b. **Warranties**: Warranties are assurances that are part of a contract.

c.   **License**: A license or certificate is a form of written approval to do a lawful thing, often issued by a division of government. Additional elements or provisions are usually added to define the extent and limits of such license. It usually gives the licensee the right to obtain certain space but not possession; therefore, the individual/organization does not become a tenant. To be a tenant, one must have exclusive possession, not mere use alone.

d.   **Lease**: A lease is a contract whereby, for a consideration called rent, one party agrees to give possession of premises to another. A lease must contain five essential elements:
1.   Contract.
2.   Exclusive Possession.
3.   Subordinate Holding.
4.   Reversion in the Landlord.
5.   Reservations of Rent.

Other formal provisions usually found in a lease include the following:
1.   Term of duration.
2.   Description of premises.
3.   Purpose for which premises may be used.
4.   Repairs and improvements.
5.   Insurance.
6.   Assignment.
7.   Security Deposit.
8.   Default and Remedies.
9.   Quiet enjoyment.

e.   **Permit**: A permit is a written acknowledgment of consent to do some lawful thing without command; it grants a liberty and professes to tolerate all legal action.

f.   **Agreement**: All contracts are agreements, but all agreements are NOT contracts. Agreements that do not include the essentials of a contract are not enforceable as a contract by law. The use of agreements therefore, should be for arrangements which are simpler in nature and duration.

g.   **Ultimate terms and conditions**: For very large and complex operations, it is advisable to include many more terms and conditions in the contract. The enforcement of certain provisions can become extremely difficult. In all cases, it will require supervision of at least one individual representing the party granting the privilege.

APPENDIX D

RELATED ORGANIZATIONS AND ASSOCIATIONS

RELATED ORGANIZATIONS
AND ASSOCIATIONS

ASAE www.asaecenter.org
American Society of Association Executives
1575 I St., NW
Washington DC 20005-1103
Phone: 202/626-2723, Fax: 202/371-8825
Email: pr@asaenet.org

APPA www.appa.org
APPA: The Association of Higher Education Facilities Officers
1643 Prince St.
Alexandria VA 22314-2818
Phone: 703/684-1446, Fax: 703/549-2772

ACME www.acmenet.org
Association for Convention Marketing Executives
204 E St., NE
Washington D.C. 20002
Phone: 202/547-6340, Fax: 202/547-6348
Email: info@giuffrida.org

ACOM www.acomonline.org
Association for Convention Operations Management
P.O. Box 659
Avondale Estates GA 30002
Phone: 404/292-3514, Fax: 404/292-2931
Email: info@acomonline.org

AIPC www.aipc.org
Association Internationale des Palais de Congrès (International Association of Congress Centres)
55 Rue de l'Amazone
1060 Brussels
BELGIUM
Phone: 32-2-534-59-53, Fax: 32-2-534-63-38
Email: secretariat@aipc.org

ACCED-I www.acced-i.org
Association of Collegiate Conference and Event Directors Intl.
Colorado State Univ., Tiley House
Fort Collins CO 80523-8037
Phone: 970/491-5151, Fax: 970/491-0667

ALSD www.alsd.com
Association of Luxury Suite Directors
636 Northland Blvd., Ste. 250
Cincinnati OH 45240
Phone: 513/674-0555, Fax: 513/674-0577
Email: feedback@alsd.com

APAP www.artspresenters.org
Association of Performing Arts Presenters
1112 16th St., NW, Ste. 400
Washington DC 20036
Phone: 202/833-2787, Fax: 202/833-1543
Email: info@artspresenters.org

ABRACCEF www.abraccef.org.br
Brazilian Association of Conference Centers (Associacao Brasileira dos Centros de Convencoes e Feiras)
Rua Barao do Rio Branco 370
 CEP 80010-180 Curitiba, Parana
BRAZIL
Phone: 55-41-322-8955, Fax: 55-41-322-8955
Email: comunicacao@abraccef.org.br

CEIR www.ceir.org
Center for Exhibition Industry Research
CEIR Headquarters
8111 LBJ Freeway, Ste. 750
Dallas TX 75251
Phone: 972/687-9242, Fax: 972/692-6020
E-Mail: info@ceir.org

CIC www.conventionindustry.org
Convention Industry Council
8201 Greensboro Dr., Ste. 300
McLean VA 22102
Phone: 703/610-9030, Fax: 703/610-9005

CMA www.cmaworld.com
Country Music Association
One Music Circle South
Nashville TN 37203
Phone: 615/244-2840, Fax: 615/726-0314
Email: international@CMAworld.com

DMAI www.iacvb.org
Destination Marketing Association International
2025 M St., NW, Ste. 500
Washington DC 20036
Phone: 202/296-7888, Fax: 202/296-7889
Email: info@destinationmarketing.org

ESTA   www.esta.org
Entertainment Services and Technology Association
875 Sixth Ave., Ste. 1005
New York NY 10001
Phone: 212/244-1505, Fax: 212/244-1502
Email: info@esta.org

EAA   www.eaaoffice.org
European Arenas Association
Sarphatikade 12
Amsterdam 1017 WV
THE NETHERLANDS
Phone: 31-20-530-4717, Fax: 31-20-530-4711
Email: eaa@eaaoffice.org

EVVC   www.evvc.org
European Association of Event Centers
Messedamm 22
14055 Berlin
GERMANY
Phone: 30-30-38-58-00, Fax: 30-30-38-58-02
Email: info@evvc.org

ESMA   www.vco.be/kd/sam/
European Stadium Managers Association
24 Rue De Commandant Guilbaud
Boulogne 95214
FRANCE
Phone: 33-1-4215-2552, Fax: 33-1-4215-1039

ESCA   www.esca.org
Exposition Service Contractors Association
2920 North Green Valley Pkwy., Ste. 414
Henderson NV 89014-0413
Phone: 702/319-9561, Fax: 702/450-7732
Email: askus@esca.org

IAEE www.iaee.com
International Association of Expositions & Events
P. O. Box 802425
Dallas TX 75380-2425
Phone: 972/458-8002, Fax: 972/458-8119
Email: news@iaee.com

IAAPA www.iaapa.org
International Association of Amusement Parks & Attractions
1448 Duke St.
Alexandria VA 22314
Phone: 703/836-4800, Fax: 703/836-9678

IAAM www.iaam.org
International Association of Assembly Managers
635 Fritz Drive, Ste. 100
Coppell TX 75019
Phone: 972/906-7441, Fax: 972/906-7418

IACC www.iacconline.org
International Association of Conference Centers
243 N. Lindbergh Blvd., Ste. 315
St. Louis MO 63141
Phone: 314/993-8575, Fax: 314/993-8919
Email: info@iacconline.org

IACVB www.iacvb.org
International Association of Convention & Visitor Bureaus
2025 M St. NW, Ste. 500
Washington DC 20036
Phone: 202/296-7888, Fax: 202/296-7889
Email: info@iacvb.org

IAFE www.fairsandexpos.com
International Association of Fairs & Expositions
P.O. Box 985
Springfield MO 65801
Phone: 417/862-5771, Fax: 417/862-0156
Email: iafe@fairsandexpos.com

IAPCO www.iapco.org
International Association of Professional Congress Organizers
42 Canham Rd.
 London W3 7SR
UNITED KINGDOM
Phone: 44-20-8749-6171, Fax: 44-20-8740-0241
Email: info@iapco.org

ICMA   www.icma.org
International City/County Management Association
777 North Capitol St., NE, Ste. 500
Washington DC 20002
Phone: 202/289-4262, Fax: 202/962-3500

ICCA   www.iccaworld.com
International Congress & Convention Association
Entrade 121
NL - 1096 EB Amsterdam
THE NETHERLANDS
Phone: 31-20-398-1919, Fax: 31-20-699-0781
Email: icca@icca.nl

IEDC   www.iedconline.org/index.html
International Economic Development Council
734 15th St., Ste. 900
Washington DC 20005
Phone: 202/223-7800, Fax: 202/223-4745

IFEA   www.ifea.com
International Festivals & Events Association
2601 Eastover Ter.
Boise ID 83706
Phone: 208/433-0950 Fax: 208/433-9812

IFMA   www.ifma.org
International Facility Management Association
1 East Greenway Plaza, Ste. 1100
Houston TX 77046-0194
Phone: 713/623-4362, Fax: 713/623-6124
Email: ifmahq@ifma.org

ISPA   www.ispa.org
International Society for the Performing Arts
17 Purdy Ave., P.O. Box 909
Rye NY 10580
Phone: 914/921-1550, Fax: 914/921-1593
Email: info@ispa.org

ISES   www.ises.com
International Special Events Society
401 North Michigan Ave.
Chicago IL 60611-4267
Phone: 312/321-6853, Fax: 312/673-6953
Email: info@ises.com
ISI www.skateisi.com

Ice Skating Institute
17120 North Dallas Pkwy., Ste. 140
Dallas TX 75248-1187
Phone: 972/735-8800, Fax: 972/735-8815
Email: ISI@skateisi.org

INTIX www.intix.org
International Ticketing Association
330 West 38th St., Ste. 605
New York NY 10018
Phone: 212/629-4036, Fax: 212/629-8532
Email: info@intix.org

IATSE www.iatse-intl.org
Intl. Alliance of Theatrical Stage Employees & Moving Picture Technicians of the US and Canada
1430 Broadway, 20th Fl.
New York NY 10018
Phone: 212/730-1770, Fax: 212/730-7809

LHAT www.lhat.org
League of Historic American Theatres
616 Water St., Ste. 320
Baltimore MD 21202
Phone: 410/659-9533, Fax: 410/837-9664

MLB www.mlb.com
Major League Baseball
245 Park Ave.
New York NY 10167
Phone: 212/931-7800

MPI www.mpiweb.org
Meeting Professionals International
4455 LBJ Fwy., Ste. 1200
Dallas TX 75244-5903
Phone: 972/702-3000, Fax: 972/702-3070
Email: feedback@mpiweb.org

AMPROFEC www.amprofec.org.mx
Mexican Assn. Of Professionals in Fairs, Exhibitions & Conventions
Ave. Benjamin Franklin, Num 166-4
Col. Escandon Mexico, 11800 D. F.
MEXICO
Phone: 55-5273-1103, Fax: 55-5273-1103

NAA www.nationalarenasassociation.com
National Arenas Association
27 Friary Ave.
Shirley, Solihull, West Midlands B90 4SZ
UNITED KINGDOM
Phone: 44-121-744-2211, Fax: 44-121-774-2211

NACA www.naca.org
National Association for Campus Activities
13 Harbison Way
Columbia,SC 29212-3401
Phone: 803/732-6222, Fax: 803/749-1047

NAAC www.accessunltd.com
National Association of Accessibility Consultants
1154 Fort Street Mall, Ste. 204
Honolulu Hawaii 96813
Phone: 808/523-3344, Fax: 808/523-3008
Email: info@accessunltd.com

NACDA www.nacda.com
National Association of Collegiate Directors of Athletes
P.O. Box 16428
Cleveland OH 44116
Phone: 440/892-4000, Fax: 440/892-4007

NAC www.naconline.org
National Association of Concessionaires
35 East Wacker Dr., Ste. 1816
Chicago IL 60601
Phone: 312/236-3858, Fax: 312/236-7809
Email: info@naconline.org

NACS www.publicshows.com
National Association of Consumer Shows
147 S.E. 102nd Ave.
Portland OR 97216
Phone: 503/253-0832, Fax: 503/253-9172
Email: info@publicshows.com

NAIA www.naia.org
National Association of Intercollegiate Athletics
23500 W. 105th St., P.O. Box 1325
Olathe KS 66051
Phone: 913/791-0044, Fax: 913/791-9555

NAPAMA www.napama.org
North American Performing Arts Managers & Agents
459 Columbus Ave., Ste. 133
New York NY 10024
Phone: 888/745-8759, Fax: 212/580-5438
Email: info@napama.org

NBA www.nba.com
National Basketball Association
Olympic Tower, 645 Fifth Ave., 15th Fl
New York NY 10022
Phone: 212/826-7000, Fax: 212/826-0579

NCBMP www.ncbmp.com
National Coalition of Black Meeting Planners
8630 Fenton St., Ste. 126
Silver Spring MD 20910
Phone: 202/628-3952, Fax: 301/588-0011

NCAA www.ncaa.org
National Collegiate Athletic Association
700 W. Washington Ave.
Indianapolis IN 46206-6222
Phone: 317/917-6222, Fax: 317/917-6888

NFPA www.nfpa.org
National Fire Protection Association
1 Batterymarch Park, P.O. Box 9101
Quincy MA 02269-9101
Phone: 617/770-3000, Fax: 617/770-0700
Email: public_affairs@nfpa.org

NFL www.nfl.com
National Football League
280 Park Ave., Ste. 12-West
New York NY 10017
Phone: 212/450-2000, Fax: 212/681-7559

NHL www.nhl.com
National Hockey League
1251 Ave. of the Americas, 47th Fl.
New York NY 10020
Phone: 212/789-2000, Fax: 212/789-2020

NLC www.nlc.org
National League of Cities
1301 Pennsylvania Ave., NW, Ste. 550
Washington DC 20004-1763
Phone: 202/626-3000, Fax: 202/626-3043
Email: inet@nlc.org

NACPA
North American Concert Promoters Association
P.O. Box 753
McLean VA 22101
Phone: 703/538-3575, Fax: 703/538-3876
Email: necpa@ix.netcom.com

PCMA www.pcma.org
Professional Convention Management Association
2301 South Lake Shore, Ste. 1001
Chicago IL 60616-1419
Phone: 312/423-7262, Fax: 312/423-7222
Email: administration@pcma.org

PRCA www.prorodeo.com
Professional Rodeo Cowboys Association
101 Prorodeo Dr.
Colorado Springs CO 80919-9989
Phone: 719/593-8840, Fax: 719/548-4876

RCMA www.rcmaweb.org
Religious Conference Management Association
One RCA Dome, Ste. 120
Indianapolis IN 46225
Phone: 317/632-1888, Fax: 317/632-7909
Email: rcma@rcmaweb.org

SCMP www.scmprof.com
Society of Corporate Meeting Professionals
217 Ridgemont Ave.
San Antonio TX 78209
Phone: 210/822-6522, Fax: 210/822-9838
Email: info@scmp.org

SGMP www.sgmp.org
Society of Government Meeting Planners
908 King St., Lower Level
Alexandria VA 22314
Phone: 703/549-0892, Fax: 703/549-0708
Email: sgmpheadquarters@sgmp.org

SC www.sportengland.org
Sport England
16 Upper Woburn Place
London   WC1H 0QP
ENGLAND
Phone: 020-7273-1500, Fax: 020-7383-5740
Email: info@sportengland.org

SMA www.stadiummanagers.org
Stadium Managers Association
525 SW 5th St., Ste. A
Des Moines IA 50309
Phone: 515/282-8192, Fax: 515/282-9117
Email: sma@assoc-mgmt.com

TEAM www.teamcoalition.org
TEAM Coalition
1101 Wilson Blvd., Ste. 1700
Arlington VA 22209
Phone: 703/741-0275, Fax: 703/524-1487
Email: jpepper@teamcoalition.org

UFI www.ufinet.org
Union des Foires Internationales
35bis, rue Jouffroy d'Abbans
F-75017 Paris
FRANCE
Phone: 33-1-42-67 99-12, Fax: 33-1-42-27-19-29
Email: info@ufinet.org

USITT www.usitt.org
U.S. Institute for Theater Technology
6443 Ridings Rd.
Syracuse NY 13206-1111
Phone: 315/463-6463, Fax: 315/463-6525
Email: info@office.usitt.org

VMA www.vma.org.au
Venue Management Association
P.O. Box 1871
Toowong   QLD 4066
AUSTRALIA
Phone: 61-7-3780-4777, Fax: 61-7-3780-4666

APPENDIX E

GLOSSARY OF TERMS

GLOSSARY OF TERMS

A

advertising campaign - The plan for advertising, promotions, and other means by which tickets for events are advertised and promoted in electronic media (radio and TV), in print, over the Internet, via direct mail, or by other means of general and/or direct contact.

ancillary revenue - Generally refers to income earned from events other than rent and expense reimbursements. Typical examples of ancillary income include concessions and catering, merchandise (novelties), parking and decorating.

ancillary revenue streams - Revenue source in addition to facility charges of rent, labor and equipment to include, but not limited to food/beverage sales, catering commissions, novelty/souvenir sales, parking fees, advertising commissions, ticket/facility surcharges, naming rights fees, sponsorships, etc.

ancillary services - Revenue sources available to facility managers by providing basic services such as food and beverage, merchandising and novelty sales, and parking services. Additional services such as equipment rentals, computer cafes, freight handling (drayage), providing box office services to other organizations, event advertising, and automatic teller machines (ATM), are just a few additional examples of such revenue generators.

audit stub - A portion of a ticket created by perforations that are retained by a ticket seller to document that the ticket was sold and at what price. Audit stubs are an inventory control device and accounting tool that identifies the price at which a ticket was sold: discount, child, full price.

avails - Dates that are available for booking.

B

back-of-house - That portion of the facility where public assess is not permitted, usually behind the stage, production area and/or other restricted areas such as mechanical rooms, dressing rooms, kitchen, etc. Beyond the physical location this term can be used in conjunction with building functions.

banquet event order (BEO) - A document that confirms a food/beverage service for a select group of people.

bar coded tickets - Tickets bearing a series of vertical bars of varying widths conforming with the Universal Product Code used especially for computerized inventory control. Bar coded tickets are now used during the admission process at numerous facilities.

billed back - The process by which one party that provides goods or services to another party bills for and receives reimbursement for the goods and/or services provided.

box office advance - Funds advanced to an event promoter from revenue derived from event ticket sales and paid in advance of the event settlement; the fulfillment of the contract by the event promoter or prior to the conclusion of the event.

box office statement - An itemized accounting of tickets distributed (sold or complimentary), or unsold and the corresponding monies collected for a specific event.

branding - Usually refers to a relationship whereby a food and/or beverage product is given exclusivity in return for agreeing to purchase advertisements and generally promote its presence at the facility via its own advertising, marketing and point-of-sale promotions in the general market area.

break-even operation - Generally refers to a public assembly facility that does not require an operating subsidy from its owner to cover annual operating expenses; operating revenue is sufficient to cover operating expenses. Debt service, capital improvement reserves and taxes are typically excluded as operating expenses.

bundling - A marketing strategy used to help promote events in public assembly facilities and used to encourage patrons and fans to make a long-term commitment by purchasing a number of events in bulk. The season ticket or subscription series of events is offered at the bulk price which is usually less than the combined individual rates of each event.

C

car-loader - A person that is hired temporarily, often a union employee (Teamsters, IATSE), to unload/load freight to and from a truck or railcar.

casual labor - Employees not holding regular positions and working only as opportunity opens (on-call). These employees may be released or furloughed when there is no work for them to perform.

certificate of insurance - Written verification of types, terms, and amounts of insurance carried by the named insured which are sent to those who require proof of such coverage.

change order - In construction or renovation, formal change made to final construction documents. A change order may affect the final cost of a construction or renovation project up or down or not al all, or it may change the length of the construction time. For a banquet, a formal change made to a Banquet Event Order changing a food service event.

changeover - The activities required to change from one stage set-up, seating configuration, etc. within a public assembly facility to another, different set-up or configuration necessitated by the requirements of different types of events or tenant's production needs.

commissaries - A warehouse or production room for food, beverage and/or merchandise. The term is also used to describe a vending room that supplies products to the hawkers selling in the seats of a venue.

complimentary tickets - Tickets to an event issued at no charge to the recipient. Complimentary tickets are specially marked, punched or printed tickets which have no monetary value. Some contracts require the promoter to pay the facility rent as if the tickets had been sold. Usually this is limited to only the number of tickets issued as complimentary in excess of the number allowed in the contract.

confirmed contract - A contract that has been negotiated, agreed to and is awaiting signatures.

contract - A written agreement between two or more parties in which it is agreed that one party will perform a desired work or provide a service for which the other will pay some form of compensation.

contracted - Contract that has been signed and returned, usually with a rent deposit.

co-promoted - Generally is a term to describe an event that the facility becomes involved with on at least a partially at-risk basis. In a co-promoted arrangement, the facility might not charge a guaranteed rent, and in some cases expenses, and earns a negotiated percentage of gross ticket sales. Some events are only willing to book a facility if the facility is willing to become an active promotional partner. By sharing in the downside risk, facilities can possibly earn more revenue through a co-promotion than a standard rental relationship.

cost accounting - Method of accounting which emphasizes the determination and the control of costs, particularly the costs of production and the final product. It deals with actual costs to be reported on financial statements. One of the principal functions is to assemble and interpret cost data, both actual and prospective, for the use of management in controlling current operations and in planning for the future.

cost estimate - A written or verbal estimate provided by a party providing goods or services to another of the resources required to provide said goods or services.

crisis management - The plan and process of responding to an emergency situation and minimizing damage to property or injuries to persons once an emergency or crisis has occurred.

cross-bounce coupon - A marketing tool used to increase sales of tickets to an event or retail product by offering a value-added benefit for the customer either in the form of a discount on the price of a ticket to an event or a discount on a retail item at a participating retail outlet or on something offered by some other promotional partner. Cross-bounce coupons are usually printed as part of a print ad for an event, but can be separately printed advertising/promotion collateral.

crowd control - General term for the combined services involved in managing the direction and demeanor of an audience.

crowd management - The planning of, and the work performed by ushers, ticket takers, peer-group security, medical teams and facility management to provide the safety and security for the general public attending events.

D

dark - A date without a performance or event and not usually available for booking.

deadwood - Unsold tickets that remain in inventory.

donor - Refers to a business, organization or individual who gives money to a fundraising drive, often to a performing arts center itself and/or one or more of its shows or to a university athletic department.

drop count - The number of ticket stubs collected for a single event at the entry point(s) of a facility. If bar coded tickets are used, a report is provided in place of the physical ticket stubs.

E

egress - The act of leaving or exiting a public assembly facility or other location.

emergency preparedness - Maintaining a plan and performing regular training to best respond to any incident, situation, or occurrence that could possibly result in the injury/death of employees, patrons, clients or visitors at a facility and/or cause any damage to the facility, equipment and its contents.

event management - The process of planning and disseminating information and communicating pertinent event production requirements to a facility's staff which results in the coordination of activities that leads to the successful production of an event.

event operations - When used as a verb, the process of running an event. When used as a noun, the various units needed to operate the event and facility, including, but not limited to, technical staff, sound and lighting operators, laborers, electricians, changeover crews, maintenance staff, etc.

event timeline - An outline or timeline used to help manage an event that lists dates when important event production details are scheduled to occur in the event management process.

exhibition - An event at which products and services are displayed.

external audit - An audit conducted by an individual or firm that is independent of the company being audited. Auditors typically are called in for an annual audit, after the completion of the company's fiscal year. Their role is to give an opinion of the financial statement's reflection of the status and operations of the company being audited. Based on what they witness during the audit, they will also produce, for management and board use, a management letter.

F

fixed assets - Those assets of a permanent nature required for the normal conduct of a business, and which will not normally be converted into cash during the ensuing fiscal period. For example, furniture, fixtures, land and buildings are all fixed assets. However, accounts receivable and inventory are not. Sometimes call PLANT.

fixed overhead - Ongoing administrative expenses of a business that cannot be assigned to a specific business activity and that tend to stay the same whether sales go up or down, e.g. rent, utilities, telephone, insurance, etc.

followspot - Spotlight mounted on a swivel socket in order to produce a sharp moveable beam of light which can travel with the subjects on a stage or ice surface as they move from place to place.

front-of-house - The area in a facility which the public typically occupies. This area typically includes lobbies, concession stands, public restrooms, ticket office and the seating area.

full-service venue - Usually refers to a facility that provides all critical support services necessary for the tenant to successfully present/produce their event.

G

golden circle - The condition in which the best seats in the house are set-aside and are sold at a significantly higher price. The difference between the golden circle price and the next highest priced ticket is considered a donation. Often used for charity sponsored fund raising events.

governing body - Typically refers to the highest authority of a facility's ownership level. Examples include city councils, county commissions, university board of regents, or a board of directors of a private corporation.

gross revenue - Total revenue generated before any expenses or taxes are applied or paid.

group ticket sales - Refers to the process of selling blocks of tickets to groups. Group tickets are usually offered for specific performances at a discount.

H

helpers - In the context of this text, entry level apprentice workers employed to assist professional craftsmen.

hotel nights - Nights in a hotel reserved and/or actually used by convention or meeting delegates. One room rented for one night is a hotel night or room night.

I

incident report - Documentation of what occurred during a situation and what steps were taken in response. Such documentation is usually made by a member of a facility's staff on a pre-printed form.

ingress - The act of entering a public assembly facility or other location.

in-house - An activity that is conducted within, coming from or being within an organization. Refers to services provided by the facility itself rather than through outside, third-party contractors. Food and beverage concessions and advertising services to event promoters are common examples.

internal audit - An independent appraisal of the financial health of a company's operation by its own employees. Employees who carry out this function are called internal auditors.

L

labor call - A specified list of required temporary personnel that must be available at a specified time and place, including stagehands with specific skills.

license application - Form completed by potential facility user demonstrating the necessary financial resources, prior experience and ability to produce an event.

limited contract - An agreement between two parties that is restricted to specific issues, such as purposes, date and time and that usually expires at the conclusion of an event.

limited view seats - Seats in a public assembly facility that offer only a partial or restricted view of the stage, performance area or playing field where the event is being held or staged.

luxury suites - Refers to a form of premium or VIP seating sold in arenas and stadiums. Suites are physically separated from the general seating and might typically offer cushioned seats, standing room for additional guests, catered meals and drinks, closed circuit TV, special VIP access including parking, restroom facilities, concierge services and other amenities.

M

market position - Refers to the relative competitive standing of a facility in its general market area.

mission statement - A mission statement defines a facility's basic public purpose, often in two powerful statements.

motor control center - That portion of the facility that is devoted to engineering and mechanical switch gear.

N

naming rights - Refers to a form of advertising and marketing whereby a business, organization, or individual, places its (his/her) name on the facility for a fixed amount of money over a period of years - or often with universities in perpetuity. In return, the naming rights sponsor is guaranteed benefits such as luxury suites, club seats, name also on the scoreboard and other inside advertising signage inventory, name on tickets, brochures, event advertising, the right of first refusal to sponsor certain events, employee group discounts and the like.

net operating surplus - Revenue that is generated and retained in excess of the total operating expenses of a facility.

O

obstructed view seats - Seats in a public assembly facility from which the view of the stage, performance area or playing field for an event is blocked or hidden from sight. Such seats my provide a view of the stage, performance area or playing field on video screens.

outsource - The act of assigning work to an outside provider.

P

packaging - Generally refers to the process whereby the facility, individually or with one or more of its prime tenants, packages respective inventory through a combined sales staff in order to offer clients the broadest possible means by which to become advertising and sponsorship partners. Income received is simply allocated on a predetermined basis.

panic hardware - A door latching assembly incorporating an unlatching device, the activating portion of which extends across at least one half the width of the door leaf on which it is installed. (UBC) Panic hardware allows anyone to open a door to permit exiting/egress even if the door is locked from the entry/ingress side.

parent organization - Refers to owner or oversight authority/entity of which the facility or operations is a subsidiary thereof.

personal seating license - Is typically used at the outset to raise funds to help finance a public assembly facility. The buyer essentially "buys" a seat(s) and has the right of first refusal to then buy tickets for all events.

petty cash - An account and location where a small amount of cash is stored for incidental expenses in purchasing or the reimbursing of inexpensive out-of-pocket expenditures.

physical plant - Refers to the equipment commonly associated with the heating, ventilation and air conditioning (HVAC) system, electrical distribution system, plumbing/sewage system, etc. within a public assembly facility.

pipe and drape - Pipe material with fabric draped from it to make up side rails and the back wall of a trade show booth or a temporary barrier.

pouring rights - Generally refers to the award of exclusive soft drink rights in return for an annual rights payment to the facility. It is generally against federal and most state laws to solicit advertising payments in return for exclusive arrangements involving beer, wine and/or alcohol.

premium seating - In arenas and stadiums, premium seating refers to the sale of individual "club" seats, the cost of which generally include tickets to all prime tenant sporting events. All other tickets must be purchased on a right of first refusal basis.

private management - Generally refers to a publicly owned facility contracting with an outside operator that specializes in the management, marketing and operation of public assembly facilities. The motivation for entering into such a relationship is often because it offers the owner the opportunity to operate, market and compete in a "business-like" manner not generally possible within their own system.

production call - A specified list of required personnel, many of whom may be temporary, that are needed to run the equipment or perform duties during the actual performance.

production rider - A document detailing an event's specific technical requirements in terms of stage location and size, sound and lighting equipment, mixer location, catering, etc. and other pertinent information.

promoter - Contracted person(s) or company(ies) responsible for costs, production and promotion of an event.

promoter packet - A pamphlet or brochure designed to familiarize a new promoter with the features and services of a public assembly facility. The contents of a promoter packet frequently includes information such as line drawings of spaces available for rent, seating diagrams, meeting room layouts, list of house-owned equipment, fire and safety codes, labor rates, maps of the area, etc. Promoter "packets" are increasingly being hosted on a facility's web site where the level of information provided is only limited by the creativity of the facility's management.

R

reconciliation - Audit reports conducted to reconcile cash and financial performance statements.

request for proposal - Process by which an outline of desired goods or services is responded to by vendors.

request for qualifications - Document issued prior to a request for proposal. The purpose is to ascertain that the respondent is qualified by knowledge, experience and financial capability to provide specified goods or services.

reserve - A date that has been tentatively held by a potential client for an event awaiting final contract negotiations. Also called a "tentative hold".

resident companies - Organizations for which the facility is their home. In a performing arts facility, it might include symphony orchestra, opera and/ or theatrical drama companies. In arenas and stadiums it typically includes sports franchises.

revocable permit - The consent or authorization to enter, occupy or for other purposes remain upon a premises that can be revoked, recalled or withdrawn.

rigger - A person who installs rigging.

rigging - General term for the rope and pulley arrangement in the grid of a theater or the chain motors and wire cables used in an arena or amphitheater.

risk assessment - The process of evaluating the severity and frequency of loss associated with a particular activity or event.

risk management - The process of identification of risk, analysis of risk as to its likelihood, frequency and severity, risk reduction/elimination and transfer, to the extent possible, of the remaining risk.

runner - Also known as Production Assistant, is usually someone familiar with the community who is employed locally by the act or promoter to provide a means of transportation for crew members and to serve as a "go for" for the acquisition of various services and sundry items needed during an event's stay in a facility.

running schedule - A schedule used to help manage an event that lists important event production elements with corresponding times when they are scheduled to occur. Elements of a running schedule for a concert include the length of time an opening act performs, intermission beginning and ending times, and the time a headliner is scheduled to appear and how long they will perform.

S

scale-the-house - The process of assigning different ticket prices to different seating areas within a public assembly facility whereby prices vary depending on the seat location.

self-sustaining - A public assembly facility that does not require an operating subsidy from its owner to cover annual operating expenses and is similar to a "break-even operation."

settlement sheet - A detailed itemization of ticket sales, production expenses, building rent, box office costs and all other event-related expenses.

show call - A specified list of required personnel, many of whom may be temporary, that are needed to run the equipment or perform duties during the actual performance.

signage - Advertising display typically located in arenas and stadiums and to a lesser extent in convention centers, performing arts center and other public assembly facilities. Signage is typically located on scoreboards and electronic message boards, outdoor marquees, interior fascia between seating levels, on concourse walls over concession stands, etc.

sponsor - Refers to a business, organization or individual that pays fees to associate its name with a special event. Various sponsorship levels are available including, for example, "presenting," "associate," and "media."

stagehand - Generic term for backstage production personnel not performing in front of the audience.

subsidized operation - Refers to a facility that has operating expenses greater than the revenue it can generate and which, therefore, requires annual financial assistance (subsidy) from its owner.

T

tentative contract - Contract that is in the process of being negotiated during the time the date is on reserve/tentative hold.

ticket broker - An individual or agency reselling tickets in a locale where selling a ticket for more than face value is legal under specified conditions.

ticket manifest - A document that is used as evidence to prove the number of tickets printed for an event when hard tickets are preprinted. Also, a statement generated by a computerized ticketing system. Both document the number of seats programmed for a specific event and includes the number of tickets sold, unsold, held, killed and issued as complimentary for a specific event or series of events.

trade show - Exposition held for members of a common or related industry and not open to the general public.

trade tickets - Tickets for an event that are offered by an event promoter in exchange for event-related goods or services such as advertising, equipment, etc.

turnstile - Device that can keep the flow of an entering crowd at a controllable level, count the number of guests passing through, and discourage or prevent unauthorized entry, usually in the form of a rotating set of arms, permitting only one guest per arm. They can be either permanent or portable.

turnstile count - The number of customers or guests who enter the facility for an event as recorded by a turnstile.

U

umbrella group - Organization that links together a larger consortium of entities.

union shop - A facility which has a contract with a union and is able to hire any person without regard to union membership, but said employee must then join the union within a specified period of time and pay dues. This does not apply in Right to Work states.

V

variable expenses - Those business expenses that usually fluctuate in direct proportion to a level of activity, such as units of production or sales volume.

volunteers - Persons who perform or offer to perform a service of his or her own free will, usually at no charge.

Y

yellow card - Refers to a union contract agreement for stagehands between show producer and organized labor which applies to traveling, touring shows.

Z

Zamboni - The given name (manufacturer) of a maintenance vehicle used for preparing ice surfaces. Often used generically.

INDEX

A

Access control, 216
Accounts payable, 140
Accounts receivable, 140
Administration, 32
Admission control, 216
Advertising and promotions, 54, 80
    Campaign, 80
    Cross-bounce coupons, 80
    In-house agency, 162
    Run of schedule, 81
    Signage, 89
Americans with Disabilities Act (ADA), 35, 230
    ADA holds, 116
Ancillary revenue, 73, 160
    Customer-related, 165-185
    Promoter-related, 162-165
Ancillary services, 36
Asset assessment, 213
Audits
    Audit stub, 107
    Cash, 139
    Internal, 141

B

Blowout, defined, 178
Bonding, 138
Booking and scheduling, 49-50, 57, 74
    Avails, defined, 56
    Booking memo, 55, 58
    Confirmed, defined, 60
    Contracted, defined, 60
    Date holds, 60
    Date protection policy, 62
    Hold date, challenge, 64
    Hold date, confirmed, 60
    License application, 55
    Policies and procedures, 49
    Qualifying the event, 54-57
    Reserved, defined, 60
    Tentative, defined, 60
Box office
    Design, 123

        Settlement, 118
        Staffing, 124
Branded items, 178
Branding, 91
Broadcast fees, 162
Budgeting
        Incremental budgeting, 134
        Line item budgeting, 135
        Performance budgeting, 134
        Planned program budgeting system, 134
        Preparation, 133
        Zero-based budgeting, 135
Business manager, 131

C

Capacity, control of, 98
Capital replacement, 233
Cash management, 138
        Audits, 139
        Petty cash, 139
        Reconciliation, 138
Certification, 43
        Certified Facilities Executive (CFE), 43
Change over, 242
Co-promoting the event, defined, 54
Commercial rights
        Inventory, 87
        Sale of, 85
Communication, 42
Communication, crisis, 217
Communication, guest, 206
        Messages, audible, 206
        Messages, visual, 206
Community relations, 78
Compliance, regulatory, 230
Contract negotiations, 143
Contracting, 65,143
Convention and visitors bureaus (CVBs), 52
Conversion, 242
Cost accounting, 136
        Cost allocation, 137
        Costs, fixed, 138
        Costs, mixed, 138
        Costs, overhead, 137-138

Costs, variable, 137-138
Crisis communication, 217-219
Crowd management, 206-208
Custodial service, 240
Customer service, 79

D

Data base management, 123
Date protection policy, 62

E

Emergency planning, 217-219
    Procedures, 217-219
Employee management
    Communication, 147
    Evaluation, 147
    Hiring and recruitment, 146
    Job descriptions, 145
    Orientation, 147
    Training programs, 147
Entrepreneurship, 41-42
Equipment needs, 197-198
Equipment rental fees, 165
Ethics, 39
Event financial settlements, 142-143
Event management positions, 201
Event planning, 191
    Event file, 210-211
    Floor plans and design layouts, 198
    Timeline, 197
Event production, 192
Event safety, 212
Event services, 241
Event tax collection, 118
Events, televised, 197

F

Facilities services manager, 210
Facility rent, 161

Festival seating, 113
Finance director, 131
Financial controls, 33
Financial performance, 8
Financial settlement, 142
Financial statements, 135
    Balance sheet, 135
    Capital expenditures statement, 136
    Cash flow statement, 136
    Event financial settlement, 142-143
    Generally accepted accounting principles (GAAP), 136
    Income statement, 135
First Amendment of the U.S. Constitution, 56
Fixtures, furnishings & equipment (FF&E), 232
Food and beverage services, 166
    Alcohol sales, 175
    Commissary, 171
    Commission agreement, 169
    Concession stands, 171
    Contracted food and beverage service, 167-169
    Contractor compensation, 169
    Hawking, 174
    In-House food and beverage service, 167
    Layout and design, 170-172
    Marketing, 172, 174
    Pouring rights, beverages, 88
    Request for proposal (RFP), food and beverage service contractor, 169
    Request for qualification (RFQ), food and beverage service contractor, 169
    Trends, 176
    Wait service, 174-175

G

Governance, 6
    Authority/commission, 15, 27
    Colleges/universities, 28-29
    Governmental unit, 27
    Non-profit organization, 15, 28
    Private management, 12-14, 29
Green management, 234
Guest communication, 206

H

Housekeeping, 240
Human resources, 144-150

I

Immigration and Naturalization Service (INS), 144
Incident command system, 218
Incident reports, 209
Independent contractors, 149
Insurance, 152
Inventory control, 141,231-233

J

Job descriptions, 145

L

Labor charge-back fees, 163
Labor unions, 247-248
Lease agreement, 144
Leasing the facility, defined, 54
Limited view, 105
Local productions, 195
Luxury suites, 83

M

Maintenance, preventive, 237-238
Management fee, 169
Management functions, 30-31
Managerial leadership, 40-41
Marketing, 71-78
    Benefits of, 72-73
    Competition, 76
    Event marketing, 73-74
    Defined, 72
    Position, 75-76

Marketing plan, 75-78
Marshalling yards, 250
Mechanical services, 236
    Systems, 237-238
Memorial gifts, 91
Merchandising, 177-181
    Flat-rate fee, defined, 179
    Per-person fee, defined, 179
    Percentage-of-sales fee, defined, 179
Mission statements, 18, 52

N

Naming rights, 85
Negotiations, 38

O

Obstructed view, 105
Occupancy codes, 100
Occupational Safety and Health Administration (OSHA), 230
Official services contractor, 231
On-sale date, 116
Operating dynamics, 17
Operations management, 241-250
    Operations manager, 210
    Engineering services, 235-236
    Staffing
        Craftsman, 239
        Tradesman, 239
Organization chart, 26
Ownership, 7, 11

P

Parking services, 182-185
    Bus, 184
    Limo, 184
    RV, 184
    Valet, 184
Patron communication, 206
Patron issues, 206

Personal seating licenses (PSL), 84
Physical plant, 211, 237
Premium access, marketing of, 82-84
Premium seating, 83, 121-122
Preventive maintenance, 237-238
Primary revenue, 161
Private management, 12-14, 29
Procurement cards, 140
Production planning, 192-194
Production rider, 195-197,243-244
Production services, 242
Productions, local, 195
Professional associations, trade association, organizations, and unions, 287-297
    International Alliance of Theatrical Stage Employees (IATSE), 248
    International Association of Assembly Managers (IAAM), 42-44
    International Brotherhood of Teamsters (IBT), 248
    Green Building Council (GBC), 234
    Leadership in Energy and Environmental Design (LEED), 234
    National Fire Protection Association (NFPA), 230
    Techniques for Effective Alcohol Management (TEAM), 175-176
    Unions, labor, 247-248
Professional development, 42
    Academy for Venue Safety & Security (AVSS), 43,216
    European Academy for Venue Management (EAVM), 43
    Public Assembly Facility Management School (PAFM), 42
    Senior Executive Symposium (SES), 43
Promoter packet, 193
Public assembly facilities (PAFs)
    Types
        Amphitheater, defined, 4
        Arena, defined, 4
        Auditoriums, defined, 5
        Commission, defined, 27
        Complex, defined, 4
        Concert halls, defined, 5
        Congress centers, defined, 4
        Convention center, defined, 5
        Exhibition halls, defined, 5
        Facilities district, defined, 27
        Performing arts facilities, defined, 5
        Special event facilities, defined, 5
        Stadium, defined, 5
        Theatre, defined, 5
Public Image, 209
Purchasing, 140

R

Rate card, 87
Reconfiguration, 242-243
Regulatory compliance, 230
Revenue collection, 99
Rigging, 245-246
Risk management, 150-153, 213-215,229-230
    Loss prevention, 151
    Loss reduction, 152
    Risk analysis, 214-215
    Risk assumption, 151
    Risk avoidance, 151
    Risk transfer, 152-153

S

Sales, 75, 85
Sales and marketing department, 75
Scaling the house, 113-115
Scheduling, 49-50
Seating
    Club seats, 83
    Festival seating, defined, 113
    General admission seating, defined, 113
    Personal seating licenses (PSL), 84
    Premium seating, 83, 121-122
    Priority seating, 84
    Reserved seating, defined, 113
    Seat location, valuing of, 100
    Status seats/holds, 116
Security planning, 213-215
Security, back-of-house, 211
Services, custodial and housekeeping, 240-241
Services, event, 241-249
Settlements, 142-143
Shipping and receiving, 231
Space rental, 164
Sponsorships, 90
Staffing, 197-198
    Back-of-house security, 210-211
    Box office, 124
    Casual labor, 147
    Front-of-house, 203-205
    Part-time labor, 147-149

Stage crew, 244-245
Standing room only, 105
Status seats/holds, 116
Subscriptions, 82

T

Technical director, 210
Televised events, 197
Tenants, 59
Ticketing services, 34-35
    Ancillary revenue, 165-166
    Group ticket sales, 80
    Historical overview, 97-98
    Secondary ticket market, 120-121
    Operations, 96
    Request for Proposal (RFP) for ticketing services, 109
    Request for Proposal Qualifications) for ticketing services, 109
    Sales, 97, 101, 117
    Scaling the house, 113-115
    Scalping, 121
    Service charges, 115
    Systems, 108-111
    Ticket process, 111-118
    Ticket revenue distribution, 118
    Ticketing manifest, 115
    Tickets
        Counterfeit tickets, 121
        Design, 101-103
        e-Tickets, 119
        Limited contract and revocable license, 103-105
        Season tickets, 82
        Walk up tickets, 118
        Will call tickets, 118
    Trends, 126-127
Timelines, event, 201-202
Traffic, 183
Transportation, 184

U

Unions, labor, 247-248
User priorities, 50-52
Utility fees, 163

V

Volunteers, 149
Vulnerability assessment, 214

Y

Yellow card shows, 248
Yield management, 124-126